The Unmasterable Past

The Unmasterable Past

HISTORY, HOLOCAUST, AND
GERMAN NATIONAL IDENTITY

With a New Preface

Charles S. Maier

HARVARD UNIVERSITY PRESS
CAMBRIDGE, MASSACHUSETTS
AND LONDON, ENGLAND
1997

Second printing, 1998

Library of Congress Cataloging-in-Publication Data

Maier, Charles S.
  The unmasterable past : history, holocaust, and German national
  identity / Charles S. Maier.
     p. cm.
  Includes index.
  ISBN 0-674-92977-2 (pbk.)
    1. Holocaust, Jewish (1939–1945)—Historiography.   2. Germany
—History—20th century—Historiography.   3. Historians—Germany
(West)   I. Title.
D804.3.M35 1988
940.53'15'03924—dc19   88-11690

For Andrea, Nicholas, and Jessica

Contents

Preface, 1997

WHAT CONSEQUENCES, if any, have followed from the inflamed German debate that became known as the *Historikerstreit*, or historians' controversy? When I wrote *The Unmasterable Past* a decade ago, I believed that the controversy had high stakes for West German political culture. Some scholars dismissed the debate as historiographically trivial: it did not evaluate new evidence or advance analysis of the National Socialist genocidal project. But that complaint was beside the point. The *Historikerstreit* was a controversy less about the past itself than about how a nation confronted a brutal and shameful past. The debate revealed that German intellectuals were divided over how centrally their country's acknowledging past aggression and genocide should underlie political consciousness. Must continued—indeed, continual—acceptance of historical responsibility underlie Bonn's commitment to democracy? Or was the Holocaust, four decades after Auschwitz and a major effort at reparations, rather irrelevant to contemporary German politics? Might not repeated acknowledgment, as some representatives of the right wing in the debate implied, actually get in the way of standing tall as a modern democracy? Wasn't it time to move on?

Of course West Germany did move on. It had the chance to fulfill the official national aspirations of almost half a century and achieve unification. It apparently left the controversy behind. Had the debate been no more than an overheated exchange? Unification demonstrated that conservatives who charged that preoccupation with the Holocaust would paralyze national energies were wrong. But results also suggested that left-wing intellectuals were also alarmist when they feared that united Germany would become conventionally nationalist. Germans have become no less repentant of their history, no more prepared to dismiss past crimes, no more cocky or chauvinist. Unified Germany was ready for responsible nationhood; it did not renounce the chance to join other countries in accepting the familiar allegiances to a territorial community, but neither did it simply resume what Jürgen Habermas, the major critic on the left, feared might become a heavy-handed nationalism, based if not on military power than on economic and financial strength.[1] Just as over a century earlier Bismarck had been careful to stress that unified Germany was a satiated power, Chancellor Kohl emphasized the European vocation of his recovered fatherland.

Do these results of 1989–1990 (if still provisional) mean, therefore, that the historians' controversy had involved just a silly clash of alarmist projections on both sides? I would, in fact, propose the opposite: namely, that the chance to air the issues immediately before unification substituted for the constitutional debate that united Germany never got around to holding once the East German state decided simply to merge with the West. To the disappointment of some intellectuals and journalists, no grand constituent assembly refounded the broader German nation in 1990. Nonetheless, the premises of national community, whether formulated in terms of legal culture, inherited collective responsibilities, or patriotic habits of the heart, had already been subjects for vigorous discussion. Unbeknownst to its participants, the historians' controversy served as a partial surrogate for the debate that an all-German constituent assembly might have appropriately scheduled as the basis for future unity.

When I wrote this book, I had another intellectual agenda as well, which encompassed problems inherent in writing history. Insofar as the debate involved important historiographical issues, they were less about what had happened than about how to evaluate or contextualize what had taken place. How else could one understand the Holocaust than by asking what sort of events it was "like"? But then how might one pose that question without diminishing its unique horror? All historical understanding must ultimately rest on comparison even though the subjects of historical reconstruction—and concerning this point German historians had long been the most insistent—retain an invincible individuality. As a historian, I wanted to probe that fundamental tension of our discipline. The Holocaust, which seemed so singular, offered the most compelling test case.

The controversy exposed other issues as well, including the problematic relationship of history to collective memory. Even if the topic by now threatens to become commonplace as an academic inquiry, as I was writing, memories of wartime roles, heroic and shameful, continued to reemerge with poignant urgency. The historians' controversy likewise opened up issues of agency and responsibility that have arisen again in the recent debates surrounding Daniel Goldhagen's book,

Hitler's Willing Executioners.[2] And it prompted other related questions that I could touch on only tangentially, but which have continued to perplex me: How could historians organize a single encompassing narrative that "did justice" (historiographically speaking) to both the perpetrators and the victims who shared an interlocking past? If history writing legitimately aspires to recover and reanimate that shared past as well as to analyze it, how can we judge the adequacy of that recovery and its freedom from illusion or sentimentality? The controversy, in short, led into the most politicized questions to emerge out of late-twentieth-century historical consciousness and narration.

The most gratifying aspect of my book's reception was its interest to readers who were not primarily historians, but who were concerned with the civic spirit of the Federal Republic and with issues of history and memory—German and Jewish—and the claims of a burdened national past. The book attempted to ask: How should Germans, and non-Germans, too, live with history when it was not just history? How should historians write history for events that they did not believe should become just history? Ultimately I wrote the book because all these were personal as well as public concerns; and readers, I believed, responded to the author's stake in his story.

This second paperback edition allows me to add a further word on the stunning development that no one envisaged in the mid-1980s, namely, the unification of Germany. *The Unmasterable Past* took the continuing existence of a divided Germany for granted. In retrospect, it implicitly suggested that the willingness to live with that division was a major test of contemporary German civic culture. Along with many West Germans, I believed that to challenge the continued existence of the East German regime would have been fruitless, provocative, and dangerous. Obviously, this proved to be a blinkered vision.

I have written elsewhere that I do not believe that social scientists were at fault for not predicting the events of 1989–1990.[3] It usually makes sense for social scientists to presuppose linear and gradual change. Since drastic upheavals take place only rarely, the logical basis of most prediction must be that the near future will be more of the same. The problem is that such a working assumption often leads us to discount mounting symptoms of crisis. We historians and social scientists were not sufficiently attuned to at least the possibility of systemic breakdown in Communist Europe. We regarded the chance of such an outcome as akin to that of a great asteroid slamming into the earth. Since 1989, I have learned that the social scientist or historian is certainly entitled to be surprised by events, but should not be surprised by surprise in its own right. There is a lot more debris in political and economic space that can head our way than in actual space. Even the health of Western representative institutions could prove vulnerable to the strains of economic transformation and inflamed ethnic loyalties.

Not every historian whom I critiqued in my book actively mourned a united Germany. Clearly the division of national territory after 1945 grieved the late Andreas Hillgruber, but it seemed to play little role for Michael Stürmer, whose writing focused not on the loss of an older unity, but on what he felt was the confused historical awareness within the postwar divided nation-state. I wrote off Hillgruber's yearnings for a German role in Central Europe too easily as "the geopolitics of nostalgia." Much of the historical work I discussed still seems politically and historically problematic; nonetheless, after 1989, I find much less nostalgia. More generally, the unification of Germany raises the issue, which I thought resolved, of whether the historians' controversy is itself just history.

What disturbed me about the work of the historians I examined, but above all the contribution of Ernst Nolte, was that it licensed, so to speak, a broader public or political relativization of responsibility. If a highly intelligent and learned historian could question whether the Holocaust was German in origin, or could come to the verge of asking whether the Jews might not have provoked events, or could at least claim that every such question involved an authentic scholarly debate, then would not the wider public be justified in throwing off any acceptance of national historical responsibility? As of 1987–1988, I believed that the great majority of the academic establishment and political leaders had rejected these implications. The Federal president then serving, Richard von Weizsäcker, explicitly condemned this strategy of reinterpretation.

The majority of vocal Germans still reject such "normalization." Unification has not led Germans to justify relativizing the evil of the Holocaust—even given such testimonies of continuing mass brutality as ethnic cleansing in Bosnia and the attempted genocide in Rwanda. The avid readership that Goldhagen's *Hitler's Willing Executioners* has found in Germany may demonstrate that younger Germans, above all, want no attenuation of historical responsibility by means of Holocaust narratives which suggest that bureaucratic structures or a merciless regime provided the momentum for the murder of the Jews. We cannot be certain. The reception of the Goldhagen volume, which many historians find intensely problematic, may also signal a new generation's confidence that it has overcome the politics of its grandparents. Even as nominal acceptance of responsibility grows, the perceived burden of historical responsibility may diminish, and Ernst Nolte's admonition that the past should pass away may in fact take place. Even if younger Germans do not believe that their country is unfairly singled out, they may not be exempt from some underlying insouciance: "Yes, let it all be revealed; it shall never be repeated. That was then, not now; it's history."

Is such an attitude to be regretted? Is it to be resisted? Intellectuals fight over the issue of memorials with the touching confidence that these structures, whose concepts and form are so intensely debated, can really keep the past present. The issue of what sort of Holocaust memorial is appropriate for Berlin has provoked intense debate now for several years. But no memorial can keep the past continually present. A fitting and authentic memorial will prompt the onlooker or participant briefly to place himself within a troubled history and envisage himself as a victim and perhaps even as a perpetrator. It should provoke tears and questions. But it can do so only for a finite moment. For most of the time the memorial testifies to irrevocable pastness.

Unification has helped to complete Germany's trajectory toward what Chancellor Kohl calls normality. Such normality includes revival among some intellectuals and politicians of a renewed national conservatism, which in Germany takes up a venerable anti-Western temptation. Some of the fashionable young conservative essayists resent being compelled to reiterate German historical responsibilities; they see the United States as a source of "multicultural" decay; they envisage an eco-holism that returns to German romantic roots and condemns Western materialism. Having continually to acknowledge responsibility for Auschwitz, as they see it, is a masochistic exercise: a sort of spiritual Morgenthau Plan imposed by America.[4] Among this circle, who freely see Ernst Nolte as a *maître-penseur,* the discourse of the *Historikerstreit* has become a discourse of current politics. Nonetheless, it would be wrong to exaggerate the importance of this provocative new conservatism, which in fact is hardly new and echoes the rightwing radicals of the Weimar republic. United Germany today does not labor under international obligations and strictures such as the Versailles Treaty imposed. It is integrated into the Western institutions of the European Community. The new right has been too much an elite affair to buttress any populistic reactions against

Maastricht; German politics has not generated a successful counterpart to Jörg Haider's Freiheitspartei, the Italian Northern League, or Jean-Marie Le Pen's Front National. Even double-digit unemployment seems to provoke little political reaction. Joblessness no longer correlates, as it did in the interwar economic crisis, with a fall in national output: societies make what they require without employing all their citizens. Only the lesson of 1989, namely, that one must be open to surprises, precludes dismissing the new right entirely.

Unification also changed the terms of the historians' debate in another respect. It provoked discussion about the comparability of Communism and Nazism and especially about the role of intellectuals in the respective regimes. Even as they drew sharp distinctions between the Third Reich and the German Democratic Republic, historians and columnists referred to two German dictatorships and sometimes attacked those who had collaborated with the second. The harsh criticism of former East German intellectuals, such as the novelist Christa Wolf, led to controversy over who was fit to take part in public life.[5] Such debate did not lead intellectuals to diminish the horror and singularity of the Holocaust. And the sharpness of the accusations soon diminished. Nonetheless, German society has also had to assimilate the legacy of repression in East Germany. A second dictatorship had to be judged alongside the Nazi experience. How much responsibility can be sifted at the same time?

Still, it remains striking that responsibility for East German abuses has been debated without abandoning scrutiny of the Nazi regime. One might have expected that once the era of German division was superseded, the evils of the National Socialist regime might have been pushed into memory's analogue of the past-perfect tense. That has not happened. It is unlikely to happen when responsibilities intrude into current debates in neighboring Switzerland or elsewhere. Memory will not fade; but perhaps neither will it afflict.[6] Maybe that is a decent enough outcome: a sense of collective responsibility less besetting than Jürgen Habermas wanted, but far more commanding than Ernst Nolte thought healthy.

I wrote *The Unmasterable Past* not primarily as a piece of reportage, but to analyze a contemporary debate as a constituent of a complicated and self-reflective history. The historians' controversy turned out to be the last major intellectual crisis of the old Federal Republic, the Bonn Republic, which had constructed a civic culture that Jürgen Habermas defined as "constitutional patriotism" because the division of Europe denied West Germany a more instinctive ethnic nation-hood. Habermas was right to see such constitutional patriotism as one of the Germans' finest achievements; it is encouraging that united Germany has largely reaffirmed this quality of allegiance to law and rights even as it has been able to recover a more traditional national framework. Therein lies the best homage to the victims of its earlier abandonment of humanity.

Notes

1. See Jürgen Habermas, "Der DM Nationalismus," *Die Zeit*, March 30, 1990, p. 62. For Habermas's early reflections on the transformations of 1989 in Eastern Europe, see his *Die nachholende Revolution* (Frankfurt am Main: Suhrkamp, 1991).

2. Daniel Jonah Goldhagen, *Hitler's Willing Executioners: Ordinary Germans and the Holocaust* (New York: Alfred A. Knopf, 1996).

3. "Wissenschaft und Wende: Grenze der Prognosefähigkeit" [Scholarship and the GDR's Transformation: Limits of Predictability], in *Einigung und Zerfall. Deutschland und Europa nach dem Ende des Ost-West-Konfliktes. 19. Wissenschaftlicher Kongress der Deutschen Vereinigung für Politische Wissenschaft,* Gerhard Lehmbruch, ed. (Opladen: Leske & Budrich, 1995), pp. 315–325.

4. For a sampling of their essays from which the phrases above have been culled, see Heimo Schwilk and Ulrich Schacht, eds., *Die Selbstbewusste Nation* (Berlin and Frankfurt am Main: Verlag Ullstein, 1994).

5. For the critiques see Thomas Anz, ed., *"Es geht nicht um Christa Wolf": Der Literaturstreit im Vereinten Deutschland* (Munich: Editions Spangenberg, 1991). I have covered some of these issues in *Dissolution: The Crisis of Communism and the End of East Germany* (Princeton: Princeton University Press, 1997), esp. chapter 6.

6. For my effort to ask why collective memory has become so major a polit-ical theme, see Charles Maier, "A Surfeit of Memory? Reflections on History, Melancholy, and Denial," *History & Memory*, vol. 5, no. 2 (Fall-Winter 1993), pp. 136–151.

Preface to the Original Edition

NO BOOK REALLY WRITES ITSELF. Occasionally, however, an issue seems to beckon urgently and overwhelms other writings in progress. *Auch wer das nicht begreift, was ihn beruft, der sei bereit:* "Even he," wrote Rilke, "who does not understand what summons him should be ready." When, in the summer of 1986, I caught up with the controversy recorded here, my sense was that the argument had serious consequences, both for historiography and for civic culture. Many of those engaged, moreover, were colleagues, friends, or at least acquaintances from a normally fraternal world of scholarship. Knowing participants on both sides, I have sought to be fair; that is, I have tried to summarize their texts as carefully as possible and to stick to sober interpretations of what participants seemed to intend by their often passionate words. I do not claim to be impartial, however. Readers will clearly understand that some positions seem repugnant to me. I find others not offensive, but certainly problematic. I have also tried to be critical of those whose views I share and admire.

Writing this book has led me to realize that issues of longer standing than the current controversy have been at stake for me. The historians' dispute has recalled questions I first confronted when, in the summer of 1955, as a sixteen-year-old exchange student of German-Jewish ancestry, I went to the Federal Republic of Germany and had to reconcile my own awareness of Nazi crimes with the decency, warmth, and affection of my host family. The question then painfully raised, and awkwardly resisted—what did you know?—has become less urgent as the generations have changed. And there have been sophisticated academic answers. But perhaps I have written this book in part because the echoes of that original silence still linger. This work is not intended as a bibliographical essay or as a contribution to the history of National Socialism, even less to that of the Holocaust. Rather, it represents an effort to think through problematic issues about the language and the use of history. I have been preoccupied with the limits of history, its reliance on analogy and comparison, and its relation to memory and to national identity.

Many people have provided important encouragement and assistance. Leon Wieseltier of the *New Republic* and Lewis Bateman of the University of North Carolina Press urged me to expand my original report on the controversy ("Immoral Equivalence," *New Republic*, December 1, 1986). West German friends and colleagues helped me collect the material that proliferated in the press: Marion Dönhoff, editor of *Die Zeit*, sent me her files of articles accumulated through December 1986; Hans Winterberg, director of the Goethe Institute in Boston, likewise had articles reproduced for me. Both helped me to keep abreast of a burgeoning literature. Hans Mommsen of the Ruhr University in Bochum provided copies of his essays; Hans-Ulrich Wehler of the University of Bielefeld sent me the manuscript of his own book *Entsorgung der Vergangenheit?* Jürgen Kocka, a former Bielefeld colleague, let me consult his files of the articles covering the debate over the planned German Historical Museum, on whose planning commission he played a major role. I have had innumerable conversations and exchanges about this controversy both in the United States and in Germany; Saul Friedländer and Jürgen Habermas were particularly helpful. Among the many people who provided constructive comments at oral presentations or encouraging responses and suggestions on chapter drafts are Carol Gluck, Leigh Hafrey, Arno Mayer, colleagues at the Harvard Center for European Studies, and two gifted former graduate students, Judith Miller and Steven Wilf. A current student, Timothy Franks, helped valiantly with the annotation; another, Günther Bischof, kept me informed about related Austrian controversies. I appreciated the chance to talk with those with whom I disagree, Joachim Fest and Michael Stürmer, as well as those whose views I largely share, at a conference sponsored by Lord Weidenfeld and Ann Getty's Wheatland Foundation at Leeds Castle in September 1987. Michael Stürmer is a colleague of long standing from whose earlier work I have learned much, and I have tried to take account of his protests about what he felt were earlier misinterpretations of his views. My wife, Pauline, and my children deserve special thanks for their unfailing patience while I wrote the following chapters.

In part this book concerns history as "reflective memory" (to use Jürgen Habermas's term). For reasons given in the chapters below, it is no accident that the theme of memory has become one of the most pervasive motifs in the social sciences, fiction, and the mass media in the past few years. One of the most painstaking recent testimonies to memory is the *Gedenkbuch: Opfer der Verfolgung der Juden unter National-*

sozialistischen Gewaltherrschaft in Deutschland (Koblenz, 1986), a two-volume collaborative work by the West German Federal Archives in cooperation with the Yad Vashem (Martyrs' and Heroes' Remembrance Authority) of Israel, which records the names, place and date of birth, and, so far as known, presumed place and date of death for the 128,091 traceable Jews from today's Berlin and West Germany who did not escape the Final Solution. Surely the most affecting memorials of recent years have been works, such as this or the Vietnam Veterans' Memorial in Washington, that can actually record the names of individuals among the masses of the slain. Because of the diffusion of other family names and uncertainties of family background, I can identify as presumptive relatives only the seven entries that bear my maternal grandfather's name, Krailsheimer, and come from his city of Nuremberg (Fürth). The youngest of the seven died at about age eighteen at Sobibor, the oldest at seventy-eight at Theresienstadt; the other five, aged forty to sixty, were apparently killed at Riga. I offer this book as a bridge between those unknown relatives who perished in obscurity and my children, Andrea, Nicholas, and Jessica. May it convey to them some of the problems that beset historians.

December 1987

The Unmasterable Past

Introduction

THIS BOOK BEGINS as the story of a controversy—what has become known in Germany as the *Historikerstreit,* the historians' conflict. The central issue has been whether Nazi crimes were unique, a legacy of evil in a class by themselves, irreparably burdening any concept of German nationhood, or whether they are comparable to other national atrocities, especially Stalinist terror. Uniqueness, it has been pointed out, should not be so important an issue; the killing remains horrendous whether or not other regimes committed mass murder. Comparability cannot really exculpate. In fact, however, uniqueness is rightly perceived as a crucial issue. If Auschwitz is admittedly dreadful, but dreadful as only one specimen of genocide—as the so-called revisionists have implied—then Germany can still aspire to reclaim a national acceptance that no one denies to perpetrators of other massacres, such as Soviet Russia. But if the Final Solution remains noncomparable—as the opposing historians have insisted—the past may never be "worked through," the future never normalized, and German nationhood may remain forever tainted, like some well forever poisoned.[1]

The issue is a difficult one. Suggesting the comparability of the Final Solution to other genocides opens the way to apologetics. It facilitates a literature of evasion. But in terms of historical method, some comparisons must be possible. Not only German nationalists but all social scientists must venture comparisons to understand even single events. What comparison is licit or illuminating? What comparison is tendentious or abusive? By the summer of 1987, such arguments had escalated into a major dispute concerning National Socialism, the role of history and national identity, the political agenda of the Helmut Kohl government, and, at its basest level, the political motivation of the contenders. And even after debate over the more specific issues becomes less passionate, the general questions it has raised will continue to divide intellectuals in the Federal Republic.

On the one side, critics—preeminently Jürgen Habermas, one of the

leading philosophers and social thinkers of the Federal Republic—
have charged that prestigious German historians were seeking to "relativize" the Final Solution as part of a new nationalist and conservative
search for a usable past. The accused—both those who produced the
original texts and their defenders—have responded that their critics
badly misunderstood history and were seeking to reinstall a repressive
leftist politics that had fallen into disrepute since the heady days of
student radicalism in 1968. So for both sides the controversy is one over
current politics as well as past history. And because all participants
have recognized that there can be no discussion of a national community without a confrontation of the darkest aspects of the national past,
the controversy is also about the German future. It resonates.

The following chapters report and reflect on the controversy. As a
historian, I am concerned most of all with the historical agendas and
approaches implicit in the contending positions. This debate, I believe, has signaled an important moment of German national self-
interrogation. It has produced the major discussion of historical responsibility and national consciousness of the last two decades. The
Historikerstreit alone is unlikely to determine the West German future
in any major sense, except for the personal enmities and methodological fractures it bequeathes to historians. Nonetheless, it reveals a wider
spectrum of loyalties and potential national orientations than were
earlier evident.

After almost forty years of West German democracy, writers on
Germany should no longer conjure up the menacing memories of the
German question on which postwar literature so often relied. The
Federal Republic remains a solid, workaday democracy. But the historians' conflict and its echoes among politicians hint that there may yet
be unsettling debate over West German strategy and alignments. It
may just be fortuitous that a bitter controversy over the legacy of the
national past has erupted at the very moment when a Soviet-American
agreement to eliminate intermediate missiles and the advent of a reformist Soviet leader are changing the variables of the East–West balance. These and other changes can exert a cumulative effect, however;
and the historians' controversy may have weakened inhibitions on
thinking through national options publicly. The revisionist theses may
yet prove to have undermined the taboos of West German civic culture. If it has become acceptable to think the unthinkable (or at least to
speak the hitherto unspeakable) about Auschwitz, then other debates
will also open. This is not to say that only the right will consider new

options. A feeling of being victimized, a yearning for national sovereignty may lead some conservatives in the Federal Republic to weigh a West German nuclear deterrent or their own arrangement with the East. So too, the hope of a neutralized Central Europe may beckon some of the left once again.[2] The debate over the national past will have served to license a debate over the German future.

These political issues, however, are not the direct concern of this book. I have addressed the historical questions in their own right. They provide enough important issues, including the following.

First, does the Holocaust, "the Final Solution of the Jewish question," have a claim to special horror in the annals of twentieth-century barbarism? If it is special, why? What are stakes of uniqueness for Germans? And from the other side (I shall touch briefly on this at the end, because it has produced equally anguished debates), what are the stakes for Jews and other victims?

Second—a question that is crucial to thinking about so much of European history between the world wars—in what respect can National Socialism usefully be considered as a specimen of a more inclusive political or ideological phenomenon, whether "fascism" or "totalitarianism"? What are the *political* implications of placing National Socialism in either of these categories?

Third, what are the *methodological* implications of assigning National Socialism to one category or the other? This question is analogous to asking about the comparability of the Holocaust. In each case, the issue is whether some more inclusive historical typology can validly encompass different phenomena. That is tantamount to asking whether historical comparison is justified. Does it have any legitimacy for reconstructing narratives of specific societies in specific eras? How does the historian or social scientist use typologies for comparative purposes—and when is comparison justified, when is it misleading or arbitrary? The problem, moreover, cuts deeper than just the legitimacy of overtly comparative methods. The historian of Germany as a field of study in its own right cannot simply shrug off the issue. Any social scientist or historian who aspires to explain the "meaning" of an event, even atrocious events, must find common categories of thought that link himself or herself and the reader with the subject. *Tout comprendre c'est tout pardonner* may not worry us if we accept that some terrible experiences will not be susceptible to historicist "understanding." If we cannot understand everything, we need not worry about pardoning everything. But, more to the point, can we understand anything without pardoning something? The current debate has re-opened crucial issues for history and the social sciences. Fittingly, it was German philosophers and historians at the threshold of the twentieth century who thought most persistently about these problems. It is remarkable that some of the historians who inaugurated the recent controversy seem not to have reviewed these earlier insights. They have hardly thought to climb onto the shoulders of the giants.

Fourth, how does this controversy fit in with the continuing argument over German identity and history? The issue is all the more timely in Germany because the current controversy has been accompanied by a government proposal to construct a museum in Berlin for German national history. The long gestation of this project has forced extensive debate over whether such a museum makes sense, how it must deal with National Socialism and longer-term trends, and what emphases should be placed upon differing aspects of national development. These recurrent questions must now be thrashed out within the context of a concrete legislative proposal.

The arguments raised by Habermas's charges and the museum debate are only the latest, moreover, in a long series of bitter disputes, each involving an effort to define national identity through history. Through the 1960s polemics surrounded Fritz Fischer's theses about German expansionism in World War I. Fischer's work and other studies of German imperialism and *Weltpolitik* raised the issue of whether Germany's international behavior was a result of class conflicts or of its geopolitical destiny as a "land in the middle." Half a century earlier the German historical community was divided over whether or not existence as a unified nation required renouncing ethical commitments to the international community. Questions of substance also implied controversies over method. At the turn of the century some scholars virtually sought to read their colleagues out of the profession over the issue of whether history might legitimately study society and community or should focus on state rivalries and ideas of high politics. Had not the triumph of the Prussian-German state implied the legitimacy of one sort of history and not of others? Historians in Germany have long understood that they legitimized national identity. They have conceded less frequently that they legitimize differing sorts of national identity. They have also not liked to admit that they have struggled for their own legitimacy as the curators of the identity they sought to articulate.

Are German historians different from their French or American or

British colleagues in this respect? Probably not. Questions of method, occasionally seasoned by biting sarcasm, have segmented French faculties. Recent British and American debates have equaled the German ones in rhetorical vindictiveness. Few Germans have outmatched the virtual accusations of cretinism thrown around in the English debates over the rise of the gentry. The intemperance of the disputes over Cold War origins in the United States was as bitter as the related polemics in the Federal Republic. Most recently, the flaws in documentation of a recent American work on the fall of the Weimar Republic generated a campaign for historiographic proscription and a controversy harsh enough to make the general press.

Nevertheless, debates in Germany seem to polarize the scholarly community more readily than elsewhere. The German community of historians is relatively small. It has often divided over methodological agendas. University places are plentiful enough to require frequent scrutiny of candidates, but few enough to make rivalries harsh. The implicit allocation of some places to historians aligned with left or right, and the involvement of the educational ministers of the federal states in each appointment also freight the choices. Although the allocation of places to adherents according to ideology is not so routinized in West Germany as in Italy, some traditional apportionment still persists. Some chairs (as in Austria) tend to stay red, some black. *Cuius regio eius religio,* the territory-by-territory establishment of Protestantism or Catholicism (updated to accommodate political as well as religious confessions) has been a way of doing business since the sixteenth century. Usually such partitioning of academic places among representatives of different approaches eases conflicts. But it can also harden party lines when conflicts intrude unavoidably. Most important, Germany has a very painful recent past. Analyzing it can never be easy, even for those young enough not to bear any direct responsibility. Historians must believe in national communities persisting through time. They feel the burden of the Third Reich as their own and seek to come to terms with it. From their confrontation derives much of the compelling fascination of the recent debate.

The controversy, however, has an importance beyond the community of historians, and it will count as part of a major intellectual debate in postwar Germany. It has raised issues that Germans have resisted facing for a long while, not merely questions of what the National Socialist experience was or meant (though these issues are momentous enough), but of what sort of national existence West Germany can enjoy. German intellectuals and politicians debated this question before they had a cohesive nation-state, and they must face the question again. In part the relation of West and East Germany provokes the issue. Of course, the Bonn government formulated a series of official answers; in the era of Konrad Adenauer it sought to claim sole legitimacy as representative of a wider historic German nation. The answer of Willy Brandt and Helmut Schmidt was different: both German states were partial representatives of a continuing nation. The East German response was simpler still: there was no continuing "nation" of Germans that glimmered beyond the two states. But these responses seemed official and stilted and had little impact on real consciousness. As the novelist Peter Schneider has written, "It's like watching the 1,011th performance of a repertory play in which actors and audience both stifle their yawns."[3]

The recent controversy over the legacy of the Third Reich suggests that there may be less yawning now. It reveals that the debate over the two Germanies captures only part of the issue of what national existence is all about. A whole other dimension had been ignored. No matter what the boundaries of the state, no matter what Germans are left outside its borders, what should a nation be after the Third Reich? What constitutes national existence: what sort of bonds does it entail? a commitment of reason and intellect to law? an inescapable community of geographic or linguistic fate? a web of unchosen connections analogous to family ties? These are inquiries about the quality of nationhood, not the boundaries of it. They have not been posed for at least a generation, that is, since the formative postwar years, when the spokesmen for the Federal Republic debated rearmament and entered the Western alliance.

Why should they be posed now? What events conspired to suspend a relatively unproblematic German approach to national existence such that painful and divisive issues erupted? On the one hand a series of commemorations—of Hitler's seizure of power and of defeat in World War II—provoked official statements that led to painful debates. But less circumstantial causes were involved. Mobilization of the peace movement in the early 1980s, activated by the decision to deploy intermediate-range nuclear missiles and by the truculent tone of American foreign policy in the first Reagan administration, also opened the national issue. Conservatives in the Federal Republic may have fitfully yearned for a less provisional nationhood, but so has the left. Some of its political and intellectual leaders have long envisioned a reunified and neutralist homeland. Nor has the left been immune from a potential for anti-Semitism, as was painfully demonstrated by the 1983 controversy over staging Rainer Fassbinder's dramatic portrayal of a Jewish slumlord. The current historical dispute centers on conservative apologetics, but the right did not open Pandora's box alone.

A generational reason may also be involved. As a German historian friend in his late thirties pointed out to me, the historians' controversy hardly mobilized his age cohort. They may have had vigorous opinions, but they did not claim the *feuilletons* (the cultural pages of the major newspapers) or take public positions. The conflict has remained the affair of those born before the end of the Third Reich. Perhaps the debate depended upon the final tug of a personally felt stake: participants needed either to redeem the honor of those they felt were maligned, or to make their own gesture of repudiation.[4] In this respect, the historians' controversy has been a last reveille for those whose lives might have turned out otherwise.

This sense of final opportunity may also be a factor in the recent surge of related controversies in other countries. "In the recent past, the memories accumulate of those who for decades could not speak about their suffering," Jürgen Habermas wrote in his second major intervention in the historians' debate; "and we do not really know whether one may really still believe in the redemptive power of the word."[5] What the Germans call *Vergangenheitsbewältigung*—mastering the past, coming to terms with the searing experiences of World War II and collaboration in Nazi crimes—has not been confined to Germany. The dispute over Kurt Waldheim's wartime service has led some Austrian historians to ask for reexamination of their country's ambiguous role after 1938; the trial of Klaus Barbie compelled yet another look at collaboration in France; the Demjanjuk trial in Israel seemed also to touch a chord. Each of these issues opened up wellsprings of emotion that one might have thought had finally been exhausted. Why this response? Was it the feeling that perhaps this would be the last occasion for direct review, the last chance to transmit memories, exact retribution, achieve reconciliation, or bear witness?

A final reason, I believe, helps explain why West Germany was ripe for the current dispute. For almost four decades the Federal Republic has lived, so to speak, by bread alone. It has pursued its economic vocation with success and single-mindedness. This was because the Federal Republic was founded as an economic unit: prefigured by the Allies' Bizone in 1947, rehabilitated in the Atlantic community as a valuable producer of coal and steel, thriving from the 1950s into the 1980s as a manufacturer of machines and chemicals, given a role in the Common Market as Europe's industrial stalwart, solicited by Washington as a financial partner. West German nationhood meant production. Nor was this a new phenomenon. In the period leading up to unification under Bismarck and arguably through the first decade of nationhood, economic union and expansion had served as sinews of German cohesiveness. But periodically the economic vocation fails to absorb German energies. Either growth falters or its successes no longer seem compelling. Then Germans have had to ask what in fact their national existence really means: an experience like that faced by Mann's Thomas Buddenbrooks, whose reading of Schopenhauer dissolved, at least for a brief interval, the certainties of his hitherto solid bourgeois life.

Perhaps we are seeing one of those collective self-examinations, the first sharply contested one since the Cold War seemed to compel the acceptance of fragmented nationhood and commitment to one bloc or the other. Not that the citizens of the Federal Republic are reappraising their foreign policy or international orientation—but they are debating what quality of nationhood is allowed them by their burdened past and by their fractured present. "Coincidence or causality: the hitherto undefinable tendency toward renewed nationalization in Germany reached its first important climax in the historians' debate," a Jewish writer living in Germany has written. "How could it be otherwise? After all the road to a nationalizing future by necessity leads via the past."[6] The economic difficulties of the 1980s may have helped set the conditions for this debate. But malaise can also spring from affluence as well as from uncertainty about the future. *Modell Deutschland,* the self-confident description of business-labor cooperation, high growth, stable prices, substantial welfare, seems less secure in the long run. But even if assured, it no longer justifies collective life as completely as it once did. For this reason, too, this controversy repays overhearing. As a debate about a difficult history it reopens the classic issues of a rich historiographic tradition. As the symptom of a present situation that has come to seem problematic for at least some, it makes West Germany interesting for more than its political economy. Ideas have come to matter at last, not just to identify some generalized advanced capitalist society, some allegory of OECD modernity, but to debate the historical possibilities for Germany—a real country in a specific time and place.

I

The Stakes of the Controversy

The Germans and their past: no really new theme there. But it is apparently not wearing thin; rather the opposite . . . the question that is now thrown open is: should the Third Reich be treated historiographically so that it no longer blocks the way to our past like some somber and monstrous monument, but rather itself becomes "history," past time, one epoch among other epochs? Or should it simultaneously remain as some admonitory memorial . . . because, in the speech of biblical simile, this stone actually became the cornerstone of the new beginning after the Second World War? And should history provide orientation, awaken pride and self-consciousness, and thus become a starting point for "identity" and "national consensus"—or is its task much more one of unsettling what is customary, throwing into question what persists, and sharpening our vision for the future?

—*Hermann Rudolph*

Bitburg History

Begin, where historical memory so often starts, with the dead. In this case just a handful of dead, whose honoring at the German military cemetery at Bitburg raised questions about the millions of dead left by the most recent German Reich and, finally, by the adversaries who combined to defeat it. At Bitburg, it will be recalled, Ronald Reagan was scheduled to lay a wreath as part of the fortieth-anniversary celebrations of V-E Day. The visit was intended as a ritual of reconciliation; it ended as catharsis manqué. It failed as ceremonial because it mobilized contrary impulses about history. Memory escaped from the control of its normal custodians—politicians who sought to play on it, and academics who lived by analyzing it—and became an unpredictable force as powerful, say, as economic discontent. The unquiet graves of the Palatinate awoke recriminations that caught up the vast audiences of the evening news in the United States and the Federal Republic, not to mention the official spokesmen for governments, veterans' and Jewish organizations, and the other constituencies crystallized around the traumatic events of the Third Reich and World War II.

Real history, painful memory, took its revenge for mismanaged pageantry.

For Chancellor Helmut Kohl and his political advisers, the American president's visit was intended symbolically to wipe away the last moral residues of probation under which the Federal Republic still labored. The pointed omission of German representatives from the 1984 D-Day commemoration still rankled. Was not West Germany the most consistently supportive ally in the North Atlantic Treaty Organization (NATO)? Was not the German Federal Republic as robust and as democratic as any other regime in the West? Had not the country sought collectively to recognize its historical responsibility by paying massive reparations to Israel and Jewish survivors? What good was served by harping on deeds that most West Germans had had no individual role in either perpetrating or even supporting? The true sacrament of reconciliation would be one that recognized the shared comradeship of arms, the sacrifices on both sides now to be hallowed as historical "tragedy."

Unfortunately, Bitburg turned out to be the resting place as well for forty-nine Waffen Schutzstaffel (SS) troops, and from this point the ritual unraveled. Chancellor Kohl felt that for the American president to back out of the visit would amount to a public disavowal. The late State Secretary from the chancellor's party, the Christian Democratic Union (CDU), Alois Mertes, a major spokesman for close German-American relations, represented the Bitburg area and did not want the visit shifted to a less encumbered gravesite. The president's advisers felt that either sloppy staff work or bad faith on the part of the Germans had placed him in an embarrassing position, so that he must either rebuff the Kohl government or face continuing protests at home. Elie Wiesel and other prominent guardians of Holocaust memories pleaded with Reagan not to travel to Bitburg.[1]

The Germans might insist on the difference among different segments of the SS—Heinrich Himmler's virtual state within a state that by 1944 embraced over a million members in very distinct divisions. The Waffen SS had served primarily as a military elite, shock-troop divisions used to stiffen the collapsing fronts as the Allied forces advanced. The extermination camps had been administered by the notorious Death's Head troops. Another major branch, the Security Services, had taken over civilian intelligence activities as well as the secret and political police, including the former Prussian Gestapo. Should not the remnant of Waffen SS forces lying at Bitburg be considered just as soldiers, entitled to share in the obsequies due the brave? The conservative CDU deputy Alfred Dregger wrote American senators that a cancellation of the visit would be an affront, and insisted later at home that all fallen soldiers were entitled to equal honor.[2] But then, it was asked, had not the Waffen SS been especially fierce in its reprisals? Might not the Bitburg graves hold remnants of the division that had massacred the inhabitants of Oradour-sur-Glane? (Indeed, Waffen SS units had been assigned noncombat guard duty at notoriously murderous concentration camps such as Mauthausen.) And in any case should the Americans undermine the determination by the Nuremberg tribunals that the SS as a whole was a "criminal organization"?[3]

Two levels of rhetoric characterized the Bitburg debate and the other statements commemorating the end of the European war. On the one hand, written speeches on both sides demonstrated acute concern for moral responsibility and for preserving a decent respect to the past. The Berlin address by the Federal Republic's president, Richard von Weizsäcker, was perhaps the noblest statement.[4] Weizsäcker has been especially eloquent on these themes, perhaps because he had the painful task of coming to terms with the role of his own father—indeed of defending him before the Allied tribunal at Nuremberg in 1946. Ernst von Weizsäcker was not a party member but nonetheless served the Third Reich as chief permanent official (*Staatssekretär*) at the Foreign Office from 1938 to 1943. The son has had four decades to reflect on the nature of that collaboration. On several occasions, most notably on the fortieth anniversary of the Reich's surrender, he eloquently recognized that Germans must always remind themselves of the Nazi past, that it continued to be a national responsibility, even if most current Germans were too young to have had even a remote role in putting Hitler into power or supporting him. Chancellor Kohl also delivered a sensitive statement at Bergen-Belsen that sanctioned no West German moral evasiveness. "Germany under the National Socialist regime filled the world with fear and horror. That era of slaughter, indeed of genocide, is the darkest, most painful chapter in German history. One of our country's paramount tasks is to inform people of those occurrences and keep alive an awareness of the full extent of this historical burden."[5] But many statements were more evasive. (President Reagan's notion that the SS boys buried at Bitburg were equally victims with those attacked by the Nazi state represented one response, to be echoed later by Ernst Nolte's view that Claude Lanzmann's film *Shoah* revealed it was probable that the SS camp crews "could also have been victims in their way."[6]) Or they reflected a sense that too much breast-beating was abject and counterproductive. Thus in May 1986, a year after Bitburg, the American ambassador, Richard Burt, told a German-American historical conference at Nuremberg that West Germany should not harp on the Nazi past but should think positively about postwar achievements: long, sustained, and well-distributed economic growth, a stable and open democracy, and international reliability.[7] His words only sanctioned what many had thought on both sides of the Atlantic. One did not have to be an aging German war veteran or unrepentant party comrade, grousing at a beer-hall table, to believe that *Mea Culpa* was unbecoming as a national motto. Bitburg, in short, became a sacrament of resentment, not of reconciliation.

This mangled ceremonial certainly did not unleash the historical controversy now under way. But it revealed a change in attitude—not a thinking about the unthinkable, but a debate over the hitherto un-debatable. Certainly scholars cannot deplore that fact alone. Neither genuine questions nor good-faith answers should be placed off limits. If historical investigation undermines the founding "myths" of one group or another, the scholar still believes that its members should revise their self-awareness and learn to live with complexity. Kant's nutshell answer to what constituted the activity of the Enlightenment is still valid: *sapere aude*, dare to know. When some knowledge is put off limits and received traditions are shielded from objective reconsid-eration, we enter the realm of hallowing and sanctification—perhaps one necessary activity for communities, but not to be confused with scientific activity. In the short run, knowledge tends to be subversive. Likewise, the validity of a historical interpretation or investigation is not to be measured by its political results. As Thomas Nipperdey, plainspoken but a historian of finesse, has written during the recent controversy: "The morality of scholarship demands that the arguments of those taking part be tested independently of their origins, motives, and consequence."[8] This does not mean that historians can find the Truth as if it were some grail retained at a scholarly Montserrat. His-torical truths will be plural and they will be political; they are answers to questions posed differently by different individuals, ages, and com-munities. They emerge from the triangle of relationships between re-searcher, data, and reader. In the social sciences, that triangle cannot be broken apart any more than quarks can normally be isolated from a proton. But the historian can usually eliminate what is not true, what does not accord with data, what stretches the normal rules of evidence and is based on no more than fancy or prejudice. What the Germans call *Wertfreiheit,* freedom from prejudicial assumptions and values, remains unattainable, but it still beckons asymptotically as a relevant norm for research and writing.

None of the reconstructions of the past discussed below, therefore, will be criticized for its author's politics as such. Granted, however, that history is not to be judged by the politics of its practitioners, this does not mean that the political contours of the debate are not interesting data in their own right. The political consequences of the debate, the starting points of the participants, thus become legitimate objects of study. Ideological preferences will shape what questions are posed, what evidence sifted and with what tests, and what formulations are likely to be offered. The observing historian can make this process into history itself. And as a historian, the observer is entitled to criticize if he or she finds that participants confuse their values with their results, if interpretations transcend evidence, or (what is almost universal) if interpretations depend upon the unequal weight given to different data. Most persistent historical debates do not finally turn upon evidence omitted, miscited, or newly found, but upon the significance to be accorded data. Ultimately, historians differ on what is important. And that is always a question of what is important for whom. So even for the process of understanding historical argument, of learning to live with a plurality of truths, one cannot avoid inquiries into historians' starting points. In West Germany, starting points, for politicians, journalists, intellectuals, and historians, may have changed—not suddenly, not merely because of an electoral swing or conservative comeback (*die Wende*), although such a shift in opinion has occurred in the Federal Republic as elsewhere in the West, but also because time has elapsed. Because the National Socialist past imposed so many limits on postwar discourse, compelled so much reticence, the passage of time must naturally corrode historical consensus. The fading of reticence must appear disturbing and often tasteless. Nor does the end of what some Germans have called the *Schonzeit,* the months in which hunting is prohibited (itself a specimen of that new tastelessness), guarantee that good history must emerge.[9] There is license for historiographic confusion as well as the opportunity for mere revision.

I use the term *Bitburg history* to refer to a multiple muddying of moral categories and historical agents. Not everyone discussed in the following pages is an offender, and it may not be possible to find any single spokesman who is an offender on all counts. Let the concept frankly stand as an ideal type of historical approach characterized by several assumptions.

First, as typified by President Reagan's effort at sympathy, Bitburg history unites oppressors and victims, Nazi perpetrators of violence with those who were struck down by it, in a common dialectic. Bitburg history courts the danger that is reminiscent of Hegel's remarkable discussion of master and slave in *The Phenomenology of the Spirit*. It confuses the formal, logical dependence of victim and victimizer (there can by definition exist no perpetrator without a victim), with a shared responsibility for the wrong committed. As Primo Levi has written, both victim and perpetrator seek to deny the memory of the crime: "we are confronted with a paradoxical analogy between the victim and the perpetrator . . . but the offender, and only he, has set and triggered it, and if he has come to suffer from his deed, it is just that he suffers; whereas it is an iniquity that the victim also suffers, as indeed he or she suffers, even after many years."[10]

Second, Bitburg history finds it difficult to pin down any notions of collective responsibility. Admittedly the latter notion is one of the most problematic concepts for ethics or history. It is hard enough to assign individual responsibility, which is one of the thorniest issues, say, for judges, biographers, and others who must confront personal action. Individual responsibility has emerged as an especially difficult concept to apply to agents of bureaucracies or military hierarchies. Obviously it preoccupied Europeans especially as they debated the appropriateness of postwar judicial sanctions and purges against collaborators.[11] It intervened as a problem in weighing the appropriateness of the Bitburg site as one for public commemoration. But it is still a somewhat different issue from that of the degree to which West Germany as a national society accepts responsibility for the Nazi past, and for how long it must acknowledge such responsibility. In what sense does collective responsibility exist? Jürgen Habermas's successive answers to that issue are considered in Chapters 2 and 5, below. The tentative and brief response, I would suggest for the moment, is that insofar as a collection of people wishes to claim existence as a society or nation, it must thereby accept existence as a community through time, hence must acknowledge that acts committed by earlier agents still bind or burden the contemporary community. This holds for revolutionary regimes as well.

Insofar as past acts were acknowledged as injurious, this level of responsibility stipulates that whatever reparation is still possible must be attempted. West German leaders have accepted that responsibility, not with consistently good grace, but to a major degree. Nor does this responsibility have a time limit. Responsibility for a burdened past can justifiably become less preoccupying as other experiences are added to the national legacy. The remoter descendants of those originally victimized have a more diluted claim to compensation. But like the half-life of radioactive material, there is no point at which responsibility simply goes away.

Now there may indeed be a difference between maintaining a decent quotient of collective memory and being obsessed by it. Few responsible Germans would deny the obligation of the former, but many think that what critics really want is the latter. Even former chancellor Helmut Schmidt argued against treating German history "only as a single chain of crimes and failure and neglect."[12] This issue underlies some of the current controversies. Bitburg history, I would suggest, comes perilously close to arguing that by now further efforts to encourage collective memory are obsessive. Ernst Nolte, a major scholar of fascism and a protagonist in the recent debates, has suggested that "talk about 'the guilt of the Germans' all too willfully overlooks the resemblance to talk about 'the guilt of the Jews,' which was a major Nazi argument." No one dared ask what would have happened had Chancellor Adenauer refused to visit Arlington National Cemetery in 1953 because soldiers were buried there who had taken part in the "terror attacks against the German civilian population." Less egregiously he argues that whereas normal past epochs, such as the Napoleonic era, can be reworked by historians but gradually lose their compelling hold, the Nazi past does not fade. It "seems to become more alive and powerful, not as model but as specter, as a past that is establishing itself as a present, or as a sword of judgment hung over the present." Has it really been only the insensitive who have sought closure, Nolte asks, so that the German past would no longer be radically separated from other national histories? Is there not some justification for resisting the demand constantly to lament the Nazi past?[13] Nolte has not been alone in this impatience. Other commentators have also implied an analogue of neurosis: fixation with earlier guilt apparently precludes a productive maturity. There is a difference, of course. The neurotic is obsessed by the guilt of longed-for, not committed, transgressions.

Finally, Bitburg history—again, an ideal type—has a third component. It suggests that the particular edge of Nazi crimes is less cutting given the general record of twentieth-century massacre and murder. Auschwitz may have been horrendous, but consider the atomic bombings of Hiroshima and Nagasaki; the conventional bombings of Hamburg, Dresden, and Tokyo; the Stalinist massacres of so-called kulaks, Crimean Tatars, Ukrainian farmers, blind folksingers, and old Bolsheviks. Recall the Turkish genocide of the Armenians, the Khmer Rouge's slaughter of fellow Cambodians. Are the Germans just getting worse marks because they mechanized the process? because gas has an aura of horror that bullets and bombs do not?[14] This issue is critical for the historian, for it raises the legitimacy of comparison, a tool he or she can never really renounce but can evidently abuse.

Thus Bitburg cast into relief fundamental questions about historical judgment. Judgment is obviously problematic, for it calls upon more than reasoning alone. It is an activity of mind and conscience, never entirely to be liberated from subjectivity, but crucial for aesthetics, for ethics, for politics, and consequently for history. Bitburg confused the possibilities for judgment along three dimensions. Once again it raised questions about individual responsibility for murderous acts. It revealed persisting disagreement over the degree to which a national community might be held responsible. And it opened the question of whether National Socialist Germany was itself so special a case in the annals of mass murder. By their inability to discriminate reconciliation from revisionism, the participants at Bitburg helped dissolve the inhibitions of historical discourse in Germany.

A "Polarized Historical Consciousness"

Early in 1986 the historian Hans Mommsen wrote of a "polarized historical consciousness" in West Germany.[15] By this he meant two different modes of interpreting the recent past. Mommsen did not say, nor did he allege later, that one was right, one wrong. He suggested that two different historiographic agendas were at stake, corresponding to different political mentalities. Conservatives in the Federal Republic, Mommsen claimed, have dealt with the Third Reich according to two successive strategies. Initially the National Socialist experience was "stylized as a fateful destiny, which though inescapable also allowed no concrete political impulses to emanate to the present."[16] In other words, it arrived fortuitously but overwhelmingly, then disappeared without a trace. More recently, according to Mommsen, conservatives have stressed a new approach. Instead of "bracketing Nazism out of historical continuity," they have sought to "relativize" it by stressing in what respects other countries have undergone comparable experiences.[17]

Opponents of this approach have sought to avoid relativism and have insisted on placing the Third Reich within the continuing stream of German history. As Martin Broszat of the Munich Institute for Contemporary History (Institut für Zeitgeschichte), one of the major historians of the Nazi state and close to Mommsen in his stress on its institutional continuities within German history, wrote in 1985, the challenge of placing the Third Reich in its historical context (what he called "historicization") lies in accounting for its contradictory elements. It involves demonstrating how administrative confusion, bureaucratic fiefs, and improvised decision making persisted alongside the claim to absolute control by the Führer. It requires understanding how elements of participation and dictatorship, or the capacity for efficiency and destructiveness, coexisted. Historical understanding also means revealing how the Nazis built upon, even as they transformed, established groups and interests and "to what degree the will of the Führer might set in motion from above only what was very concretely motivated from below." For Broszat, the old notions of a mass dictatorship, coordinated from above and based upon radicalized ideological adhesion, have yielded to a new picture of a regime that was opportunistic, populist, and authoritarian, hardly coherent or ideological. Even more unsettling, Nazi social-welfare projects sometimes resembled those of the Western democracies, while its domestic adversaries, no matter how brave, sometimes shared antiparliamentary and anti-Semitic assumptions. " 'Normalization' of our historical consciousness," Broszat finally argued, "cannot spare the Nazi era in the long run, cannot succeed only by circumventing it. Even the global rejection of the Nazi past is a form of suppression and taboo treatment."[18]

But certainly Ernst Nolte could not have disagreed. In a contribution to a British volume in 1985 he prefigured much of the argumentation that aroused so much clamor when published in the *Frankfurter Allgemeine Zeitung* a year later: "The Third Reich should be taken out of the isolation in which it still finds itself even when it is seen within the framework of the 'Epoch of Fascism' [that is, even in Nolte's 1963 comparative framework] . . . The demonisation of the Third Reich should be opposed . . . A thorough investigation and penetrating comparison will not eliminate the singularity of the Third Reich, but they will make it appear nevertheless as a part of the history of mankind which not only reproduced traits of the past in a very concentrated form, but which at the same time anticipated future developments and tangled manifest problems of the present."[19]

Thus two claims of historical understanding are at stake, two approaches to "comparison," two sorts of "normalization." The issue does not separate those who urge historical comparison from those who resist it. It initially separates those who want the Third Reich compared with other regimes—preeminently Stalinist Russia—from those who want its policies and support compared with the other epochs of a continuous German history. Let us call the one "horizontal" comparison, across frontiers; the other, "vertical" comparison, through time. Nolte has consistently championed the former; Mommsen and Broszat, the latter. Mommsen sees the former approach as serving a conservative political agenda that wishes to rehabilitate a German national identity, the latter as serving a critical stance that emphasizes democratic reform and commitment. In fact the politics of historiography is more complex than this initial distinction allows. Some forms of horizontal comparison have become taboo for conservatives in the Federal Republic, namely neo-Marxian or even liberal efforts to interpret Nazism and Italian fascism as authoritarian responses to crises of capitalism. Legitimate horizontal comparison, in the conservative perspective, emphasizes the commonalities between the Soviet regime and the Third Reich. Italian fascism is brought into the equation only if its parallels with Marxism are stressed. The political agendas of comparative history are explored below in Chapter 3. The point for now is not that some comparisons are correct, some false, but that they correspond to the historians' ideological starting point. Although comparisons can overcome subjectivity, they nonetheless must begin with it.

Just as the plea for comparison covers at least two historiographic projects, so the concept of historical "normalization" implies opposed interpretive programs. For Nolte, the idea implies that National Socialism can be treated dispassionately, nonobsessively, along with other nations' episodes of terror. Auschwitz need preoccupy the Germans no more than Hiroshima or antebellum slavery, say, haunts Americans. Normalization for Broszat and Mommsen likewise means that Nazism should not be treated as an extraordinary, metahistorical event. The Third Reich was not a parenthesis in German history but a substantive component. History thus teaches the need for a continuous democratic critique of German institutions. Hence Mommsen and Broszat regard those resisting this approach as nationalist and conservatives. Ironically, however, the other dissenters are often those Holocaust historians who remain fixated by the ideological ferocity of Nazism. For Mommsen and Broszat the crucial aspects of the National Socialist experience must be analyzed in terms of elites, bureaucracies, the coexistence of continuity along with violent change. Too great an emphasis on ideology gets in the way of their social-structural historiography.

Two factors caused all these issues to emerge in the spring of 1986: the aftermath of Bitburg and the anniversaries; and the fortuitous cascade of works by Nolte and the Cologne historian Andreas Hillgruber, which West Germany's most noted social philosopher, Jürgen Habermas, criticized as a conservative, nationalistic, and Cold War–oriented historiographic offensive. In effect, Habermas mobilized the critics of what he construed as an encroaching apologetics. One specific stimulus was the publication in early 1986 of Hillgruber's small volume *Zweierlei Untergang. Die Zerschlagung des deutschen Reiches und das Ende des europäischen Judentums* (Two sorts of demise: The shattering of the German Reich and the end of European Jewry). Hillgruber is a careful student of diplomacy and World War II; he has focused his documentary research above all on the strategic concepts that led Hitler to his fatal attack on Russia in 1941. He is admittedly conservative, but he cannot be suspected of harboring apologetic intentions toward Nazism or any problematic concerns about the Jews. Indeed in earlier works Hillgruber had even suggested that Hitler insisted on continuing the Russian war, after he had so evidently been set back in the winter of 1941–42, primarily to control the area most densely settled with Jews so that he could liquidate them. Hillgruber regarded Hitler as possessed of a monomaniacal ideological commitment to win *Lebensraum* and complete his genocidal project. Nor has Hillgruber ever sought to seal Hitler off from the rest of German history. Like the historians of the left in the 1960s, he has pointed out the harbingers of Hitlerian concepts in General Ludendorff's expansionary aims during World War I. Why should his book have aroused such concern?[20]

The major essay in this slim volume concerns the defense of Germany's East Prussian front in the winter of 1944–45. Hillgruber sought to justify the Wehrmacht's bitter resistance against the advancing Soviet forces. To convey the Wehrmacht's terrible mission in the winter of 1945, he claimed, is among the most difficult challenges a historian can face.[21] Hitler had given orders for impossible defenses of fortress cities. Soviet troops arrived with apparent license to rape and assault. Indeed it was the revulsion against this evidently sanctioned brutality that so alienated Alexander Solzhenitsyn, who was serving with the Russian invaders. Millions of German civilians and soldiers waited for occasional trains in bombed-out stations. Others sought to sail precariously across the Baltic from Danzig to Jutland or cross the narrow spits of land along the coast. Those who did not flee in time were expelled at the end of the war from Prussia, from the Sudetenland, from Silesia. Anyone who has spent any time in postwar Germany has listened to firsthand stories of these harrowing months. During my own first visit in 1955, I was told of the progress of a winter wagon caravan through the forests of East and West Prussia; in the summer of 1985, an archivist in her mid-fifties related her scarifying adventures as a child alone, somehow crossing the lines on the Baltic littoral, being whipped across the face by a panicked Polish farmer whose cart she sought to ride, harassed by self-important local Nazi officials for traveling alone as a youngster, and finally reaching relatives in western Germany.[22] Hillgruber rehearses these conditions in his essay essentially to defend the German army against the charge that by resisting Soviet troops they were abetting Hitler's work of massacring the Jews. He also wants to make their fighting explicable, justifiable, even in a period after many of their most decent colleagues had sought to assassinate Hitler. How could the mass of soldiers be defended for carrying on when the moral leaders had felt it preferable to kill Hitler and seek peace?

But this tragic task of defending the German population was not the only justification for the Wehrmacht's bitter fighting. Hillgruber claims that Stalin, Roosevelt, and, above all, Churchill had long harbored plans to dismember Germany. He cites the wartime concepts for dividing Germany and recalls British resentments against a vigorous German competition from the turn of the century on. In fact the Allies did not consistently plan partition of Germany. Although they agreed upon breaking up the federal state of Prussia, brief thoughts at Yalta about actually dividing Germany were firmly rejected, by Stalin as well as the Western leaders. Given the magnitude of the war effort that Nazi aggression had unleashed, the Allies' postwar plans for Germany seem rather moderate. The Morgenthau Plan for razing German industry appealed to Roosevelt only during the last six months of his life. The

Allies never ratified it, and it lasted only as one strand among several confused guidelines during the first year of occupation. British and American leaders did consent in effect by stages, from Teheran to Potsdam, to amputation of Germany's eastern provinces. De facto partition of the remaining territory was not a military objective, was resisted as official policy through the initial stages of the occupation. Some American policymakers, such as George F. Kennan and Walter Bedell Smith, envisaged it as a possibility soon after the victory. It is unclear when the Soviets decided that a divided Germany was more desirable than a united, pro-Soviet state. In any case, the increasingly unbridgeable division came about only with the Cold War after the occupation began.

Of course, the German military did not need to know what plans for a defeated Germany actually governed Allied policy to fear the worst. Given the vastness of the combat in the East, the fact that Germany had been able to mount so tremendous a military effort barely more than two decades after World War I, the ferocity of the fighting and appalling losses of Soviet soldiers, the systematic Nazi and Wehrmacht killing of Communist Party cadres, any soldier forced back through western Russia and Poland had to suspect that defeat meant catastrophic consequences. Under such circumstances it is comprehensible that some officers would act to get rid of Hitler and seek a negotiated settlement, and that others would fight as obedient soldiers to delay or perhaps fend off being overrun. What is curious is not that Hillgruber explicates these cruel choices, but that he demands that his reader take a stand: "If the historian gazes on the winter catastrophe of 1944–45, only one position is possible . . . he must identify himself with the concrete fate of the German population in the East and with the desperate and sacrificial exertions of the German army of the East and the German Baltic navy, which sought to defend the population from the orgy of revenge of the Red Army, the mass rapine, the arbitrary killing, and the compulsory deportations."[23]

In fact few historians or commentators, German or non-German, have belabored the "ordinary" soldiers of the Wehrmacht with their combat. To argue that the defense of the winter of 1944–45 was waged as a cover for killing Jews would be implausible. The crematoria at Auschwitz were dismantled by late November 1944; the Soviets had liberated the other Polish extermination centers before then. (In theory ordinary soldiers were not supposed to know of their grisly work.) The charge can be made that the German winter combat nonetheless preserved a monstrous regime and allowed prolongation of suffering and hundreds of thousands of further Jewish or other civilian deaths. "Life" in the concentration camps within greater Germany did grow crueler as deportations ceased: Anne Frank, like so many others, perished inside Germany only a couple of months before she might have been liberated. Moreover, forced marches of surviving Jews from camps shut down in the East to those still functioning in the West took the lives of tens of thousands, as did the deportations among what remained of Hungary's Jewish population in the last winter of the war. German courts sentenced 5,764 countrymen to death for crimes of opposition during 1944 and at least 800 from January to May 1945. Buckled to the guillotine or dangling in slow nooses, the victims probably identified less with the Wehrmacht than has the historian. Nonetheless, despite these tolls of the Third Reich's final months, neither historians nor Allied governments have laid these crimes at the feet of the army—any more than they have charged the German soldiers who delayed the Americans at the Bulge in December 1944 with a criminal act. It might indeed be argued that the Wehrmacht, short of fuel and bereft of air cover and engaged on fronts across Eastern Europe, France, and then the Lowlands and Italy, fought most impressively during the last winter of the war.

These considerations, however, do not force "identification" upon the historian. One of the historian's tasks is to recreate the choices that historical actors faced, to convey the objective and the perceived alternatives confronting his protagonists. This involves what Germans have called *Verstehen,* an empathic penetration that has been crucial to the German historicist program. But the *Historismus* to which Hillgruber evidently appeals also insisted on the plurality of viewpoints. It was developed precisely to counter the notion that some standards of judgment should be more privileged in history than others. Even by the historicist canons, the scholar must lavish hermeneutic or interpretive penetration upon all conflicting viewpoints and perceptions. For Hillgruber to say that he picks one at the cost of, say, the perspective of those who sought to rid the country of Hitler in 1944, or those, like Speer, who had at least sought to moderate the scorched-earth fanaticism of the 1945 defense, is a one-sided exertion. As such, no matter how great the *bona fides* of the historian (and Hillgruber's is not in question), the way can be opened to apologetics. And not only to historiographic apologetics; for in a country where the Resistance movement still seems to some a betrayal of the fatherland, Hillgruber's insistence on a choice between faithful soldiers of the Reich and the others must further devalue those who chose differently from the historian.

Hillgruber's little book raises other problems. Are the "two sorts of demise" really to be grouped as two sorts of one phenomenon? The destruction of the German Reich was of a state, a public, national community, admittedly with deep roots in East Central Europe, ancient settlements along the Baltic, into Masuria, Poznan, Silesia, and the Sudetenland. Its destruction was attended by loss of life for perhaps a couple of million and expulsion for over ten million. Hillgruber chooses the noun *Judentum* (Jewry) rather than the word *Juden* (Jews) to set the collective concept in parallel with that of the Reich. But the destruction of Jewry under the Third Reich was the destruction of individual Jews as much as of any corporate existence. The choice of language obscures the difference. Moreover, the small essay on the destruction of the Jews was published as a pendant to the larger piece on the defense of East Prussia. It must seem pallid after that emotional exercise in identification. The sufferings of Jews are not evoked: no sealed freight cars, purposeful starvation, flogging, degradation, and final herding to "the showers" parallels the accounts of the evacuation of East Prussia. If indeed these two experiences are two sorts of destruction, one is presented, so to speak, in technicolor, the other in black, gray, and white.

This is not to suggest that there is an anti-Semitic agenda in Hillgruber's work. Indeed Hillgruber insists how deeply anti-Jewish attitudes were rooted in Germany before the Final Solution. He suggests that even a non-Nazi, authoritarian regime would have deprived Jews of rights and imposed legislation similar to the Nuremberg laws. Hillgruber seems overwhelmed by the fury of Nazi anti-Jewish measures; they go beyond the historian's power of explication and belong to the realm of pathology.

Books take on a life of their own. Hillgruber did not intend his essay as a right-wing apologia, but it must abet a conservative orientation. It confesses a national identity; it rehabilitates the military vocation. Its allegations concerning arguments about Allied war aims recapitulate an older Prusso-German historiography, according to which the Wilhelmine Empire was pushed into war by British encirclement and frustration of legitimate national goals. Hillgruber laments that after 1945 Prussia and Germany were no longer able to fulfill their mediating role between East and West. This is the geopolitics of nostalgia. The

role of the Germans as a "bridge" or mediator represents another
conservative trope of the prewar era—one with both a Hohenzollern
and a Habsburg variant.[24] According to this nostalgic view, only the
old Central European empires prevented dangerous confrontation between the Western powers and Russian despotism; they alone kept the
volatile, lesser peoples from constant quarrels. Imposing peace has
provided a justification of empire since Virgil. But by what means?
Magyars and Austro-Germans united to rule their respective "barbar-
ians." A common interest in perpetuating the partition of Poland con-
joined Prussian and Russian interests under Bismarck (and briefly
under Hitler and Stalin).

The "land of the middle" is central to the historiography of the
conservatives. The recent controversy has remobilized—but also reworked—two venerable paradigms for German history (discussed in
Chapter 4). On the one side is a model of the *Primat der Innenpolitik,*
the primacy of internal politics: a scenario in which class divisions lead
to authoritarian regimes that in turn rely upon expansionist foreign
policies to reinforce domestic elites. With different emphases this
model informed Marxist analysis and what might be termed the social-
democratic historiography of the 1960s and early 1970s. It has served as
the implicit orientation of the journal *Geschichte und Gesellschaft* and
has been most identified with some of the historians drawing upon the
framework of "organized capitalism" in the mid-1970s. Some of its
adherents have insisted that German particularities produced particularly aggressive results. The Germans did not have a bourgeois revolution; feudal and precapitalist *mentalités* and bureaucratic forms persisted alongside the newer inequalities produced by capitalism. Junker
arrogance combined with capitalist hegemony.

The other major paradigm is the even more hallowed *Primat der
Aussenpolitik* (primacy of foreign policy), an approach undermined by
Fritz Fischer's critique of German expansionist war aims in 1914, further eclipsed during the reformist ebullience of the 1960s and 1970s,
then defended anew in the pages of the prestigious *Historische Zeitschrift.* Its champions include Hillgruber; another historian of Nazi
foreign policy, Klaus Hildebrand; and, most trenchantly, Michael
Stürmer. After able studies skillfully drawing upon the analysis of internal coalitions, Stürmer has increasingly insisted that Germany's historical fate has been molded as "land of the middle." The country's
alliances, its domestic structures, ultimately its division have resulted
from the seismic pressure of her great neighbors: Russia on the one

side, France and Britain on the other. From this perspective foreign policy thus tends to be a defensive reflex. That is why, no matter how maniacal Andreas Hillgruber may believe Hitler's ambitions really were, the Wehrmacht's defense of the eastern marches can still be envisaged *sub specie necessitatis.* The controversy over Hillgruber's book thus resumes disputes more than a century old: on the one side the establishment's focus on geopolitics and the primacy of international pressures—the historiography of Ranke, Droysen, Sybel, and the younger Meinecke; on the other side, the dissenting (at least until the 1960s) historical culture attributing foreign and domestic policies to the ramifications of inequality—the legacy of Marx and Engels, Mehring, and Kehr.

Did those earlier debates, it might be asked, have to remain so polarized? Must the newer ones remain polarized today? In fact there are what the Germans call *Ansatzpunkte,* intellectual footholds, so to speak, that would allow some differences to be overcome. The legacy of Otto Hintze provides one, that of Max Weber another—sociological and historical simultaneously. To be sure, the work of Hans Mommsen and Broszat remains attuned to the study of bureaucracies and authority, charisma and routinization. Their reliance on these concepts has led to its own debate about the nature of the Nazi regime and its sources of support. Nonetheless, the recent public controversy over National Socialism has not focused on their work, nor has it been informed by the legacy of Hintze and Weber. In fact it has been an atavistic controversy in methodological terms, the antagonists drawing upon forebears who loom as great figures in German historical writing, but not necessarily the most useful ones. Hillgruber has pressed into service a flawed historicism; Ernst Nolte has asserted a problematic Hegelianism.

Helping the Past to Pass Away: Nolte and Auschwitz

Nolte, who was trained in metaphysics, made his mark as a historian of political ideas in 1963. His major study, *Der Faschismus in seiner Epoche* (Fascism in its epoch),[25] examined the protofascism inherent in French reactionary thought (a scholarly project carried out in further detail by Zeëv Sternhell), the full-blown fascism of the Italian movement, and then its radicalized German "fulfillment." The three stages incorporated elements of thesis, antithesis, synthesis—with the German variant recapitulating the racism of Action Française, which had been largely absent in the Italian version. The book revealed that Nolte's objective was less to provide an analysis of causal development (ideas were causative by implication) than to try out various definitions of fascism until a sufficiently expansive and dynamic one could be reached at the end of the final case study. In effect, the three fascisms each embodied a partial realization of a fascist ideal type. Although the program was Hegelian, aspects of Heidegger's metaphysics also informed the approach. For Heidegger, the existence of things in the world represents a "falling away" (*Verfallen*) from being as such; mortality and perceived time embody the pathos of this ebbing from real being. For Nolte, each variant incorporated a closer approximation to the most fully developed fascism; the philosophical historian's task was to work through historical examples to arrive at that core. On the other hand, fascism did not exist as some Platonic ideal out of time. Since it emerged through historical stages, learning what it was meant following how it developed, studying the phenomenology of the movements as they presented themselves in their concrete circumstances, that is, in their epoch. The result was a history full of brilliant *aperçus* and comparisons backward and forward in time, illuminations of one movement in terms of the other two. Nolte's program imparted a coherence and even dignity to the stock of nationalist and fascist ideas that the often opportunistic contradictions of the leaders did not always reveal. And although the work did not rely upon party archives or other manuscript documentation, it did reflect broad reading. Historians interested in comparison were cheered by the defense of the comparative method, its brilliant application, and the demonstration that fascism—for all the differences among national movements—still served as a coherent concept. Indeed, many of Nolte's political allies today have spent a good deal of effort seeking to undermine the validity of a concept on which Nolte has always insisted.

In retrospect one can find in the original master work an emphasis on the kinship of fascism and Marxism that would serve as an intellectual gangplank to the right. For Nolte, fascism ultimately was defined as a radical reaction to the "transcendence" implicit in the modern world. Transcendence has been a key Nolte concept. It refers to a sort of metaphysical modernization, to the progressive emancipation[26] of humanity from existence as contingent creatures defined by family, village, workplace, or national loyalty—all the rich specificity of roles that conservatives celebrate—to being autonomous individuals, unconstrained by traditional roles—but atomistic and existentially lonely. The industrial revolution brought practical transcendence; the era of revolution brought political and spiritual transcendence. Marxism, in effect, made the fullest claims to transcendence, dissolving the economic constraints of capitalism. Nolte argued, as had other conservatives, that in fact the weak individual was not prepared to stand so radically denuded of the fabric of loyalties and roles that had been intellectually constraining but spiritually nurturing. Consequently, fascism emerged as an answer to transcendence—a program of counter-transcendence that could answer Marxism in its own terms: a counter-revolution that relied upon democracy to defeat democracy. For this reason fascism—and here Nolte seconded the Marxists—was not merely an antiliberal or anticapitalist program. It was the response to the most radical claim to transcendence, namely Marxism, and thus could not fully emerge until after the Russian Revolution. Simultaneously a counterprogram to Bolshevism and to nineteenth-century liberalism, it was keyed to a particular epoch in world history—that is, it depended upon 1917.

It is worth recalling how brilliant and intriguing Nolte's study appeared a quarter-century ago. Although it was not a study of institutions, it seemed to accomplish many intellectual tasks at once: it related fascism to both its liberal and its Marxist enemies; defended the overarching concept, staked an ambitious claim for the comparative method; took seriously what was obviously a momentous and compelling if often incoherent ideology; integrated along a continuum (but also kept distinct) movements that were verging on fascism but were not fully fascist—that is, demonstrated that it was ahistorical to see Action Française as fascist because a key aspect of fascism was precisely its epochal signature, its being tied to the interwar and post-Bolshevik decades. It also suggested that with the Nazi defeat and the division of Germany, fascism as such could not again be a real threat.

In light of Nolte's subsequent output, however, the work reveals problematic aspects. Nolte has increasingly insisted that communism and fascism are less radically opposed doctrines than twin products of the industrial and bourgeois revolutions—two revolutionary answers to the homelessness of the liberal age. This represents a subtle shift in the original emphasis.[27] Second, Nolte's intervening work of 1976, *Deutschland und der kalte Krieg* (Germany and the Cold War), incorporated several murky and suspect arguments. The target of this long historical rumination was the strident left-wing German student movement of the late 1960s, "the party of the GDR [German Democratic Republic]." Nolte was badly scarred by their militant, often abusive critiques before he left the University of Marburg for Berlin. He also felt that his left-wing colleague at Marburg, Wolfgang Abendroth, had signally failed to support his right to assert his views without harassment.[28] In *Deutschland und der kalte Krieg* Nolte sought a world-historical significance for the Cold War and defined it as "the ideological and political conflict for the future structure of a united world, carried on for an indefinite period since 1917 (indeed anticipated as early as 1776) by several militant universalisms, each of which possesses at least one major state."[29] In this polarized world Germany played a special role. Just as the Third Reich had incorporated the most radical stream of countertranscendence, so now, with the era of fascism closed, the two Germanies were bearers of the two streams of triumphant transcendence: of American liberalism and Soviet Marxism, respectively. In effect a truncated Germany had found, even in defeat, a world-historical role of even greater significance than its earlier mission of fascist countertranscendence. In the 1976 book Nolte seemed curiously obsessed with Israel—the nation of the former victims, whose army had attained territory and statehood while the state whose policies had contributed to Israel's birth, Germany, had to renounce both.[30] He accepted the necessity of Willy Brandt's *Ostpolitik* although he felt it represented "self-surrender" (to the subversive student movement at home) as well as mere territorial renunciation. However, the alternative of resolute nonrecognition of the East (the course chosen by, among others, the Arabs vis-à-vis Israel) had to be renounced because Germany was on the front lines of the Cold War.[31] In his most astonishing formulation Nolte called for a new historical awareness that could rehabilitate the reputation of the Bismarckian Reich as a moderate state (fair enough), but would further recognize that every major nation with claims to power (the United States and Britain excepted) has had "its own Hitler era, with its monstrosities and sacrifices."[32]

Nolte's recent works have increasingly insisted on these problematic interpretations. He cannot resist the provocative coupling of Israel and Nazi Germany: "We need only imagine, for example, what would happen if the Palestine Liberation Organization, assisted by its allies, succeeded in annihilating the state of Israel. Then the historical accounts in the books, lecture halls and schoolrooms of Palestine would doubtless dwell only on the negative traits of Israel; the victory over the racist, oppressive and even Fascist Zionism would become a state-supporting myth."[33] To be sure, Nolte insists that such a conclusion would be a travesty of Zionism, which originated as a resistance to European anti-Semitism. But if the comparison is flawed, why tease us with it? Should not the recent history of the Germans impose a certain reserve and sense of taste? Or is there a heavier implication? Nolte also asserts that "it can hardly be denied that Hitler had good reasons to be convinced of his enemies' determination to annihilate him much earlier than when the first information about Auschwitz came to the knowledge of the world," and he cites Chaim Weizmann's "official declaration in the first days of September 1939, according to which Jews in the whole world would fight on the side of England."[34]

Were it not for the fact that such ideas take on a tenacious life of their own, this charge would not be worth pausing over. It seems hard to believe that Nolte's major academic supporter, Klaus Hildebrand, even took note of this passage when he praised the essay as "trailblazing."[35] After all, despite the desperate rising of the Warsaw Ghetto in 1943, the Jews of conquered Poland were hardly in a position to "annihilate" Hitler when he moved to annihilate them. Nor was it surprising that after six years of systematic persecution of German Jews, their exclusion from professions, virtual reghettoization, and the Kristallnacht pogrom, Zionist leaders should support those arrayed against Hitler.

The suggestion that Hitler might be acting preemptively against the Jews did not find its way into Nolte's controversial 1986 essay in the *Frankfurter Allgemeine Zeitung,* "Vergangenheit, die nicht vergehen will" (The past that will not pass away). This piece was prepared for a prestigious annual conclave of intellectuals, the Frankfurt Römerberg Conversations, but Nolte found his invitation withdrawn before his presentation "for unknown reasons." The thrust of his argument, he claimed, was to put into context the National Socialist terror, to help Germans deal with their past in a more productive and less obsessive manner. Nolte cites the revulsion of one of Hitler's early colleagues, Erwin Scheubner-Richter, killed in the abortive Munich Beer Hall Putsch of 1923, at the massacre of the Armenians in Turkey: a reckoning "in an Asiatic manner far from European civilization." Did not Hitler actually fear, Nolte asks, that the Russians might seek to carry out such an " 'Asiatic' deed" against the Germans?[36]

It is a striking deficiency of the literature about National Socialism that it does not know about, or will not take account of, the degree to which everything the National Socialists later did—with the sole exception of the technical procedures of gassing—was already described in a voluminous literature of the early 1920s: mass deportations and shootings, torture, death camps, extermination of entire groups according to mere objective criteria, public demands for the destruction of millions of guiltless human beings regarded as "hostile."

It is probable that many of these reports were exaggerated. It is certain that the "white terror" also carried out fearful deeds, although there could be no scope equivalent to the postulated "extermination of the bourgeoisie." Still, the following question must be deemed admissible, indeed necessary: Did the National Socialists carry out, did Hitler perhaps carry out an "Asiatic" deed only because they regarded themselves and their kind as the potential or real victims of an "Asiatic" deed? Wasn't the "Gulag Archipelago" more original than Auschwitz? Wasn't class murder on the part of the Bolsheviks logically and actually prior to racial murder on the part of the Nazis?[37]

Following Jürgen Habermas's resounding critique of this article (see Chapter 2), Nolte's view was endorsed in August by the editor of the paper that printed his original essay, Joachim Fest, author of a major biography of Hitler and a good collective biography of Nazi leaders published in English as *The Face of the Third Reich*.[38] It was also supported by the Bonn historian of Nazi foreign policy, Klaus Hildebrand. How, Fest asked, could Habermas have overlooked Nolte's chief concern, the connection between Bolshevik and Nazi mass murder? To suggest that genocide is a widespread occurrence, Fest illustrated his piece with a photograph of skulls accumulated by the Khmer Rouge. And he quoted a Cheka leader that the bourgeoisie must be exterminated as a class. Not only were Nazi and Bolshevik murders equivalent, Fest implied, but also Hitler was probably influenced by reports of atrocities from Russia. In postwar Germany the core of truth in these reports gave Hitler's "extermination complexes a real context." Nazism, however, would get the worse press because it was more visibly "mechanized."

These charges are tendentious. It is not mechanization alone that makes historians pause over Nazi crimes, unless centrally issued policy directives, the pursuit of Jews all over Europe, and systematic internment followed by phased deportation count as mechanization. It is not a preference for pastoral slaughter that makes Auschwitz appalling.

Nor did the Russians prefigure the Final Solution in the early 1920s. Granted that both sides perpetrated widespread atrocities in the Russian civil war, the killings under such conditions were different from those carried out in the concentration camps. It is not clear that Hitler ever actually got detailed reports—indeed, Fest says only that he might have got them. Hitler himself spoke and wrote about the pre-1914 roots of his anti-Semitism, especially of his sojourn in Vienna, where he encountered kaftaned Jews and could learn from Mayor Karl Lueger's anti-Jewish rabble-rousing. Recent biographies have unearthed other potentially formative influences up through his recuperation from a gas attack in the hospital at Pasewalk.[39] But none of these investigations cites reports from the Russian civil war or the early Soviet use of terror. The direct quotation on which Nolte relies to allege the impact of such reports derives only from 1943. Nor do Nolte, Fest, and Hildebrand claim what might be more plausible, namely that the Stalinist purges of the 1930s provided the inspiration for the Final Solution, although Hildebrand later cited the Stalinist persecutions through World War II as the comparable experience.[40]

Nolte has since denied that he meant that the Bolsheviks intended physically to kill the bourgeoisie. "Annihilation of the bourgeoisie" need presumably have involved only the denial of a political role for a tiny minority and the nationalization of enterprises and in no way a physical liquidation. He emphasizes that Hitler went from ascribing class guilt to ascribing biological guilt. Presumably only the latter required biological extinction. Still, insists Nolte, the Gulag Archipelago is "more original" than Auschwitz because Soviet terror provided an example for the architect of Auschwitz, not the other way around. Granted there was a qualitative distinction between Auschwitz and Bolshevik terror, it is unacceptable to deny the connection.[41]

But the issue is not one of perceiving a connection. After all, many hallowed historical concepts rest on the commonality of mass movements, authoritarian regimes, the application of arbitrary power. They include "totalitarianism," "the age of the masses," "the age of dictatorships," "the era of world wars"—all typologies reminding us how human life in the first half of the twentieth century has been repeatedly hammered on the anvil of politics. Comparability is there to be discovered, or shaped, or sometimes imposed. The issues that comparison raises for historians are: What knowledge does it advance? What question does it help resolve? And—the issue cannot be avoided—whose concepts does it privilege?

To control the terms of comparison is to control the parameters of historical—and sometimes political—discourse. Historical interpretations must simultaneously be *political* interpretations in that they support some beliefs about how power works and dismiss others. But they need not be *politicized* interpretations; they need not be weapons forged for a current ideological contest. For leading adversaries in the contemporary West German debate, however, they have become politicized.[42] They are stakes in a struggle. This is what Nolte and the conservatives have recognized: "The situation of the Federal Republic, characterized by the non–passing away of the past, can lead to a qualitatively new and unprecedented situation in which the National Socialist past becomes a negative myth of absolute evil, prevents relevant revisions, and is therefore hostile to scholarship. Simultaneously this has the political consequence that those who fought most decisively against this 'absolute evil' were the most correct."[43]

But what is the struggle about? For Nolte, the bracketing of Auschwitz and the gulag means freeing historical consciousness from "the tyranny of collective thought." It means being able, as Hillgruber was able, to suggest that the historian might identify with the role of the Wehrmacht and not necessarily with that of the Resistance. It means lifting the burden of "absolute evil" from the German past and reconstructing a usable identity. It means precluding a leftist interpretation of twentieth-century history, rolling back what has been condemned as the self-righteous political and academic intimidation of the late 1960s. On a general level, this means sanctioning a political discourse that can accommodate anti-Western overtones. It opens the door for a conservative nationalism among the "successor generation" of West German politics.[44] Bonn is not yet Weimar and is unlikely to become so, but intellectually it has become a bit closer than it was. The historians on the right would deny this intent; certainly Michael Stürmer would insist that he seeks only a more decisive Western orientation. But in the historiographic depiction of Germany as a victim of great-power partition, planned by the Anglo-American allies as well as by the Soviets, some of the conservative historians justify those who may yet call for a new German *Eigenweg* (Hildebrand's phrase).

On a more academic level, the struggle to control historical comparison is not really about National Socialism, but about the last twenty years of German cultural politics. The left has long since lost whatever power it might have had selectively to control historiographic agendas, university politics, evaluation of examinations, professorial appointments, or general cultural reputations. Only some of the historical categories on which the left relied in its earlier effort to shape historical discourse still stand, like deserted garrison towers, no longer able to dominate the historiographic landscape but provocative reminders of an earlier claim to hegemony. Is there not the danger, too, that, left to stand, they might one day serve again as strongholds? Even though unoccupied, should they not be razed? The *Historikerstreit* has really been a struggle over those remaining towers.

2

Habermas among the Historians

I consider the debate opened by Habermas to be a misfortune. The terrain of scholarly dispute is very sensitive, the moral and political commitments are strong, the subtle distinctions and attempted boundaries collapse in confusion, the German penchant for ultimate thoroughness triumphs. Rifts are torn open; the historians' guild, along with the public, becomes polarized. The ground on which scholarship and liberal culture stand is thin enough. For that reason we need the virtues of history, sobriety and distance; we need pluralism beyond moralistic suspicion and political partisanship. We need pragmatism against moral absolutism, and precisely for moral purposes.

—*Thomas Nipperdey*

Conservative Recovery

Nipperdey's disillusioned judgment was certainly correct in one sense. Controversies require at least two sides. Had Jürgen Habermas not seized upon the Hillgruber book and then upon Ernst Nolte's essay, Germany's "polarized historical consciousness" might not have exploded into warfare on the cultural pages. The historians themselves had not responded with particular indignation. Indeed if there was any noticeable intellectual trend among them in the decade preceding the controversy, it was a broad recovery of conservative interpretive possibilities.

The last bitter controversy had broken out early in the 1960s, when diplomatic historians turned to the analysis of internal elites to account for German imperialism and aggression. Fritz Fischer's original exposé of German war aims in 1914 widened into a critique of the Wilhelmine social order and eventually into an attack on the academic elites.[1] But the process of historical revision usually leads to a blurring of harsh alternatives. By the 1970s, diplomatic historians concerned with the eras before Hitler stressed the complicity of other states and not just German expansion. Historians such as Hillgruber, Hildebrand, and Lothar Gall, author of a successful new biography of Bismarck and editor of the *Historische Zeitschrift*, were openly criticizing the social history that had seemed so triumphant a decade earlier. They stressed traditional approaches to political decision making and the history of international relations, the old *via maesta* of German historical studies. Efforts to explain foreign policy as an outcome of domestic struggles were condemned as modish or leftist. Certainly it was legitimate to argue against advocates of the "primacy of domestic policy" that Berlin's response to international crises might have had its own momentum and did not represent just a manipulative response to working-class advances at home. But conservative historians such as the elderly Walther Hubatsch or the then young Klaus Hildebrand did not merely insist on a methodological point. They also claimed to discern influences from East Germany or the student movement's extraparliamentary left.[2]

Political attacks in general grow more strident as an adversary falters. By the mid-1970s, despite vigorous rebuttals, the "critical" historians, those deemed to be on the historiographic left, were no longer producing the major studies that had opened up the discipline in the 1960s. The dissidents of the previous decade, such as Fritz Fischer and Immanuel Geiss, were no longer making the same impact. (Indeed Geiss was evolving politically and would support the conservatives in the Habermas dispute.) Alternative approaches in the classic arena of diplomatic history, such as Heinrich Boehme's political-economy analysis of unification or Hans-Ulrich Wehler's study of imperialism, had no sequel.[3]

This does not mean that methodological trends that seemed so exciting in the 1960s have been abandoned. In part they have simply become established enough to lose their political edge. Their advocates no longer imply they offer a privileged access to historical truth. Furthermore, the problems afflicting the West (though milder in Germany than elsewhere) through the 1970s—a decade of persisting inflation and growing unemployment, of disillusion with détente and of intensive arms competition—suggested that the realm of international relations could not easily be analyzed just as a function of domestic politics and society. The ascendancy of Kissinger and Brezhnev abetted the revival of Ranke.

A generational transition was also at work, its tempo imposed first by the renewal of academic culture soon after World War II, then by the great expansion of the university system in the 1960s. Some of the major historians who had helped reconstruct the profession after 1945 were passing from the scene: the late Werner Conze, who had encouraged investigations in social history, relinquished his Heidelberg chair in the mid-1970s. The late Theodor Schieder, concerned with the comparative development of nation-states and teacher for a remarkable cohort of successors, retired in 1970. These and other "elder statesmen" were certainly conservative by temperament. But they never had an outright ideological ambition for history. Had they still been active, it is doubtful that they would have pursued so concerted a campaign for "normalization" of the past or been so preoccupied with shaping a receptive public opinion.

Another impetus to conservatism was the delayed effect of the roughly fourfold expansion of university positions from about 1960 to the mid-1970s. The new infusion initially awarded perhaps half the chairs to academics in their mid-forties or younger, but then tended to delay subsequent rotation.[4] The outspoken recruits of social history or sociologically based analyses have become professorial executives of a less ebullient establishment. Some of them no longer press their claims with their earlier youthful enthusiasm. Quantitative history and demographic history found their niche but did not sweep all before them. The major "social democratic" typology of "organized capitalism," identified largely with the Bielefeld historians Wehler, Jürgen Kocka, and Hans-Jürgen Puhle and their Freiburg colleague Heinrich August Winkler during the 1970s, had been accepted for certain analytical tasks, and its champions no longer defended it with the same claims for universal validity. Intellectual support for their critical approach (exemplified most sharply by Wehler's harsh assessment of the German nation-state from 1871 to 1918)[5] from outside Germany had always been important. Cross-connections with America—their own studies in the United States, the influence of émigré Hans Rosenberg, the earlier connections between Charles Beard and Eckart Kehr—had exerted a formative influence. Now the support from abroad was undercut, as younger British historians, especially, criticized the model of Germany's supposedly persistent premodern social structure and resulting divergence from the West (*Sonderweg*).[6]

Sometimes, too, new approaches could accommodate conservative agendas. Social history research flowed into *Alltagsgeschichte*—the history of everyday life, an effort to capture the experiences of ordinary women and men, often through oral history. *Alltagsgeschichte* could occupy those young researchers who two decades ago would have been militants on the left; but it could equally serve conservative advocates of "normalization." Building upon anthropological and ethnographic models, the historians of everyday life often forswore imposing any value systems that their subjects did not develop: workaday life in the Third Reich could be remembered as no more than workaday life. Hierarchies of domination and exploitation that had impressed social historians through the 1960s might be evoked by young researchers concerned with the collective memories, say, of the working class. But historical ethnographers, armed only with a tape recorder and a sympathetic ear, could easily construct a reassuring pastoral past: call it, after Edgar Reitz's impressive cinematic rendering of a half-century in the life of a Palatinate village, *Heimat* history.[7]

It would be misleading to discern a coherent ideological orchestration of the new trends. Some historians openly insisted on the political stakes of contending interpretations. But given the usual process of historical argument and revision—the professional rewards for superseding the last wave of interpretation—it did not take a right-wing "project" to accumulate scholarly findings with conservative implications. Nonetheless, to many moderate historians it appeared as if the conservatives felt that their moment had come to shape historical consciousness. *Praeceptor Germaniae* has always been a tempting role and would beckon all the more once Chancellor Kohl expressed a keen interest in German history. Even before Kohl's accession, what by the late 1970s was termed the *Tendenzwende,* or shift in trend, was hard to resist. Similar conservative tendencies have marked other disciplines, and the influences spill over. The undermining of Keynesian theory has had a major impact on the interpretation of the Weimar Republic. Knut Borchardt, the economic historian at Munich, challenged received wisdom on the left by suggesting that Chancellor Heinrich Brüning—long criticized as feckless and reactionary for his deflationary policies during the depression—had had no real alternatives. No Keynesian salvation for the Weimar Republic, Borchardt insisted, had been possible. German workers had priced themselves out of world markets. Because businessmen saw the republic as inherently structured in favor of the organized working class, it was almost inevitable that they should aspire to supplant the regime. Here was a historical treatment that perfectly suited the new economic-policy preoccupations of the late 1970s and early 1980s. The demands of an international economy beyond the control of policymakers, the diagnosis of excessive wage levels as the underlying difficulty, the burdens of public spending and the dangers of an "overloaded democracy," the general mood of iron constraint: the bugaboos of 1980 had all shaped the disasters of 1930. Borchardt's approach acutely discomforted the historical defenders of Weimar democracy and of the welfare state in general.[8]

The historiographic scene in Germany during the last years has thus been a complex one. Traditional approaches have found new and powerful advocates. Enthusiasts for social science approaches have sometimes insisted upon findings that would earlier have counted as conservative or nationalist. Historians once associated with the left have enjoyed a certain refulgence and sometimes settled into a rather whiggish centrism. By and large, pluralism has prevailed. It was not always accepted gracefully, indeed had to be fought for. (By the late 1970s Hans-Ulrich Wehler felt that a mean-spirited resurgence was inhibiting "public argumentative discussion" and cowing younger historians. Departments had fought bitterly over appointments.[9] Conservatives, for instance, also resented Wolfgang Mommsen's vigorous administration of the prestigious German Historical Institute in London. And the edgy disputes in Germany sometimes found partisan echoes among the historians of Germany in the United States or Britain.) Nonetheless, there was variety enough by the mid-1980s; a hundred flowers had bloomed. Hence although different approaches might be exploited for political argumentation, moderate conservatives such as Nipperdey could take comfort from the fact that not every methodological choice, not every scholarly achievement, had to have a partisan implication. Nipperdey's own skillful work on the political culture of the nineteenth century, Reinhart Koselleck's contrapuntal examination of legal thinking and institutional realities in the late eighteenth and early nineteenth centuries and his continuing history of key political concepts, Klaus Tenfelde's textured studies of coal mining communities transcended narrow agendas and enriched the discipline.[10] The ground for scholarship may have been less thin than Nipperdey later claimed. (Even as he stressed vulnerability, he also pointed out an underlying democratic commitment. Of course, since no real political alternative was feasible, such a commitment hardly "committed" any substantive stance.)

It is tempting to conclude that the Federal Republic's historical community was enjoying what in the United States has been termed a postrevisionist consensus—or, if not a consensus, at least an unresolved tug-of-war. Chancellor Kohl's appeal to historical awareness, the projects for history museums in Bonn and Berlin (discussed in Chapter 5, below), brought debate but constructive engagement from conservatives and progressives. Clio was enjoying, if not a tranquil moment, at least the stimulus of an open market in the Federal Republic. Such trends were hardly unique to Germany. They also characterized developments in France, Britain, Italy, and the United States. (One of the sad legacies of the Third Reich has been that much of postwar German historiography has been reactive—thorough, sometimes daring in application, but still attendant upon innovations abroad.) If there has been a historiography of "the shift," *die Wende*, it has prevailed throughout the West.

Habermas's Indictment

Did Habermas, as Nipperdey suggests, really throw an apple of discord among the historians? Certainly his challenge to what he saw as an encroaching apologetics was written with verve, irony, and a sometimes provocative reading of the texts. It was also written by an outsider. Those stung by his polemic carped that if he were a history student he would certainly fail his exams; he could never have sat through a history seminar. True enough, Habermas is not a historian—but historians have never claimed a hermetic discipline. To distort what an opponent has written violates intellectual argument in general, not just the historians' supposed reverence for texts. In any case, as West Germany's leading contemporary social philosopher, Habermas has long been concerned with problems of history, politics, language, law, and economics. He is at home with English, has taught in the United States and is appreciative of its liberalism, yet continues a clearly German tradition of philosophizing. His ideas draw upon Kantian normative liberalism and tackle anew the conundrum of in what sense one can guarantee objectivity in the social sciences. Though sometimes described as an heir of the Frankfurt school, Habermas tends to reject much of the critique of the Enlightenment developed by Max Horkheimer and Theodor Adorno. Discussing the mood of reaction he saw prevailing by the end of the 1970s, Habermas did not just take the right to task. He also distanced himself from tendencies toward romantic irrationalism among a disillusioned left.[11] In the current dispute Habermas has allowed no ambiguities about the Western Enlightenment tradition, renewed in the United States:

> The political culture of the Federal Republic would be worse today if it had not adopted impulses from American political culture during the first postwar decades. The Federal Republic opened itself for the

first time to the West without reservations; we adopted the political theory of the Enlightenment, we grasped the pluralism which, first carried by religious sects, molded the political mentality, and we became acquainted with the radical democratic spirit of the American pragmatism of Peirce, Mead, and Dewey.[12]

This "opening without reservation" is what Habermas has praised in the recent dispute. The offending historians, on the other hand, represent a dangerous current of neoconservatism in which

The modern world appears as the world of technical progress and capitalist growth; all social dynamic, which is ultimately based on private investments, is modern and desirable, the motivational resources on which this dynamic thrives are in need of protection. Danger lies in cultural transformations, motivational and attitudinal changes, and shifts in patterns of values and identities, which are attributed to the entry of cultural innovations into more or less traditional forms of life. Therefore the legacy of tradition has to be preserved as far as possible.[13]

Since Habermas engaged the revisionist historians as an extension of his quarrel with the West German neoconservatives, much of his rhetoric echoes his earlier critiques. Moreover, the responses he has incurred from Hillgruber and Hildebrand seem tailor-made to confirm his own diagnoses, blaming, in effect, the intellectuals for a disorientation of national values.

The other major thread of Habermas's ideas has been a post-Marxian analysis of the sociology of knowledge. For Habermas, all forms of inquiry have their respective *Erkenntnisinteresse*, their cognitive stake or "interest" in the knowledge they seek. In his major work of the late 1960s, *Knowledge and Human Interests*, Habermas differentiated three spheres of inquiry, each with its characteristic interest. The empirical and analytic sciences maintained a technical cognitive interest that sought to master the outer world. The hermeneutic and historical sciences sought to reconstruct "meaning" and develop a "practical" interest in forming the good society and advancing communication. Finally, Habermas identified a self-reflective search for knowledge with an interest in "emancipation," that is, with an "interest" in furthering the conditions of free inquiry needed for its own progress.[14] Habermas's categories suggested that some approaches to knowledge were superior to or more objective than others if the interest served was that of emancipation, the development of a mature autonomy and responsibility (*Mündigkeit*), an attainment that has beckoned German thinkers on the left since the Enlightenment. *Knowledge and Human Interests* provoked enthusiasm and critique, and Habermas progressively revised his position over more than a decade, finally to reach a new synthesis in his 1981 *Theorie des kommunikativen Handelns* (*Theory of Communicative Action*).[15] Here the starting point is no longer the undeservedly privileged perspective of the epistemological subject, the knower, but the more general conditions governing language and communication. Habermas, however, still envisages an ascendant progress of knowledge and insight; still proposes that certain conditions of discourse allow more objective knowledge and assure more rationality than do other, more constrained conditions. But how does Habermas escape the long-standing difficulties of trying to guarantee one group of intellects or policymakers a privileged epistemological stance—whether Plato's philosopher king, or Hegel's bureaucrats, or Mannheim's "free-floating," non-class-affiliated intellectuals? What guarantees the superior insight of the philosopher's friends?[16] Whether successfully or not, Habermas seeks a firmer ground by focusing, not on the individual thinker's qualifications for objective knowledge, but on the conditions governing the community of language users and the arena of discourse. Emancipatory knowledge emerges only out of public discussion unconstrained by political pressure or economic power. Habermas's work presupposes that knowledge and politics must be shaped in conversation, not in isolation. For Habermas, any serious partner in a conversation presupposes *ipso facto* that rational discourse is possible, that society can develop a notion of rational consensus—agreement on how to argue, if not over final results. Such conditions assume further that groups and participants can develop an ideologically undistorted insight into their needs.[17] Overcoming such deformations, imposed as they are by powerful monopolies, including the mass media, or by general tendencies such as consumerism and a narcissistic culture, or by the nationalism revived by the conservative historians, is difficult; but Habermas's beliefs are characterized by an evolutionary optimism. On the one hand, communities of discourse, public spheres of opinion, are continually widened. On the other hand, societies can develop higher levels of collective learning, and not merely scientific, but moral knowledge. The creation of a bourgeois reading public brought one epochal opening, which he described in an early, classic case study.[18]

Habermas has been a major representative of what is undoubtedly

the preeminent thrust of European social thought in the last generation: a reorientation which originated with interwar intellectuals, but
which gained ground on the left, at least, through successive waves of
disaffection from Soviet Marxism. The philosophical counterpart of
this postwar trend involved a redirection of social and philosophical
thought. The critical focus shifted from class structure in its own right
to the conditions governing communication and speech as fundamental attributes of political society. To be sure, philosophy as a formal
discipline had long been preoccupied with linguistic analysis. But in
contrast to the heirs of Wittgenstein, Habermas has refused to accept
language as a gamelike analogue in which meaning, ultimately, must
be anthropologically derived from an almost tribal context of usage.
And in sharp contrast to Michel Foucault and French historians he has
resisted viewing language as an instrument of power and domination.
Nor has he accepted the claims of semiotics or deconstruction, in
which the fascination of language derives from its opaque testimony to
man's irrevocable separation from some primal community.[19] Foucault, Derrida, Heidegger, and Nietzsche he views as intellectual sirens
of a disturbing countertradition that undermines the Enlightenment
project. This earnest, progressive standpoint has led to his most recent
philosophical dispute with Jean-François Lyotard, who has criticized
Habermas for seeking to provide a new "metanarrative," that is another grand didactic scheme of an unfolding rationality, whether in the
spirit of Hegel, Marx, or Freud. According to Lyotard, the postmodern mind rejects these unfounded and unnecessary appeals, and
Habermas appears as slightly anachronistic, unresponsive, for instance,
to an art that is not anchored in a metanarrative of reason.[20]

Habermas honed his views of history in a major debate with the
conservative philosopher of hermeneutics, Hans-Georg Gadamer. In
line with a long German tradition, whose nineteenth-century elabora-
tion culminated in Wilhelm Dilthey, Gadamer insisted that historical
interpretation rested upon "understanding" (*Verstehen*), the historian's
effort to penetrate his subject's value system and to perceive it, so to
speak, from the inside out. This is the tradition to which Hillgruber
appeals when trying to justify the Wehrmacht's combat in the winter of
1945. The key problem for hermeneutical interpretation is usually construed as establishing the meaning of words and acts for one's historical subject. For Gadamer, interpretation is not problematic (it is an act
between conversing adults, one of whom is usually dead); but understanding what it involves is. Following Heidegger, Gadamer insisted

that the necessity of hermeneutical interpretation emerged from the finitude and historicity of human existence. The shared language of tradition—the process of conducting a conversation with the subject by treating the text he or she left behind as a question to be answered—guaranteed adequate understanding. Habermas sympathized with Gadamer's stress on dialogue, and he certainly felt that hermeneutical understanding was one of the basic forms of knowledge. But he feared that Gadamer's emphasis on deriving meaning from the text on the basis of shared "tradition" amounted to surrendering unreflectively to the prejudices of the protagonist. It recapitulated the historicist sin of acknowledging only those values inherent in the object of historical study and abnegating any possibility of a critical perspective. Instead, Habermas called for "critical reflection," just as he has called upon "reflective memory" in the recent controversy. Moreover, Habermas argued, understanding social and economic structures allows us to curb hermeneutical excess; we need not just interpret symbol systems but can cross-check them by analysis of social and economic and political arrangements.[21]

The early debate with Gadamer suggested that Habermas was bound to be wary of any hermeneutical search for identity. Historicism (*Historismus:* the demand for *Verstehen* and empathy) had to be suspect, especially after justifying German power politics for over a century. Certainly Habermas was provoked initially by the substance of what he read, by the message, not the methodology. Nonetheless, the new historical accounts exemplified the possibilities for abuse he had earlier discerned in theoretical debate. Scathing though his attack was, Habermas's vigorous statement did not represent any new militance on the left. If the ideological spectrum had become wider, the shift was on the academic right. The climate of opinion Habermas wished to guarantee no longer retained any post-Marxian or even Frankfurt school residues. What he saw menaced was the liberal-democratic community of the West—paradoxically, however, what Michael Stürmer also claimed to be defending.

Stürmer is a historian, formerly at the University of Erlangen and now the new director of the government-financed think tank, the Ebenhausen Foundation for Science and Policy (Stiftung Wissenschaft und Politik), who has written trenchant analyses of Weimar politics, the Second Empire, and even eighteenth-century furniture guilds.[22] After social contacts helped enable him and Chancellor Kohl to discover a shared concern for history, Stürmer helped serve as a speechwriter until, reportedly, Chancellery officials grew wary of his intrusion. Stürmer starts from the hypothesis that the Federal Republic does not have a readily available historical identity: the interest in historical museums, centennial expositions, even such kitsch as the televised "Holocaust" spectacular, testifies to the public's longing for orientation. Whether "the search for a lost past" reflects a positive reawakening of a historical sense and a search for traditional culture or whether it arises from contemporary insecurities is not crucial. "Both determine the new search for an old history. Loss of orientation and the search for identity are brothers. But anyone who believes that this has no effect on politics and the future ignores the fact that in a land without history whoever supplies memory, shapes concepts, and interprets the past will win the future."[23]

According to Habermas, Stürmer's quest for historical identity (or orientation)[24] provided the unifying thread for the revisionist assessments of the Third Reich offered by Nolte and Hillgruber. History for Stürmer, Habermas wrote, amounted to a sort of spiritual insurance payment to compensate modern man for the damages entailed by modernization. He cited Stürmer's belief that even academic history was driven by collective, largely unknown needs for an endowment of spiritual meaning (*innerweltliche Sinnstiftung*). And he dismissed the significance of Stürmer's simultaneous concession that history had to apply scholarly rigor and shun mythmaking. The historian, Stürmer wrote, had to walk a narrow path in his search for spiritual significance and his effort to demythologize. Habermas hardly felt that the offending historians had kept to the straight and narrow.

Why did Stürmer's formulation of the historian's dual task excite so critical a reaction? After all, at the same time that Stürmer was urging historians to provide societies with an underpinning of meaning, the then president of the American Historical Association, William H. McNeill, devoted his presidential address to a plea for restoring the role of myth in history.[25] Many (including this author) felt uncomfortable with such an appeal but it created no anguished reaction. (Not that historical myth has not exerted harmful consequence in the United States: think of the received version of the history of post–Civil War Reconstruction and its impact on racial attitudes.) But how much more problematic must be the appeal to some deeper significance of history in a country where the previous regime had invoked ideologies of irrationalism, of race, blood, and obedience. Was there a stable line, Habermas asked by implication, between endowing with meaning and nurturing dangerous myth? For Stürmer, on the other hand, the search for meaning has been a natural reaction to the continued uprooting of German society—the agrarian and industrial revolutions, the political upheavals of 1848, and Bismarck's modernization from above, long before Hitler "made the unthinkable thinkable and barbarism into a regime."[26]

Of course what also separated Habermas and Stürmer was the particular meaning to be endowed. Two concepts of national identity and Western community were in conflict. For Stürmer, the Federal Republic's connections with the West are institutionalized primarily through the Atlantic alliance. Aspirations for Central European reconstruction, notions of *Mitteleuropa,* he sees as "Green" reveries. The claim that the Soviets had ever been willing to trade unification for neutrality was utopian. Historical evocation of a broad left-wing "antifascism," either during the early 1930s or under the aegis of the "Antifa" committees, which emerged as the Nazi regime collapsed, represented a sort of boozy Popular Front nostalgia. Endless pining over these unrealistic alternatives, constant reproaches over lost opportunities, Stürmer felt, could only make West Germany's allies doubt their NATO partner's resolve and maturity. "The Federal Republic has economic and world-political responsibilities. It is a keystone in the European defense arch of the Atlantic system." Nonetheless, the search for a "lost history" was not only legitimate but also politically necessary. "For it is a question of the inner continuity of the German Republic and its calculability in foreign policy. In a land without memory anything is possible."[27]

For Habermas, such ideas threaten to resurrect both a traditional nationalism and an anticommunist reaction. Not the military alliance, but the liberal political values of the West, furnished the proper nexus for loyalty. Unreserved acceptance of Western political culture was the great intellectual accomplishment of the postwar era,[28] and it would not be stabilized by any *deutschnational* NATO philosophy:

The only patriotism that does not alienate us from the West is a patriotism of commitment to constitutionalism [*Verfassungspatriotismus*]. Unfortunately, a loyalty to universalist principles of constitutionalism, one anchored in conviction, could be inculcated in the cultured German nation only after—and by virtue of—Auschwitz. Whoever wants to suppress the blush of shame about this fact by resorting to slogans such as "obsession with guilt," whoever wants to summon the Germans back to a conventional form of their national identity, destroys the only reliable basis of our Western loyalty.[29]

Having provided a conceptual alternative to Stürmer's alleged view of history, Habermas went on to a devastating and often sarcastic critique of Hillgruber's and Nolte's work. He asked why Hillgruber had not taken advantage of the passage of forty years to impose a more objective perspective (one that in any case he could not avoid having). This would have allowed him to take into account the selective perception of the participants, to balance their respective views and add the knowledge of hindsight. But it would have meant involving moral considerations—weighing defense of the East against continuance of a murderous regime. Despite the publisher's claim, Hillgruber's book failed precisely in its refusal to bring together the collapse of the East and the destruction of the Jews. When some judgment on the destruction of the Jews had to be delivered by the historian, charged Habermas, Hillgruber fled to "the anthropological-universal" and pleaded that a moral reckoning outran the competence of the historian because it escaped the realm of the unique event.

Habermas implied that Hillgruber was as confused as he was conservative—unable or unwilling to make the methodological distinctions needed to confront such painful history. Nolte, however, was "cut from entirely different wood." Habermas scornfully discussed the Heideggerian concept of transcendence that Nolte had refurbished in his *Historische Zeitschrift* article. It was a doctrine of Pop profundity, an undifferentiated process that evoked a montage of Californian modernity.[30] What was even more pernicious, it made an antimodernist reaction all too justifiable and misleadingly bracketed "Marx and Maurras, Engels and Hitler with all due emphasis to their differences, [as] still related figures." Marxism and fascism, so Habermas read Nolte, were similar reactions to the "anxious realities of the modern."[31]

Habermas smelled a lingering brown-shirted Heideggerian metaphysics. "Still, one might let this scurrilous background philosophy of a significantly eccentric mind rest in peace, if neoconservative contemporary historians did not feel compelled to exploit precisely this form of revisionism."[32] Habermas then went on to recite the images of Israeli annihilation and Weizmann's declaration that Nolte had alluded to, and he cited the Berlin historian's argument that Nazi crimes followed Bolshevik ones and might have been a response to a real feeling of threat. In 1985 the *Frankfurter Allgemeine Zeitung* had correctly protested the staging of Rainer Fassbinder's play about a Jewish slumlord as anti-Semitic; why had they printed this piece, given that "Nolte left Fassbinder in the shade by far"? Habermas's answer was that Nolte solved the conservatives' dilemma, articulated by Stürmer, of creating a national identity without a nation. Nolte removed the stigma of uniqueness from Nazi crimes and evoked the persisting danger of the Bolshevik, "Asiatic" enemy.

By all means, Habermas argued, let Germans distance themselves from the Nazi past. But they must do so precisely to carry out Broszat's program of "historicization," of mastering historical understanding—not to advance the revisionism recommended by a Stürmer or Hildebrand, "not to cast off the burdens of a past happily no longer morally constraining." Habermas continued: "I do not want to ascribe evil intentions to anyone. But there is a simple criterion that sorts out the two attitudes. Some of us assume that the work of gaining distance and understanding liberates the power of reflective memory, thus enlarging our capacity to work out ambivalent legacies on our own. But others want to use a revisionist narrative to equip a conventional identity with a national history."

An "Intellectual Civil War"?

Certainly Habermas must have realized that this declaration would evoke an angry response. It scornfully dismissed the historical efforts of Nolte and Hillgruber. It also ascribed to his targets a calculated campaign to encourage a new conservative identity that merged Cold War NATO militance with traditional German nationalism. It designated Stürmer's essays on the public's thirst for history as evidence of a coherent strategy for the "endowment" of identity. And it proposed that, whether intentionally or fortuitously, Hillgruber's, Nolte's, and other revisionist assessments were the chief weapons in this campaign. Such charges left few friends on the right.

For Habermas's adversaries the issue was not any alleged apologia for Nazism, but the left's supposed effort to censor scholarship. Turning over their columns to Hillgruber for an extensive reply in December 1986, the editors of *Geschichte in Wissenschaft und Unterricht,* the leading journal for history teachers, declared that Hillgruber had been pilloried without precedent: "Those opposed have to speak out. Anyone who seeks to outlaw in advance or declare taboo particular reflections about our (certainly very sensitive) relationship to the National Socialist past, anyone who wants to slander and bring into public disrepute those who do not agree, does not just commit a fatal blow to the spirit of scholarship, but also damages the political culture of our country."[33] Hillgruber himself charged that Habermas had misleadingly compressed what he had written, and he pointed out—justifiably—a few instances in which his critic had misleadingly cast his statements in the worst possible light.[34] Habermas had also not deigned to explain that the reason the book's second essay on the extermination of the Jews was relatively brief was that it was the revised text of a summary report to a historical congress. Habermas had also willfully neglected Hillgruber's effort to convey the pathos of the army's obligations. (The point here, however, was that indeed Hillgruber had built his argument upon mood music and tragic atmospherics—precisely a method the philosopher could not accept.) If Habermas wanted to play the role of Enlightenment spokesman, so Hillgruber waxed sarcastic, one might have expected at least a breath of the tolerance that was so central to the eighteenth century. No trace of Lessing's Nathan the Wise informed Habermas's attack; instead, Hillgruber discerned elements of the play's fanatical patriarch, who answered to all objections: "It doesn't matter. The Jew will be burned!"

Nor, argued Hillgruber, had his own work included one word about NATO: "How does he get around to categorizing my work as part of a so-called neoconservative trend? For decades I have never concealed my deepest mistrust of all left-wing and other world-improvement utopias, which arises from my basic conservative stance. I am happy to count as a conservative even if it is meant as a term of defamation." As for hostility to the West, it was far more likely that the left's aversion to NATO would unleash the political and cultural process that Habermas claimed he wanted to hinder.

What motivated Habermas? asked Hillgruber as he concluded with real fury. Perhaps he sought to offer assistance to the Social Democrats in the 1986 electoral campaign; more probably he wanted to reinforce his dominating role on the left. (Similarly Klaus Hildebrand would later claim that Habermas was trying to recapture the influence he had been losing since 1968.)[35] For decades Habermas and his fellow travelers had insisted that Nazism and the German people during the Third Reich were all of a piece. Any effort at differentiation was suspected of apologetics. The only pluralism that Habermas really defended was one within the left. Hillgruber recalled the "agitation and psychic terror" of the student movement, abetted by professors such as Habermas. "If it is Habermas's goal to recreate the intolerable atmosphere that then prevailed in the West German universities, he is deceived.

History does not repeat itself at will according to the imagination and desires of failed 'prophets' and political agitators."[36]

Hillgruber had apparently not taken to heart Christian Meier's intervention, in which the head of the West German historians' association had just declared the dispute ended! But choleric though he was, Hillgruber still differentiated his views from those of Nolte and Fest, observing that any comparison of Stalin's crimes with the far-better-documented Nazi killings faced many problems, in both quantitative and qualitative aspects. As for the notion that reports from Russia about "Jewish-Bolshevik" atrocities after World War I had motivated Hitler's anti-Semitic program, Hillgruber rightly emphasized that the origins went back to Hitler's prewar sojourn in Vienna if not to an even more basic psychopathology.

And even sympathizers had questions for Habermas. A perceptive Italian interviewer asked how he believed the conservatives' alleged view of Germany as the "land of the middle," with its traditional overtones of hostility to East and West, was compatible with a "German-national NATO philosophy." Then, too, might not Habermas's search for a "postconventional identity" prove too abstract? Habermas admitted that it should be articulated more thoroughly: it was a concept to which he had to return.[37] According to Habermas, the very ebbing of conventional national identification—which German public-opinion pollsters traced with such alarm—revealed that young Germans had not thrown away the opportunity for moral renewal that the national catastrophe had provided. Still, others also questioned whether a legal order—*ubi constitutio ibi patria*—really provided a tangible enough object of allegiance. The Berlin historian Hagen Schulze suggested that no matter how attractive the appeal to constitutional patriotism might appear as a *raison d'être* for the Bonn Republic, it was not sufficient. The good German constitutional patriots of the Weimar Republic had had no emotional bulwark against traditional nationalists.[38] For the historian, moreover, national identity hardly appeared as such a bogey. The concept really just amounted to an explanation of why a given country turned out one way and not another. And unless West Germans accepted some idea of national identity, how could they be asked to accept any historical responsibility for Nazi deeds—"that is precisely why the DDR [Deutsche Demokratische Republik] denies its identity with German history in general." An important response—but what Habermas feared was not so much this minimal notion of historic outcome and linkage as a reinfused mystique. Admittedly, he did not adequately specify what other alternatives for identity, either conventional or postconventional, might exist.

Furthermore, Habermas probably attributed far too cohesive an organization to the conservative offensive.[39] As Nipperdey wrote, the fact that political claims might be made on memory "is not a Machiavellian idea of Stürmer's, but a simple truth."[40] Moreover, it did not take a conservative campaign to raise issues about the uniqueness of Nazi crimes. The half-life of remorse was bound to be finite. Germans—especially those who did not enjoy what Chancellor Kohl had described (without an effort at irony) as "the grace of being born late"—were bound to ask about the uniqueness of German crimes. Americans who have spent time in Germany have often encountered critical, sometimes smug questions about the bombing of Dresden. *Tu quoque*—the apologetics of supposed equivalence—has long been resorted to as an unofficial response. Did it take an orchestrated, neoconservative campaign to give this approach official sanction? Wasn't Bitburg sufficient?

But if there were no conspiracy, many conservatives certainly shared the conviction that their time had come and the hour of the left's "false prophets" had passed. Now, forty years after defeat, with a CDU government in power and a widely shared mood that Germans could take pride in much of their history,[41] the historians of the right could try to cast off the restraints that had kept some formulations off limits. What was new was that German "culture bearers" should lend respectability to such a response. The editor of *Der Spiegel*, Rudolf Augstein, offensive to many for his sometimes messianic poses, still had a point when he vented his stupefaction: "What is currently taking place among historians, philosophers, and sociologists would have seemed hardly possible five years ago." Now we have to concern ourselves with the following questions: Did Hitler have to feel threatened by world Jewry because Chaim Weizmann declared war alongside England? Does it really pay to know that the Allies bombed Hamburg without knowing of Auschwitz? Did the Allies intend to dismember parts of Germany even without knowing of the exterminations? (Yes, answered Augstein to the last, but only after the country had fought two wars of expansion.)[42]

"Mirror, Mirror on the wall, Who was the unfairest of them all?" *Der Spiegel*'s sarcasm provoked harsh comments from those who felt that Nolte and Hillgruber were being defamed. Surprisingly enough, a diplomatic historian once of the Fritz Fischer school, Immanuel Geiss, rushed to their defense. Habermas had sought to use scare tactics; now Augstein, Geiss charged, was seeking to read the conservative historians out of the democratic community. Habermas and Augstein together, Geiss charged, "threaten our scholarly and political pluralism"; they had implied that those who thought differently from them were close to Nazism, and were threatening the "intellectual civil war that Stürmer had hitherto conjured up only allegorically."[43] Klaus Hildebrand, a historian of Nazi foreign policy at Bonn, charged Habermas with utopianism and "unfamiliarity with the process of historical research" and defended Hillgruber with quotations from Malraux, Camus, Wilhelm Röpke, Solzhenitsyn, Elie Halévy, and Raymond Aron.[44] Hillgruber was right to point out that Allied ambitions to dismember Germany were not merely a response to genocide. Why should Habermas mock such revelations? "Unfortunate historians," a conservative columnist in *Die Welt* wrote with heavy irony: did they not understand that Habermas was unconcerned about facts and sources, but sought only to establish new dogma that every historian had servilely to accept? The new dispensation had three propositions. First, crimes committed by the Germans and in their name were and would forever remain "totally unique, without model or analogue in history"; second, "all Germans were 'liberated' in 1945, whether or not they were thereby killed, starved to death, raped, imprisoned, driven from their homes, taken away, or oppressed under a communist dictatorship"; third, "anyone doubting one of the first two propositions or seeking to relativize it through so-called facts, is a fascist."[45] It did not take long for the debate to degenerate.

The most explicit endorsement of Nolte came about six weeks after Habermas's critique, from the editor of the *Frankfurter Allgemeine Zeitung* itself, Joachim Fest.[46] Little in Fest's collective biography of Nazi leaders, *The Face of the Third Reich,* or in his massive life of Hitler would have signaled his position. But since the end of the 1960s, Fest declared, it had been customary to tar every historiographic deviation from fashionable left-wing trends with the brush of fascism. What was decisive for such critics was the motive, not the scholarship. "For this wretched practice, there has recently been a new variant. It derives from Jürgen Habermas." Habermas had assembled a pastiche of quotations to place renowned historians under "NATO suspicion." He was trapped in his conspiracy theory, stuck with outmoded categories of progressives versus conservatives, liberals versus German nationalists.

Would it not be more accurate to divide those for whom history confirmed a pessimistic view of man "governed by hatred, fear, and extermination, without sense or purpose," for whom Auschwitz appeared as a ' technical innovation," from those who believed in human perfectibility? For the utopians, Auschwitz was an aberration; for the pessimists, it was apparently just one genocide among many, "not the first and also not the last." Of all the participants in the controversy Fest took the palm for cosmic equanimity!

Fest clearly supported Nolte on the substantive issue of historical precedent and comparability. Witness the first leader of the Cheka, who in 1918 had claimed that the Bolsheviks would "exterminate the bourgeoisie as a class." For Nazis or Bolsheviks, Fest wrote, the principle was the same: attack enemies not on the basis of guilt or innocence, but on the basis of simple membership in a social group: "Here a race, there a class." Fest did not ask whether the rhetoric of destroying the bourgeoisie as a class might not have referred to collectivization of private property rather than to the physical extermination of all bourgeois. He also denied any other uniqueness to National Socialist crimes. Could one really believe that Stalin's gulag was less "mechanical" than the concentration camps? As for those historians who contended that Nazi crimes were especially horrifying because Germany was a cultured and developed nation, Fest argued that they were just updating National Socialist arrogance. Not to rate Turkish, or Russian, or Khmer Rouge atrocities as equally horrible was patronizing and racist. One did not, Fest proposed, actually have to accept Nolte's suggestion that Hitler's destructive will was predominantly inspired by the atrocities of the Russian revolution. One only had to understand that he was unlikely not to have been influenced. Reports of murders, deportations, and eradications were doubtless exaggerated; "nonetheless they contained a nucleus of truth that was enhanced in credibility by the pathos of the imminent world revolution. Despite all the distortions they gave Hitler's extermination complexes a real background." By what right, then, could critics object to Nolte's statement that the events in Russia were the "logical and de facto predecessor for Auschwitz"?

This logic proved too much even for those who felt uneasy with the tone of Habermas's polemic. Eberhard Jäckel, an editor of Hitler's writings and a historian of Nazi ideology who has dissented from the Broszat-Mommsen approach to Nazi "polycracy," declared that Habermas had been unfair to Hillgruber, but that Nolte and Fest had gone too far. The debate, he felt, had been characterized by veiled accusations on each side: Nolte had insinuated that some (unspecified) historians did not wish to weigh Stalin's crimes against Hitler's. Hildebrand had murmured that some wanted to impose political "questionnaires" (as the Americans had done to weed out Nazis) and impose orthodoxy—likewise without identifying who; Fest had insinuated that it had become customary since the late 1960s to inquire into motives rather than evidence. But Fest himself was perfecting this tactic: "He does not say there is a causal connection [between Soviet crimes and Auschwitz]. He says only that it would not be impossible to impute one. And if his observation arouses dissent, he does not ask whether this might be explained by the fact that the sources contradict it. No, he turns to the practice he has himself criticized and asks about motives." In any case, Jäckel declared that he would stick to the issue. Taking up the proposition—stated even more baldly by Fest than by Nolte—that the murder of the Jews was not unique, Jäckel declared: "the National Socialist killing of the Jews was unique in that never before had a state with the authority of its responsible leader decided and announced that a specific human group, including its aged, its women, its children and infants, would be killed as quickly as possible, and then carried through this resolution using every possible means of state power."[47]

As for the implication that Auschwitz was a response to the gulag, Jäckel pointed out that it rested on Nolte's fanciful interpretation of Hitler's 1943 reference to the "rat cage" that might await captured German officers. Jäckel pointed out, however, that Nolte's refusal to believe that Hitler's "rat cage" referred simply to Lubianka flew in the face of Hitler's repeated declarations that he meant the notorious Moscow prison. "What this all has to do with the killing of the Jews, initiated in 1941," Jäckel wrote, "Nolte must still explain." In fact the whole argument was merely *post hoc, ergo propter hoc.*

Ultimately, asked Jäckel, what difference did it make whether German crimes were unique? Even if Nazi genocide was comparable to other massacres, would this fact have justified, for example, canceling West German reparations to Israel? So too, Hagen Schulze—who was friendlier to Nolte and Fest and critical of Habermas—asked, would National Socialist crimes be somehow deemed less reprehensible even if some comparisons were possible? And did not a denial of comparability also lead to evasive moral judgments? The absolutely singular case could be seen only as an aberration, outside history, and thus as not morally binding any more than the crime of someone clearly insane.[48] What Nolte and Fest tended to obscure was that claiming the Holocaust was unique did not mean it could not be compared with other genocides. Insisting on its special nature did not preclude recalling Stalinist terror. Every event is singular in some respects, a member of a broader category in others. As Jürgen Kocka wrote a few weeks after Jäckel, "There is nothing to object to in historical comparisons, rather the opposite." But in that case, compare Germany with the Western societies among which Germans usually liked to be counted. To argue that the comparison with Western countries was implicitly arrogant or racist, as Fest maintained, was wrong. It was just to take the European tradition of the Enlightenment seriously.[49]

What sort of comparison is licit, or decent, has not been conclusively answered in this controversy. Nolte, Fest, and Hildebrand argue that of course the Holocaust was unique, as are all historical phenomena—but what are important are its comparative aspects. Their opponents argue that of course elements can be compared, but what is essential is its singularity. The purpose of comparison is what is at stake. Despite Jäckel's, Schulze's, and, later, Christian Meier's argument that the murder of 6 million people would be as reprehensible even if the crime were just one among others, comparison or uniqueness remains a major issue. Not to be alone among the societies perpetrating genocide apparently dissolves a whole interconnected chain of inhibitions. Nolte apparently feels that it dissolves the paralysis imposed by the past. By the electoral campaign of 1986–87, it dissolved many historical inhibitions, as journalists and politicians suggested that the Final Solution might even have been implicit in the program of the Enlightenment. Certainly it sanctions historical reassessments and political implications that were hitherto off limits. Let us accept that no question should be out of bounds. Does that mean that every answer must be honored?

The Limits of History

Has there been closure to this debate? Or was there only exhaustion? By December 1986, the chairman of the German Historical Association, Christian Meier, who had evoked the origins of politics among the Greeks,[50] sought to dampen the excess of politics among the historians.[51] Meier suggested, prematurely it turned out, that both sides had softened their position. He also ventured that in light of Nolte's later article, "the problem of uniqueness is no longer contested." Although

Meier tactfully praised Nolte for making the public more aware of the century's multiple genocides, he also insisted that no comparative reckoning would alleviate the oppressive legacy of the German past. "The consciousness of these misdeeds is burned too deeply in the foundations of the Federal Republic." Much as one might wish to overcome the "hypnotic crippling" of the National Socialist era, trifling with the Holocaust was no solution. It amounted to evasion. Echoing Kocka, Meier pointed out that it was hardly an example of *Herrenvolk* mentally to point out that Germany was the only Western country to have practiced genocide. And echoing Jäckel, he maintained that uniqueness was not the principal issue. "What good is it to us, if the destruction of the Jews is part of a chain along with the liquidation of the kulaks or Pol Pot's exterminations?" The Final Solution must not be made into a question of bookkeeping.

Nonetheless, the issue of uniqueness, Meier felt, remained important from a different viewpoint. The Holocaust had to be deemed unique, and therefore its brutal history had to be kept vivid. Better for Germans to tell it to themselves than always have it told to them. Here the question of identity intervened. The controversy was, and remained, less about the past than about the present and the future. The Federal Republic was the only German successor state that made recognition of and regret for Nazi crimes part of its fundamental law. On this count, Habermas was alarmist: none of the writers he had attacked could be accused of trivializing Nazism. None had desired to " 'cast off a past that has happily been divested of its moral burden.' " Admittedly Michael Stürmer reflected a widespread conservative attitude when he sought to ground a national consensus in the whole of German history. Habermas was right to lay his arguments at Stürmer's door; but "it would have been better had he read him more carefully." Stürmer did not long for *Mitteleuropa*; his stress on exposed eastern and western borders was no "geopolitical incantation"; unlike Hildebrand, he did not call for "endowment with meaning."

Finally, asked Meier, could West Germany subsist only with a patriotic constitutionalism? Was it not allowed to claim a meaningful national identity? "With all due sympathy for a postnational identity, can it suffice when we live among nations?" Habermas's second article, in November 1986, had suggested that the legacy of Auschwitz still bound those too young to have been involved, even those born recently, because they shared "life forms" or common origins that had made Auschwitz possible and were still potentially available. Too abstract, argued Meier. After forty years of democracy the danger of recurrence was not the issue. Yes—Auschwitz still weighed on German youth, but because there existed a real national identity. "For if we continue to behave in many respects as Germans, is it really [the recognition of life forms] and not rather the fact that we are German, that lets us have hope?"

Meier claimed to offer no more than an "interim balance," and he ended by pleading for the moderate center. But not all voices were moderated. Nolte wrote tartly to the *Frankfurter Allgemeine Zeitung* to say that he had not softened his position, he had only tried to correct some abusive misreadings.[52] Hillgruber did not temper his own response;[53] and Hildebrand could not be restrained from writing: "The fact that the chairman of the German Historical Association, the historian of antiquity Christian Meier, seeks to excuse such a procedure [Habermas's skewing of quotations] is incomprehensible to me and writes another page in the 'chronique scandaleuse' of this debate . . . To seek understanding for Jürgen Habermas's 'declaration of war' may or may not honor the person who tries, but to want to justify his treatment of texts contradicts everything normal in historical scholarship and in life in general. Any student who dealt with literature according to Habermas's procedure would fail his exam."[54]

Habermas had published his second major essay before Meier's effort to transcend the *Historikerstreit*. He found no reason to retract what he had written. The lengthening interval since the Third Reich necessitated some form of historicization—one way or another. The traumatic commemorations of the mid-1980s—the fiftieth anniversary of Hitler's coming to power on January 30, 1933; the fortieth anniversaries of the plot of July 20, 1944; and the surrender of May 8, 1945— finally opened the floodgates of memory and made the public realize that the past was not simply fading. But how should Germans work through these memories? Habermas cited some ugly manifestations: CDU parliamentary leader Alfred Dregger's opposition to dwelling on the past; efforts to disqualify a witness in a euthanasia case because his having had a Jewish grandparent might prejudice his testimony: were these and other expressions a coincidence, or "is there gradually spreading in this republic a spiritual climate that accommodates all this?" Bitburg had already brought such trends into play: "The aura of the military cemetery was to awaken national sentiment and historical consciousness. The proximity of the mound of corpses in the concentration camp to the SS graves in the military cemetery—in the morning Bergen-Belsen, in the afternoon Bitburg—implicitly contested the uniqueness of the National Socialist crimes; and the handshake of the old generals in the presence of the American president finally confirmed that we had always been on the right side in the fight against Bolshevism."[55]

For Habermas, all these expressions—callous, insensitive, or manipulative—testified to a deeper trend. In this respect, his view was bound to be one-sided. After all, the handshake of old adversaries can seal the conclusion of a real battle as well as indicate a covert alliance. Still, Habermas raised a profound problem. Was there no sense of responsibility for past evils that might inhibit these ugly political phenomena? Forty years earlier, Habermas reminded readers, Karl Jaspers had wrestled with the issue of what collective responsibility was borne by Germans who had not resisted the regime. "Today," Habermas noted, "those who at the end of the Second World War had already been too young to have any personal burden of guilt have grandchildren."[56] Did those born afterward still bear any responsibility? For Habermas they did, and not merely a formal corporate liability because West Germany claimed continuity as an institutional entity. "The simple fact is that even those born later have grown up in a context of life [*Lebensform*] in which *that* was possible." An inextricable mesh of family and of local, political, and intellectual traditions provided even the youngest Germans with a historical legacy. "None of us can escape that milieu, because our identity as individuals and as Germans is indissolubly woven into it."[57] Because all Germans grew up in a psychological and institutional framework that had once succumbed to barbarism, they were apparently still potential perpetrators.

As a serious thinker, Habermas's political interventions have reflected the issues of his major theoretical work. The division between constitutional patriotism and the concept of "life-forms" echoed the discussion of "life-world" and social systems that was central to Habermas's 1981 magnum opus, *The Theory of Communicative Action*. In that two-volume work Habermas returns to the classic sociological agenda of rationalization and proposes a twofold theory of society: first as a "life-world" constructed by actors who share and renew symbols and culture; second as a set of functional systems built around purposive rationality. Under ideal conditions language and communication should enable society to develop the different systems (economy, politics, and so on) required for collective life and should simultaneously allow a general advance of law, rationality, and individual liberty without sacrificing the solidaristic orientation represented by the life-world. Rationalization as such did not have to desiccate or distort community. Nonetheless, some developments, such as modern capitalism or bureaucracy, advanced not a generalized liberal order, but tended virtually to metastasize as subsystems that "colonized" the life-world.[58]

The Theory of Communicative Action served as an extended argument for hope against the bleak scenarios of disenchantment and domination that characterized Max Weber and Theodor Adorno. But the danger that Habermas perceived among the historians was somewhat different. Their neoconservative nationalism was less a systems orientation run amok than a threat to the general evolution of the lifeworld toward new forms of "postconventional" identity. The constitutional patriotism that Habermas envisaged was not only a functional system for nation-state organization, but was evidently envisioned as an emancipated stage of a lifeworld. Habermas has not renounced the idea that a German community provided a matrix for tradition and culture. Neither in *The Theory of Communicative Action,* nor in his November 1986 discussion of "life forms," nor in his third major essay of summer 1987, the Sonning Prize address (discussed below in Chapter 5) did Habermas relinquish the idea of a formative cultural tradition that participants were born into, drew upon, and renewed. The "life forms" proposed during the *Historikerstreit* were only a special case of the theoretically elaborated lifeworld.

The problem was that the German life-forms had earlier been terribly distorted by the nationalism Habermas felt was reemerging among the allegedly neoconservative historians. Habermas drew upon the life-forms argument to suggest that the proclivities for Nazism from 1933 to 1945 lay embedded in a culture that might still transmit them in 1986. This was an implication that seemed unfounded even to sympathizers. Christian Meier, for example, rejected Habermas's dualist concept and said simply that it was better to admit that a conventional German national identity existed and continued to impose a legal and historical liability. Habermas apparently felt that the potential for Auschwitz was still inherent in every German's cultural inheritance. For that reason the Holocaust remained as a mutual, and not merely collective, responsibility. This responsibility entailed in the first instance an obligation to remember, and not with the head alone, the dead murdered at the hands of Germans. These dead had a claim on a solidarity that those born afterward could provide only by renewal of memory. If Germans failed to live up to this legacy of Benjamin, "then Jewish citizens, the sons, and daughters, and grandchildren of the slain, would no longer be able to breathe in our land." By virtue of this need for constant renewal of memory, relations with Israel could not be entirely (or merely) normalized in the foreseeable future. In effect, Habermas suggested that the Holocaust must be as fundamental to German identity as it was to Israel's.

The current conflict, Habermas continued, centered on how Germans should relate to their own traditions. Until now the official answer of the Bonn Republic had been clear: "After Auschwitz we can create our national self-awareness only out of the better traditions of our not unexamined, but critically assimilated history." Now this premise was being attacked by the right. Conservatives feared that such a critically examined history undermined collective identity, social integration, and consistency as an alliance partner. It hindered rehabilitation of conservative traditions, such as Heideggerian philosophizing that had seemed tainted after the National Socialist experience. Thus forty years after Jaspers had arduously resolved the conflict over collective responsibility, it had broken out again.

> Can one claim to be the legal heir of the German Reich, can one continue the traditions of German culture, without taking historical responsibility for the form of life in which Auschwitz was possible? Can one take responsibility for the interconnected origins of those crimes with which our own existence is historically woven in any other way than by means of a solidaristic memory of what is now irreparable, in any other way than by means of a reflective, critical attitude vis-à-vis the traditions that endow our identity?

This passage from Habermas's second essay is among the most difficult but important in all the literature generated by this controversy. It is also one of the most problematic. To establish his sense of continuing historic responsibility, Habermas evoked an almost Burkean concept of national society with its organic "contract" between the living and the dead. He proposed a society of mutual, not merely corporate or collective, responsibility. And he sternly insisted that living up to that responsibility meant renouncing the spurious consolation of a historical sense that searches for traditional identity. German history must remain painful history. But even if it drew upon the concept of lifeworld in his *Theory of Communicative Action*, how did Habermas's sense of a formative national community, a "form of life"—in effect, of a deterministic influence extending through time—

accord with his concept of *Verfassungspatriotismus*? Constitutional patriotism, after all, is a loyalty of reason alone to liberty and law, in effect to a transnational liberal republic. What West Germans were to be praised for, in the first essay, was having forged a nationality based upon Kantian ideals. But what he insisted they recognize, in the second essay, was a national matrix that determined gestures, traditions, habits, and moral legacies. To be fair, these ideas were thrown out in journalistic form—responsive to current controversy, rapidly drafted, purposely polemical. And *The Theory of Communicative Action* had proposed an evolution from lifeworld to rational community. Still, his philosophy comprises a series of asymptotic efforts to reconcile antinomies. No single statement has been without internal tensions.

Habermas insisted, I believe correctly, that the question of comparability was not just a scholar's issue. If comparability was exploited to diminish national responsibility, it was a civic question, and he resented Nipperdey's and Hildebrand's very disparate efforts to present the controversy as exclusively a historians' dispute. At stake was not some recondite argument about a value-free social science (*Wertfreiheit*), but the public use of history. When newspapers took over historians' disputes about comparability, then it became obvious what an impact they must have. Had the dispute been confined to scholarly journals, Habermas claimed, he would not have intervened. For the *Frankfurter Allgemeine Zeitung* to publish Nolte was not a sin, but it was an innovation in the political culture and self-comprehension of the Federal Republic. And it was perceived as such abroad.

Let me be fair. Habermas's position appeals to me first as a historian contemplating Germany, second as an American liberal thinking of analogous debates in our own public life, whether over race or foreign intervention. The formulas he invokes are resonant of the Enlightenment; they eschew the problematic subjectivism that too often tempts the West German Left. I am afraid that Nolte's or Fest's tortured reasoning could open the way, not to a Holocaust (that is hardly possible), but to some form of ugly politics, some infringement of dissent or attack on diversity: the political fantasies of the *Bildzeitung* rationalized in the language of *Existenzphilosophie*. Even if no practical consequences followed from the revisionist view, if West Germany remained as robust a democracy as it has been, its civic culture would be degraded by the distortions of historical memory involved.

Nonetheless, Habermas's stand raises three sorts of difficulties. First, he overemphasizes a NATO-nationalist agenda: he implies the existence of a clique of Germans and Americans conspiring to prosecute their alliance and burying the Nazi past to do so. But the NATO's *raison d'être* has more to do with the wall dividing Berlin than with the wall around Bitburg. It has been Brandt's alliance as well as Kohl's and Stürmer's, Carter's as well as Reagan's. Second, as we have seen above, Habermas proposed two differing approaches to German identity that seem hard to reconcile (although his 1987 Danish address attempted to do so). Third, Habermas's ambitious claims for historical rhetoric may raise a difficulty that some of the less partisan participants in this debate have suggested but find hard to prove.

Habermas is a brilliant debater about history, but—aside from the accusations of distortion levied by his opponents—his polemics raise the problem pointed out by Thomas Nipperdey at the outset of the chapter. Nipperdey pleaded that history was fragile. Does his preoccupation with the vulnerability of liberal inquiry really represent, as Habermas has charged, a mandarin desire for "an ideologically closed milieu, unreachable from reality"? I do not think so: concern about historiographic overload is legitimate. Although every contender— Habermas as well as Stürmer—recognizes that history is the craft with which the ideological and political waters of the Federal Republic must be navigated, the vessel is a frail one. It can easily be swamped. It can accommodate only so much conflict among those riding it. Does not— so Christian Meier and Thomas Nipperdey both ask, and with justice—history need to enjoy a certain immunity from being overloaded, if it is to serve as a vessel for collective navigation?

Habermas would doubtless respond that this metaphor merely echoes Nipperdey's historical "quietism" and is a utopian stance. The broadest ideological challenges cannot be excluded. Willy-nilly the boat takes water. But even if one grants that Habermas is correct, historiography need not simply echo ideological conflicts uncritically. The question becomes how history can mediate ideology methodologically. By mediate I do not mean just cover over, or state indirectly. I mean incorporate but transcend. For the historian this requires a rigorous analysis of presuppositions from all contending points of view, indeed the effort to see the stakes even for parties who may have been muffled or absent. Two analogies may help define the role of the historian in dealing with ideological controversy; one is to the courtroom, the other to the nature of politics, domestic or international. Anglo-American judicial proceedings rely on an adversarial procedure to construct the most plausible narrative of disputed events. No lawyer is responsible for truth but only for a stylized text or dialogue that places his or her client in the most favorable light. Most historians, however, would feel uncomfortable with such a description of their own mission. They see their role as akin to that of either the detective or the judge (even more akin to a French judge, with the right to question witnesses, than to an Anglo-American judge).[59] The judge's commitment transcends that of either party to the conflict; he represents the interest of the community in arriving at as close an estimate of the truth as possible. In this sense, the historian's resort to adversarial procedures must be limited. Admittedly, a dispute carried on in the culture pages of major newspapers may have different ground rules from one conducted in scholarly journals and at conferences. But even in the daily press, the historian should be committed to a role different from that of the lawyer.

Consider the second analogy: Politics—*pace* Carl Schmitt—is not reducible to civil war. Nor is Clausewitz's famous dictum readily reversible: the fact that politics can dissolve into violence does not mean that it is just a continuation of warfare by other means. Not all political systems must incorporate the societal tensions and latent ideological conflicts of the Weimar Republic. Likewise, the international system is not just a Hobbesian state of nature, even if, in the final instance, no common sovereign can prevent wars. For most of the time nation-states exist in a state of quasi-cooperation. They seek to avoid war; they encourage commerce and travel and cultural exchange; they recognize wider, transnational links; and, if catastrophe threatens, political leaders seek to shift the blame they know will follow. Such a view of international society, which recognizes conflict but does not presuppose an unremitting struggle for power, has been termed, after the seventeenth-century philosopher of natural law, Grotian.[60] From the Grotian perspective nation-states or international systems are not merely the expression of frozen conflict or of "structural violence." They embody cooperation more than a stalemate of naked force disguised by ideological moralizing. Civil society and political institutions have their own genuine infrastructure of sociability; they rest on real needs for comradeship.

So, too, the social sciences and historiography should be able meaningfully to supersede ideological partisanship—not by denying that these scholarly activities are conditioned by politics, but by recognizing their commitment to a shared project of knowledge. Of course, this requires a preliminary effort at self-reflection, of thinking through how the historian's own views of the past are shaped by political or psychological preferences. This is the equivalent of the psychoanalyst's own analysis. Once that essential clarification is carried out (often it is omitted or rejected outright!), a scholarly project cannot simply be dismissed because of its politics. The social sciences, the *Geisteswissenschaften,* exist in the analogue of a Grotian, not a Hobbesian, realm. At the very least the writer of history requires a reader prepared to be open-minded. The text negates solipsism. The writing and reading of history must rest upon intellectual sociability.

Of course Habermas would respond that this claim for history is analogous to his view of discourse in general: the willingness to enter a conversation implies a commitment to the possibility of rational consensus. It thus provides the possibility for reasoned knowledge. But a political conversation may have different qualities and "interests" from a historical one. Certainly the latter should be a truth-seeking procedure and the reconstruction of "meaning" in the human sciences. Ideally, political argument is also a truth-seeking procedure, but it can be just an exercise in compelling assent. Even in a liberal democracy, where political debate involves some level of commitment to truth as well as power, participants are still granted the right of pleading an *ex parte* case. Political discourse in modern conditions rests on adversarial argumentation: the society presupposes that policy is chosen out of the clash of partial views, not because each participant undertakes to present all sides to every question. Although historiographic activity often becomes an adversarial procedure, it theoretically involves a more inclusive commitment. Hence the linguistic commitment in historical conversations may have to be of a more sociable and inclusive nature. The concerns voiced by Nipperdey are not those of a utopian— although the fault for overburdening historical discourse does not rest primarily with Habermas. Habermas was not offering a historical reconstruction; he was writing a political response to a conservative mobilization of historical rhetoric for political ends.

Does the Grotian analogue mean that all historical positions are admissible and must be accorded equal validity? Christian Meier objected when Habermas termed Fest's defense of Nolte a bad, even evil (*schlimm*), article. Habermas presumably meant that it was not good-faith history, that it was manipulative and not part of an effort really to advance knowledge or enlightenment. It is all very well to claim that historiography rests upon a certain sociability so not every issue need threaten ideological conflict; but some political positions only mas-

querade themselves as genuine scholarly efforts. Most of us do think
some projects are out of bounds. A *Journal of Historical Revision,* which
endeavors to prove the Holocaust did not really happen, blatantly
racist anthropology—do these efforts enjoy the rights that are implied
by a community of discourse? That question can be answered only on a
case-by-case basis. By and large, though, the historical community
probably does better to accept marginal cases as good-faith efforts,
subject to thoughtful rebuttal, rather than as merely evil positions.
Better to admit than to anathematize, to take Nolte and Fest as reasoned historical discourse.[61] (Neither has sought to deny what happened, only to put a different light on it.) At the same time, Habermas
was right to point out that the Nolte-Fest position has gone
significantly beyond what used to be regarded as the decent historical
and intellectual discourse of the Federal Republic. It has attenuated
German responsibility, whether by diminishing Nazi initiative in the
Final Solution or by diminishing the special aura of the events. The
Nolte-Fest position has given academic credentials to what hitherto
was the underground discourse of the *Soldatenzeitung* or SS reunions.
It was not improper for Habermas to point out this innovation in the
social structure of scholarship.

The Habermas debate has been important because the issues are
painful. But once raised—and they were raised on the right—they
must be argued through. They concern some of the most difficult
moral and historical questions of our time. But the debate has been
almost impossible because of the demands placed upon history writing. Political engagement and scientific accuracy are not necessarily in
conflict. Absolute separation of a supposedly sterile scholarship from
political passion is an untenable dichotomy: impossible to achieve in
any case, and not always valuable. But the discourse of reasoned answers and the discourse of public conscience may have divergent objectives. Habermas insisted that the debate over the Nazi past engaged
both levels at once, the political and the scholarly. He was right. But he
did not find it easy to conduct it on both levels at once, and perhaps we
must have two linguistically differentiated debates. Perhaps there is a
tension between the immersion in complexity that historical judgments
require and the simplification needed for political argumentation.

We are left, therefore, with three questions. How much polemic can
history bear before it is deformed? This is not a mandarin's concern.
Even if it cannot be answered by a general rule, the question is justified
by the passion of the *Historikerstreit* and compels reflection on the

boundary conditions of historical discourse. The second question involves "doing history" and is the classic concern of Weberian social science, namely how typologies are utilized, when they are legitimate in history and social science. This is the question which the issue of comparability has raised in a new form and which is addressed in the next chapter. Finally there is the issue of German identity, taken up in Chapter 5. On one level this is an issue that German history has continuously addressed: What state or states do the German people construct? For Habermas it is less a question of national framework than of national values: What is the quality of identity? "Our mother country is not where we find happiness at last. Our mother country, on the contrary, is with us, in us. Germany is alive in us, we represent it, willy-nilly, in every country to which we go, in each climate. We are rooted in it from the beginning, and we can never emancipate ourselves from it." Habermas could have written those lines, not in his first, but certainly in his second major contribution to the controversy. So of course could Michael Stürmer. They come, however, from the youthful Leopold von Ranke, whose preoccupations still overshadow much of this controversy.[62]

3

A Holocaust like the Others?
Problems of Comparative History

Question from the audience: And do you believe it's possible to come to grips with the events that you write about?

Answer: No. (The deaths of six million Jews, twenty million Russians, six million Poles.)

In that case—follow-up question—what's the use of bringing it up again and again?

—*Christa Wolf*

Indeed one cannot do scholarship at the open grave of the slain. But no grave is so large and remains so fresh that after the passage of years or decades it cannot become—or must not become—the theme of scholarly inquiry.

—*Ernst Nolte*

FOR CHRISTA WOLF'S PROTAGONIST, memories of the Nazi past keep coming back precisely because she cannot master them. "Who would dare to say at any particular time: We have come to grips with it?"[1] Ernst Nolte, in contrast, believes that Germans can get a grip on even the most traumatic events by "historicizing" them, in effect mastering them with historical and philosophical perspective. *Nihil humani* . . . "there is nothing human that stands outside history. For this very reason it must be thoroughly understandable. What is not understandable would exist as an 'absolute evil' or an 'absolute good' outside history and could not be a matter for the historian."[2] To make comprehension possible, Nolte has proposed two strategies. The one, comparative, suggests that even though it was unique, the Final Solution was one terrible deed among others. The massacre of the Armenians by the Ottoman Turks, the atrocities of the Russian civil war and later of Stalin's purges, the decimation of Cambodia, even, by implication, the bombing of Dresden—all these events share the quality of mass murder. They do not excuse the Nazi crime, but they must alleviate its special stigma. Invoking the wider genus of genocide can dissipate the clinging aura of the unspeakable. As Klaus Hildebrand verges on saying, the sin then becomes that of modern man or twentieth-century society.[3]

Once this sort of comparison begins, no distinction is likely to remain intact. For Joachim Fest, only the more mechanized killing of prisoners distinguished the German camps from the Russians': Zyklon B represented a technological but not a moral watershed.[4] But if the technology of death alone distinguishes, must we not agree with Alfred Schickel that "even the use of gas was ultimately no more 'singular' than . . . using climate as a murder instrument in Stalin's camps north of the Arctic Circle."[5] No difference remains.[6]

In fact Nolte is not content with insisting on comparability. He argues further that the Holocaust might be understood as a defensive response, misconceived but provoked by fear of the now notorious "Asiatic deed"—the phrase borrowed from Erwin Scheubner-Richter's description of the Armenian massacres in 1917 but applied (by Nolte) to the menace of Bolshevik atrocities that Hitler might have felt could befall the Germans. (By extension, Hitler's attack on the Soviet Union, though unnecessary and therefore criminal, still retains some characteristics of a preventive war.)[7] So, too, Chaim Weizmann's declaration of Jewish support for Britain after the outbreak of war in September 1939 might have justified or explained the interning of Jews in German-held territories.[8] What Nolte actually proposes—and what Fest's supportive article endorsed—is often unclear. Is he offering the historian's judgment, or just a possible reconstruction of how the National Socialist leadership may have viewed the world? We are summoned in the name of scholarship to accept, at least as a thought-experiment, the recurring arguments of neo-Nazi publicists. Implications take refuge in question marks, hypotheses, and subjunctives. For this prose we need to invent a new grammatical mode: the pseudo-interrogative.[9]

A decade ago such argumentation would have emerged only from the rank undergrowth of neo-Nazi literature. It is hard to believe that the historian must still list the objections to Nolte's reasoning: first, that Jews were stateless and could not in any official sense wage war as a coherent unit; second, that they were hardly in a position to mount de facto resistance as a people; third, that Weizmann's "declaration" followed upon six years of the Third Reich's persecutions[10]—the original boycotts and violence of 1933, the exclusion from the professions, the Nuremberg laws of 1935, the destruction, arrests, and confiscations attendant upon Kristallnacht in 1938. The officially organized German

Jewish community (and racially defined German Jews who had not been affiliated) had already had to endure brutality, legal segregation, confiscations, and general degradation. Who had declared war on whom?[11]

Moreover, even Nolte can invoke only internment as the response justified by the laws of war. At the most extreme, the logic proposed would have allowed the treatment of Jews as California Nisei, that shameful chapter of American racist panic. If the motive were the dread of Bolshevik terror, the fear of the "Asiatic deed" from the steppes, what grounds could there be for exterminating Jews already penned up in Warsaw or Łodz, Drancy, Salonika, or Theresienstadt, or those ferreted out of Hungary or Holland? Fest insisted that Nolte was justified in proposing that reports of the bloody Russian civil war were reaching Germany in the early 1920s and might well have frightened the Nazis. The Munich Soviet Republic, installed briefly in April 1919, with Jews among its Bolshevik leadership, had also reported to the shooting of hostages. The fears, visions, and longings of the early Nazi leadership may have been confirmed by that local civil war. But Hitler's fierce loathing of Jews was created before World War I. Vienna in 1905, not Munich in 1919, was the more decisive crucible. His paranoid reductionism was confirmed by the German capitulation of 1918. We just have no evidence that he was significantly politicized by the events of the Russian civil war.[12]

This is not to argue that there is no connection between the Russian Revolution and the rise of Nazism. As Nolte's first book proposed, fascism (including its National Socialist variant) was the new political signature of the epoch shaped by World War I.[13] The war radicalized the claims of left and right. It enabled Lenin to triumph in Russia, and it also generated protofascist movements. These fused an exaltation of the combat experience with contempt for both bourgeois liberalism and Marxist internationalism. In the interwar period, fascism and communism each recruited partly on the basis of the danger from the other. Obviously, without the specter of the Bolshevik seizure of power, the constellation of contending forces in the German revolution and its aftermath would have been profoundly altered. But Nolte now claims far more than this general interconnection to which most historians would subscribe. He is suggesting that the Nazis feared that Soviet terror would be used against Germans, and that the Final Solution can even be seen as a sort of preemptive defense. The gulag is the precedent for Auschwitz, and not merely in the weak sense that modern history all hangs together so that if one strand is removed, all must have been different. It is the precedent in a far more direct process of imitation. But the evidence for this influence (the possibility that the Nazis got exaggerated reports of Bolshevik reprisals during the civil war; the truly tortuous exegesis of Hitler's fears expressed at the time of Stalin-grad) is indirect at best and occasionally flies in the face of known records.[14] It can hardly explain the different forms and targets of Nazi killing. As much precedent lay in the euthanasia program, which had already exploited the concept of *lebensunwertes Leben* (life unworthy of life) to terminate 60,000 to 80,000 lives, some by means of carbon monoxide gas chambers. As early as 1935, Hitler had confided that he might use the opportunity of wartime to remove remaining impedi-ments to euthanasia programs.[15] The Nazi murders had their own momentum.

The fact that genocide was conceived at home does not, however, preclude comparison. To compare two events does not entail claiming that one causes the other. Comparison is a dual process that scrutinizes two or more systems to learn what elements they have in common, and what elements distinguish them. It does not assert identity; it does not deny unique components. The issue to be resolved is under what circumstances comparison adds to knowledge. First, it must have a plausible basis in fact.[16] Just as important, however, comparison should go beyond mere taxonomy and offer perspectives that the single case might not suggest. Then it can help reveal a wider historical process at work.

Cases of mass killing offer a valid enough starting point for compari-son. But comparison for what end? Some of what we understand of terror and genocide in general can be learned from any *one* of the cases, Stalinist, Nazi, or Cambodian. Comparison is hardly necessary to un-derstanding how pervasive were, say, the isolation or atomization em-phasized by Hannah Arendt,[17] the fear of intervening when friends were dragged away, the destruction of human solidarity. Likewise, comparison is not strictly necessary to understanding how crucial was the fragmentation of responsibility among the perpetrators. The entre-preneurs of genocide are like the organizers of Adam Smith's pin factory who have discovered the division of labor. Ideologues conjure up a monstrous conspiracy and insist that some groups partake of lesser degrees of humanity; ambitious administrators define target cat-egories and compete for jurisdiction; different officials pass sentences or create administrative authorities; others arrest, some load onto trains, others unload, some guard, others herd people to the killing ground or into the gas chambers; still others shake cyanide crystals into the vents. (We cannot fall back upon this fragmentation of tasks, however, for the *Einsatzgruppen*, the SS killing squads that shot thousands upon thousands of Jews before the gas chambers were in operation. They did not merely carry out one task on an assembly line, but hunted Jews or partisans with zeal. Some machine-gunned rows of naked, depersonalized targets; others shot one by one.)[18] Mass murder as a vocation does not depend upon sadism. It may be facilitated by ideological indoctrination; it may require no more than the motivation to do a "good" job and be a "good" soldier. Certainly it requires a radical skewing of perceived solidarity. Any sense of connection with the target fades; the only obligation that motivates unites the murderers.[19]

Understanding this process, to the degree that it can be "understood," does not require comparison so much as reflection on any particular genocide. Why, then, compare holocausts? What "interests" orient this research, in Habermas's terminology? Several motives are possible: scientific, exculpatory, and even proprietary.

The scientific interest has several components. Comparison will enable the historian better to understand the specificity of each such murderous episode. Marc Bloch emphasized that historians exploit comparison precisely to learn what aspects of a historical situation were singular,[20] and, it will be argued below, any comparison that fails to emphasize the persisting differences is probably undertaken in bad faith. But comparison may also help the researcher to discern a common causal mechanism otherwise unrevealed—to diagnose, in a sense, a human illness, or develop a sociology of genocide. Whether comparison can yield such regularities is unclear. Nevertheless, social scientists strive to understand the causes and course of modern wars or revolutions. In the same spirit, a social science of comparative holocausts might produce new insights. Finally, the student may just possess a taxonomic passion, the urge to understand the variants among genocides, to develop a classificatory expertise in the dark side of history.

The second underlying motivation—to remove the emotional or moral burden of singularity and uniqueness—is more problematic. This alleged search for "normalization" is what is at stake in the current controversy. The difficulty, of course, is that no historian or social scientist will admit that the need for moral unburdening has operated as a motive. Thus the question arises as to whether some "objective" test can be devised that allows us to decide when scholarship is so motivated, and, if it is, whether it must thereby be invalidated. Subjective orientations, as Weber suggested, lie behind all social-scientific questions. The problem is to determine at what point they render the results untrustworthy.

The final interest also has a moral dimension, and likewise raises troubling questions, which will be explored in the Epilogue. It is the reverse of the exculpatory motive, namely the desire to share in the moral, political, or material compensation that Holocaust victims now claim from the rest of humanity.

No matter what the motivation or "interest" in the research, the test of the comparison must be its relevance and explanatory power. To some degree validation must remain subjective. But are there no criteria to test whether comparisons are fruitful and illuminating? Or at least no objective criteria that can test whether or not they are trivial, arbitrary, or misleading?[21] Some guidelines to resolve this problem will be suggested at the end of the next section.

Preserving Distinctions

Start, however, with Nolte's specific comparison. To what extent was the Holocaust one among other genocides? To what degree was it worse than or different from other acts of tyranny or totalitarianism? Can its evil be compared, weighed, or calculated on some moral index? What should be the relevant universe of comparison? Here, to be fair, we must examine Nolte's subsequent efforts to clarify his original position. With the *Historikerstreit* behind him, Nolte has published two volumes: a collection of responses to his critics[22] and a massive synthetic essay that Nolte sees as a sort of epilogue to his "trilogy" on fascism, communism, and the Cold War.[23] In this last book Nolte insists, "The Final Solution is singular in a certain, not merely trivial sense, but that does not mean it cannot be compared."[24]

Those who objected to Nolte's and Fest's articles argued that the comparisons with the Ottomans, the Khmer Rouge, or even post-revolutionary Russia were superficial and invalid. Only Germany had been a cultured Western state, heir to Enlightenment values, developed politically and economically. Fest replied that this objection concealed an implicit racism, an updated *Herrenvolk* mentality. It patronized non-westerners and alleged that they need not be held to common ethical standards. Not so, responded Jürgen Kocka. The issue was Germany's own points of reference. In all important respects, including the rule of law, Germans had sought to be compared with Western nations. But among that comity theirs was the only country that had lapsed into so murderous a policy.[25]

Kocka's argumentation is well taken, but wanton murder is not a crime only by Enlightenment standards. The Cambodia slaughter was not just a savage eruption in a remote tribal society. It was a complex product of ideological zealotry and ethnic prejudices. In proportional terms, Jews and Armenians suffered a greater toll (from "others"). But considered as the aftermath or prolongation of a civil war, the Cambodian massacres from 1975 to 1978 probably claimed a greater share of victims than any other twentieth-century conflict—up to a million or more victims in a country of about 7 million. Nor was Cambodian society, with its French-educated elite, its episodic intolerance of minorities, and its revolutionary cadre obsessed with an ideology of Kampuchean purity and economic development, untouched by the impulses that emerged in Russia and Germany. The Khmer Rouge turned its fury first on all sources of potential opposition, including so-called intellectuals, professionals, and city dwellers in general; then on ethnic minorities; and finally on its own cadres. There may have been less time to establish a secret police or other terrorist bureaucracy. But, as is often the case elsewhere, the Cambodian revolutionaries characteristically demanded that their former comrades and current victims undergo self-abasement and confession. Woe to those summoned by the Khmer Rouge to write their autobiographies.[26]

The Turkish slaughter of perhaps a million and a half Armenians presents a closer parallel to the National Socialist targeting of Jewish victims. Here, after all, was a deliberate massacre of an ethnic minority, ordered by the Ottoman minister of the interior in 1915, organized under government supervision, and carried out by frequent pogrom-like slaughters in local communities, followed by mass deportations to concentration camps in the Syrian desert, where the victims were left to weaken and die of exposure and starvation or to be attacked anew by their persecutors.[27] In many respects the Armenian slaughters read like a curtain raiser for the Final Solution, rehearsed among a less Westernized population where doctrines of holy war allowed a mass fury for which the Nazis had to substitute the bureaucratic indoctrination of the SS. Savage though it was, the Ottoman crime did not yet possess killing institutions such as Auschwitz or Treblinka. The point, however, is not that the genocide of the Jews was somehow worse, but that it had its own unique characteristics. The Ottomans resented the racial minority in their midst, and government officials envisaged the Armenians as a fifth column for the Entente in 1915, much as the Jews appeared as the fomenters of a global coalition against Germany. Nonetheless, important differences remained. The German regime saw much of its *raison d'être* in combatting Judaism and Jewish bolshevism throughout Europe; it was collectively obsessed by Jewish issues; anti-Semitism played a general role as a doctrine of hostility against liberal and Enlightenment values throughout the Western world. None of this is to dismiss the cruelty of Turkish policy or the sufferings of the Armenian communities.

As Nolte insists, the parallel that seems most relevant is that of Stalinist terror. Only Stalinism has allowed Nazism the possible consolation of taking second place among exterminations. The Russian civil war from 1917 to 1921 may have sacrificed millions of victims, but the killings of the 1930s could no longer claim even the alibi of being wartime reprisals. Repression in both Stalinist Russia and Nazi Germany went far beyond the pogrom model. (The organized destruction of Kristallnacht, however, bore some similarity to the Russian government's acquiescence in—or indeed encouragement of—the devastation by the Russian Black Hundreds after the 1905 Revolution.) Both the Third Reich and the Soviet regime proceeded methodically. In both cases huge bureaucratic apparatuses understood that their mandate called for arrests, deportation, and death.

Still, it is not clear what devastations are comparable. Should one count the victims of the Ukrainian famine of 1932–33 as part of the terror? Did the famine involve a deliberate Soviet policy of preventing food from reaching the Ukrainian population—a victory of attrition, comparable to the German conduct of the war against the Herero in Southwest Africa in 1906, or to the Nigerian suppression of the Biafrans in 1967–1969? Or is one to count only executions and deliberate deportations? Even without the estimates of the famine, the death toll under Stalin probably outnumbers that of the Nazi camps.[28] The following list provides rough estimates of the Soviet and Nazi victims, grouped as far as possible in parallel categories, including the number of official death sentences. Death sentences in court accounted for only a small number of victims. The Nazis, of course, did not use judicial proceedings to carry out the murder of Jews as Jews. Moreover, even in cases in which courts did not impose the death penalty but sentenced offenders to labor camps (in Russia) or concentration camps (in

Germany), death often followed as a matter of course. In the Soviet camps, Robert Conquest reports, one third of the prisoners died within the first year, and by 1938 the death rate for all camp prisoners was about 20 percent per annum.[29] Mortality figures for the German camps are estimated at about 33 percent per annum before the war, at least 45 percent thereafter.[30]

Estimates of Soviet Victims, 1926–1953

Deaths and/or deportation of "class enemies" (kulaks)
during collectivization
  7 million dead in the 1932–33 famine
  c. 4 million deaths (3 million Ukrainian kulaks and 1 million Kazakhs) after
    deportation, 1926–1937
  perhaps another 3.5 million deported before 1937 but dying later

Political purges
  1937–1939: 7–8 million arrested, with perhaps 1 million of these sentenced to
    death and executed in prison or later in camps
  1936–1953: perhaps 12 million deaths in camps from mistreatment and hard-
    ship

Arrests and deportations of Poles, 1939–1942
  1.06 million, of whom 270,000 died

Deportations of ethnic enclaves in the USSR after 1940
  200,000 from the Baltic republics
  200,000 Bessarabians, c. 1.5 million Volga Germans, Crimean Tatars, etc.
  Deaths involved unknown; perhaps 500,000

Estimated total deaths: c. 20 million[31]

Estimates of Nazi Victims, 1933–1945

Executions following judicial proceedings
  Civilians: 16,560 estimated overall, about 12,000 of which occurred in the
    years 1940–1944 (includes up to a couple of hundred summary executions
    during the Roehm Purge of June 30, 1934, and at least 200 prominent
    members of the Resistance leaders after the abortive plot of July 20, 1944,
    although Ministry of Justice figures record 5,764 death sentences for 1944,
    800 for January–April 1945). Military: 40–50,000 German soldiers (follow-
    ing courts-martial).[32]

Deaths in concentration camps aside from mass exterminations
  Perhaps 1 to 1.8 million (population of concentration camps: approximately
    25,000 by September 1, 1939; approximately 700,000 by January 15, 1945;
    perhaps 8–10 million prisoners of all sorts passed through the concentration
    camps in 1933–1945)[33]

Executions by German armed forces and mobile SS Einsatzgruppen in Russia, 1941–1945
　1–2 million

Executions of Jews, gypsies, and Slavs in conquered and disarmed territories under German control, 1940–1945 (i.e., in ghettos and extermination camps)
　4–5 million[34]

Estimated total deaths: 7–8 million

This list excludes the German executions of alleged partisans or related reprisals during the war. It also excludes the mistreatment, shooting upon surrender, and killing by attrition of perhaps 2 million German and 3.3 million Russian prisoners of war;[35] the decreed executions of POW officers attempting to escape from German captivity (British and American officers were spared); or the perhaps 2 million or more Germans who died during the expulsion of about 12 million Germans from East Prussia, the Sudetenland, Pomerania, and Silesia at the end of the war.

No matter how stupefying, the numbers remain important. Too often the issue of numbers is treated slightingly. The liberal historian who lives in more peaceful times is troubled by civilian deaths that take a far smaller toll, such as those of My Lai, Beirut, or even Hiroshima. Is not the difference between them and Auschwitz only quantitative? Even were the differences "merely" quantitative (which is not the fact), numbers matter. Most people accept that murdering upward of a million people is a different order of crime from unjustly executing several hundred. Nonetheless, the tolls of both the German and the Russian regimes are so massive that the issue of uniqueness cannot turn on numbers alone. What sets apart the National Socialist crime—not necessarily making it "worse" but making it different, and appalling and unassimilable—is ultimately the murder of Jews. Without the Jews, the *furor teutonicus* might have raged in the conquered regions of Russia, and tens of thousands would still have died in the concentration camps in Germany and Austria. But the great extermination centers in Poland—Auschwitz, Belzec, Chelmno, Majdanek, Sobibor, and Treblinka—would not have been established. Without the Jews the mass shootings at Babi Yar, Kamenets-Podolsk, Riga (first of the native Jews, later of the German Jews sent to the ghetto emptied by the initial wave of killing), Rovno, Odessa-Dalnik (a contribution by Rumanian forces), and elsewhere would not have taken place.[36] As Eberhard Jäckel has written: "never before had a state . . . decided that a specific human group, including its aged, its women, its children and infants, would be killed as quickly as possible, and then carried through this regulation using every possible means of state power."[37]

It is true that Stalinist terror also targeted broad groups of victims who were defined not by their deeds, nor even by their imagined crimes, but by ascriptive group characteristics alone. Nolte, Fest, Hildebrand, and others have argued that whereas Hitler's regime proscribed by virtue of "race," Bolshevik ideologues called for the liquidation of the bourgeoisie "as a class." Liquidating a class usually meant removing its social-structural underpinning, that is, expropriating private capital. In the aftermath of the Russian civil war and during collectivization, however, it often did mean physical liquidation, as some groups of allegedly nonproletarian origin were denied access to cities, jobs, and food. Kulak status—passed on to children regardless of their actual socioeconomic condition—could mean starvation. In other cases, relatives of those under arrest themselves came under official suspicion. Like Nazism, Stalinism often took its vengeance by category.

Both doctrines, too, indulged in a discourse that allowed a ready transition to violence. What the exact intention of violent rhetoric might be was not always clear. In a notable Reichstag speech of January 30, 1939, Hitler announced that a new war would entail the destruction of the Jews, and in August he allegedly asked his generals, who still talked about the extermination of the Armenians? Nonetheless, we cannot be certain to what degree figurative language and literal plans mingled in his thinking.[38] Legal segregation, exile from Germany, mass murder—the options chosen would depend upon opportunities and the exclusion of alternatives. Nazi discourse accommodated, even encouraged, murder. It prepared the leadership to effect physical extermination without agonizing over any intervening moral threshold. Once the briefly held idea of shipping Jews to Madagascar proved a mirage, poison gas hardly seemed a step different in kind. The seductive formula of "life unworthy of life" facilitated a glissando from euthanasia to genocide. But liquidation of the bourgeoisie as a class could also license murder. Given the abusive potential of ideology, the distinction between the categorizing of right and left may be less robust than liberals like to believe.

Nonetheless, important differences persist. No Soviet citizen had to expect that deportation or death must be so inevitable by virtue of ethnic origins. "Unlike the case with any other group, and unlike the massacres before or since, *every single one* of the millions of targeted Jews was to be murdered. Eradication was to be total."[39] Nor did the Soviets establish facilities purely for extermination. The conditions of labor in the Siberian camps were lethal enough that only a quarter of inmates might survive. But no camp such as Treblinka existed, precisely just to kill masses of human beings on arrival. Nor did the Soviet regime dedicate itself to the dragnet of victims, wherever it might reach them. Only the Nazis defined the Jewish communities of Europe as their game, bargaining even with would-be allies of the New Order to lay their hands on even the smallest Jewish settlements.

Claude Lanzmann has captured the quality of this mission by returning almost compulsively to the role of railroads and trains in *Shoah*, which starts with repeated views of the locomotive creaking into the country station at Treblinka. The emphasis on trains and stations, followed by an extensive discussion of how the Reichsbahn mundanely organized this human freight service, is fitting. For the Final Solution depended upon transports. The railroads connected the overcrowded centers of population and resettlement with the establishments of death. A string of boxcars would arrive regularly, for example, in the center of Westerbork to pick up a consignment of several thousand Dutch Jews, thence to take them on their slow lethal journey to Auschwitz, where they would be sorted into those immediately to be killed, and those to be used temporarily for labor. As one of the chroniclers of Auschwitz wrote, "The transports swell into weeks, months, years. When the war is over, they will count up the marks in their notebooks—all four and a half million of them. The bloodiest battle of the war, the greatest victory of the strong, united Germany. *Ein Reich, ein Volk, ein Führer*—and four crematoria."[40]

Still, some of these distinctions seem less clear-cut than they did earlier. Testimony from the Soviet Union erodes the Nazi specificity. Solzhenitsyn describes the "zek" cars leaving the Moscow Northern prison at 1700 hours on odd-numbered days and at 600 hours on even-numbered days, or the red trains for mass deportations; the trips lasting for weeks with little water and food, the deaths en route.[41] Evgenia Ginzburg and other witnesses recall the "Stolypin cars" wandering around central Asia, leisurely taking their thirsting and fetid cargo to the frozen north. Ginzburg, Nadezhda Mandelstam, and Vasily Grossman allow little sentimentality about Russian conditions.[42] For too long Western intellectuals hung on the difference between Stalinist excesses committed in the name of historical progress, and Nazi crimes carried out to abet the most backward aspirations. In a sense they sought to relativize Communist terror vis-à-vis Auschwitz, even as Nolte and others have sought to relativize Auschwitz vis-à-vis the gulag. Insisting on the distinction between the ideological objectives of Communism and Nazism is not the problem. Raymond Aron was able to preserve the difference without excusing either regime: "Of course, I do not ignore the fact that Stalin probably massacred more people as enemies of the revolution than Hitler did in the name of the purity of the race . . . Hostility based on the class struggle has taken on no less extreme or monstrous forms than that based on the incompatibility of races. But if we wish to 'save the concepts' there is a difference between a philosophy whose logic is monstrous and one which can be given a monstrous interpretation."[43] It is indeed crucial to "save the concepts." Every historian would have to regard it as crucial even were she or he writing as the last survivor on a dead planet. Much of the *Historikerstreit* is precisely a contest over moral distinctions, which, if clouded, license barbarism. But if we insist on distinctions, it cannot be to rehabilitate Stalinism.

Nor can we easily chalk up the differences that did exist to the advantage of one regime or the other. In terms of moral bookkeeping both experiences were appalling. Consider the relationship of legal proceedings to punishment. The Soviets may have passed a larger proportion of their victims before some form of tribunal. Sometimes quotas of victims were suggested for particular regions or camps. The security forces apparently knew intuitively that, say, 5 to 10 percent of the party members in a given area were dangerous wreckers and merely asked the local bosses to find which ones they might be! Of course, when trials did take place, as in the case of the Nazi *Volksgerichte*, the proceedings were travesties. Nazi jurisprudence, however, did not have the same need to have the victims confirm their guilt and the beneficence of the regime: judges were content with the opportunity merely to degrade, denounce, and sentence their victims. Moreover, the Nazi courts usually tried cases that, no matter how monstrously, were still construed as acts of real opposition—even if by the war years, such crimes might represent only petty complaining, offhand comments, predictions that the war might be lost, or slackness on the job. The Soviet courts imposed more readily the jurisprudence of the Red Queen. Only after arrest could the victim know he or she had been guilty of "wrecking" or abetting Trotskyite conspiracy. The crimes were fanciful: anti-Soviet agitation, counterrevolutionary activity, *sus-*

picion of espionage (surely a self-proving category), even family relationship to someone convicted.[44] Arrest might follow as an interrogated prisoner was persuaded to denounce possible collaborators among his friends and colleagues. (Ethnic groups and kulaks could be consigned to the gulag without trial.) In terms of the means of interrogation, and then of brutality by camp guards, it would be hard to distinguish degrees. But Nazi Germany relied less on major purges. There were continuing arrests and imprisonments, widespread confinement before trial in concentration camps, increasing recourse to the guillotine against complainers and doubters—but only one major judicial purge. In the repressions following the July 20 plot, the People's Court tried and executed about 200 from the networks of the conspirators. (In the wake of the June 30, 1934, arrests of the Sturmabteilung [SA] and other potential anti-Nazis, perhaps 100 victims were shot summarily.) But this was only a small portion of the approximately 6,500 death sentences meted out for opposition to the regime or the war in 1944–45. In all, the courts probably ordered from 20,000 to 25,000 executions for political crimes during the twelve years of the Third Reich.[45] Estimates of Soviet executions in 1937–38 included half a million political prisoners and half a million thieves.[46] Which is worse, a regime that hardly bothers with trials, that just turns over to the police, the army, or the security forces the power of life or death; or one that insists on parodies of trial and confession?

Distinctions remain, but they are not the sort that can be used to establish special medals for victimhood. Hannah Arendt emphasized the common role of terror in totalitarian systems:

> Total terror, the essence of totalitarian government, exists neither for nor against men. It is supposed to provide the forces of nature or history with an incomparable instrument to accelerate their movement . . . terror executes on the spot the death sentences which Nature is supposed to have pronounced on races or individuals who are "unfit to live," or History on "dying classes," without waiting for the slower and less efficient processes of nature or history themselves . . . The inhabitants of a totalitarian country are thrown into and caught in the process of nature or history for the sake of accelerating its movement; as such, they can only be executioners or victims of its inherent law.[47]

Terror was essential to keeping a population atomized, invertebrate: "Isolation may be the beginning of terror; it certainly is its most fertile ground; it always is its result."[48]

Nonetheless, terror functioned somewhat differently in Stalin's Russia and under Nazism. The studies that sought to demonstrate the barbarism common to totalitarian regimes, including Arendt's imposing but problematic work, failed to emphasize some revealing distinctions. Arendt rightly says that arrests of real opponents could never have sufficed to keep the camps filled either in Russia or Germany. The system required innocents.[49] But the issue is not only whether terror struck at innocents (a language that unfortunately implies that the so-called guilty were guilty of real crimes). It is also important whether there might have been predictability about which innocents were chosen and therefore which innocents might be spared. In the German case, the innocents replenishing the camps were generally Jews, and Aryan innocents were largely spared unless slandered by personal enemies. Nazi terror operated against opponents of the regime or those who verged on dissent. It also culled Jews from the Aryans. But non-Jewish political figures could survive unmolested if they stayed clear of any organized opposition. Not every former opponent was spared, but many were left merely to vegetate. Social Democratic trade union leaders and Center Party figures such as Konrad Adenauer waited for the storm to pass. In effect terror circumscribed the German racial community, confirmed those who might belong, and moved implacably against those who would not, or for "racial" reasons could not. Moreover, after the suppression of the SA there was no major purge of members of the National Socialist movement. While the Führer was declared to be the source of law, and thus an arbitrary concept of legislation was enshrined in jurisprudence, rules remained consistent. This situation was significantly different from that in the Soviet Union, where constitutional norms were formally inscribed, but opinions that were within the range of orthodoxy one year might be declared retroactively subversive the next. By the late 1930s the cadres of original revolutionary leaders had been largely liquidated. When Hitler consolidated his position over the military establishment in 1938, he removed two principal generals, which in one case required an elaborate trumped-up case of homosexuality. Stalin had up to half of his officer corps liquidated. In Nazi Germany law might be officially oracular, but practice was consistent if brutal. In the Soviet Union no consistency could be expected. Quirks of fate doomed people or saved them. German terror worked to enforce a protected community and move ruthlessly against those outside the *Volksgemeinschaft*; Soviet terror aimed precisely at eliminating any such predictability. When Hitler enacted what he intended to be the legislation for arrest due to strike most terror—the Night and Fog decree of December 7, 1941—it was directed at subjects in the occupied territories, not at German citizens.

The principle of German terror (when practiced inside Germany) was to enforce an iron law of predictable consequences, any deviation from which was likely to consign the deviant (and Jews were deviants) to the realm of arbitrary power, torment, and dehumanization. The principle of Soviet terror was to enforce the arbitrary discipline of nonpredictability. Stalinism was stochastic. After an arrest, acquaintances would decide that the victim must have done something, gone too far, had a bad character. Mandelstam's widow recalls:

> We never asked, on hearing about the latest arrest, "What was he arrested for?" but we were exceptional. Most people, crazed by fear, asked this question just to give themselves a little hope; if others were arrested for some reason then they wouldn't be arrested, because they hadn't done anything wrong . . . "*What for?*" Akhmatova would cry indignantly whenever, infected by the prevailing climate, anyone of our circle asked this question. "What do you mean, *what for?* It's time you understood that people are arrested *for nothing!*"[50]

History, the Party, was always right, but wherein correctness lay was not easily known. As its agents used to say, "Give us a man and we will make a case." One need not hold everything to be true, Kafka's priest tells Josef K.—only to be necessary. " 'A gloomy opinion,' K. answered. 'It makes the lie into the order of the world.' "[51] Hidden gods, however, do not lose their appeal by virtue of inscrutability.

This distinction between predictive and stochastic terror may be overdrawn. The specter of friends and colleagues being arrested at night, brutally interrogated, and then incarcerated in one of the dozens of concentration camps was hardly calculated to make sensitive Germans feel cozy in the *Volksgemeinschaft*.[52] In both the Third Reich and the Soviet Union, the length of time in a camp or the rigor of the experience was uncertain. Informal expressions of opinion had to be circumspect; no one could be certain of his friends. Both systems encouraged denunciations and informers and destroyed trust. Still, the quality of disciplinary fear created was of a different order. If we distinguish among different forms of democracy, we should classify forms of terror. Increasingly during the 1930s in the German Reich there was certainty of exclusion, hardship, and degradation for Jews; there was the likelihood of cruel interrogation, internment at a camp, perhaps

death, for those contemplating opposition. After 1941 there were deportation and usually death. But the loyal or the passive non-Jewish
subject did not have to live with terror as did the Russian intelligentsia,
party members, functionaries, or factory managers. And some unfortu-
nates managed to be exposed to the menaces of both regimes: "The
way we have scurried to and fro in the twentieth century, trapped
between Hitler and Stalin!"[53]

Why, given this invidious competition, does it seem important to
insist on the uniqueness of the Nazi crimes? Why is there still a resonance to Auschwitz that Vorkuta or Kolyma does not possess? Because, nowhere else but in German-occupied Europe from 1941 to 1945
was there an apparatus so single-mindedly established to carry out
mass murder as a process in its own right. And not just mass murder,
but ethnic extermination—killing, without even a pretext of individual
wrongdoing, an entire people (if gypsies are counted, two peoples),
including its children and its aged. The Russian system was wantonly
brutal, cynical in its demand for punishment and confession, cruel,
sycophantic, a perversion of any ideals that once motivated the revolutionaries. And yet despite all the blood, it did not set out to exterminate as an end in itself. Physical extermination may not have been the
initial objective of the Nazis, at least not one they could envisage as
possible. Circumstances led to the Final Solution as a murderous one.
But the logic and rhetoric of Nazism easily sanctioned murder. It so
dehumanized Jews that murder, at the end, seemed hardly a new
threshold. The witness is appalled above all by the killing itself; but the
agents themselves had already crossed the threshold of moral consciousness. By 1941 genocide became a technical objective. It motivated
a zealous bureaucracy, prevailed against what would have been a more
"rational" use of slave labor, diverted energies from a desperate war
effort. That single-minded orientation to killing a target population
did not grip the Soviet regime, although it wanted absolute subordination of any potential or imagined dissent.[54] No one in Germany cared
whether Jews dissented—who could have expected otherwise, except
the administrators of the camps who needed their services and expected their cooperation?

There is another valid reason to reject the Noltean comparison. It is
more methodological, less about the Holocaust per se. Historians do
not usually believe it acceptable to judge questions according to their
intent or their possible political implications. Not every historical
finding will please the liberal or the conservative: let the political chips

fall where they may. This returns us to the issue of the "interests" or motivation behind comparison. Even an exculpatory intent does not *ipso facto* invalidate a historical comparison. Nonetheless, two criteria do help us decide whether or not the interest in "normalization" has undermined the legitimacy of scholarly inquiry.

First, some inquiries are not open-ended questions, but disguised theses, proposed in a pseudo-interrogative mode. If that is the case, then proofs and argumentation must be offered to substantiate them; they cannot just be thrown out as open-ended hypotheses. Otherwise they travel under false passports. This seems to me the case of Nolte's argumentation. Who, however, decides whether a question is genuine or a disguised thesis? Nolte, Fest, and Hillgruber argue that the historian who objects is substituting taste for truth, aestheticizing a political argument. But there is a test. A genuine historical question will not influence opinion unless it is actually answered. A spurious one is designed to sway opinion by virtue of its just being asked. It asks not about the truth of a proposition, but whether a proposition suggested as true can be uttered. It pretends to test a hypothesis but actually tests the limits of acceptable discourse and achieves its effect because liberal societies do not like to limit discourse. "Was Auschwitz like the gulag?" is a genuine, if clumsy, question. "Can't we possibly say that Auschwitz was like the gulag?" seems to me a spurious historical question, and cannot really claim the privileges of authentic historical inquiry.

The second methodological criterion has less to do with language and more with results. Comparisons cannot be declared intrinsically valid or invalid, right or wrong. They are tools whose utility depends upon the question being posed. An open-ended comparison of Soviet and Nazi prison camps is certainly a useful tool for thinking about how the two regimes resembled each other. But if comparisons are not intrinsically right or wrong, they can be productive for scholarship, or unrewarding, or actually misleading and tendentious. How do we decide?

There are two possible tests. One can be only retrospective: a fruitful comparison generates further hypotheses and research; later researchers build upon its insights to advance knowledge, and we ultimately know that the comparison was not a dead end but a new departure. The other test can be applied without waiting for a verdict. It will not establish that a comparison was fruitful, but it can at least guarantee that it was not tendentious or spurious. Any genuine comparative exercise emphasizes uniqueness as much as similarity; it establishes what is common in contrast to what is distinctive. Ever since Aristotle, comparison has been understood to be an exercise in classificatory logic in which what is generic can be understood only in relation to what is specific. Comparison must be a two-edged sword. A historian's unwillingness to acknowledge both aspects of the venture and a tendency to minimize distinctions at the cost of what is similar may indicate a partisan intent. Nolte's first book was impressive precisely in the continuing tension between an overarching typology of fascism and the variations among the cases chosen. But the emphasis in the recent essays has been to minimize distinctions, to resort to "logical" connections when actual similarities seem abstract at best. In Nolte's scheme the differences would overstrain the framework of comparison; hence the discomfort with working them through. Raymond Aron's notion of "preserving the concepts" or Bloch's insistence on underscoring distinctions thus has a special importance. It is a moral demand upon the researcher; that is, it keeps the comparative historian honest, and it offers a guideline for testing the quality of comparative work offered by others. It is not incompatible with comparative history; indeed it remains the condition of its validity.

"Fear of Fascism"?

Usually those writers who stress the commonality of terror also emphasize the similarity of terrorist regimes. "A fundamental difference between modern dictatorships and all other tyrannies of the past," Hannah Arendt wrote, "is that terror is no longer used as a means to exterminate and frighten opponents, but as an instrument to rule masses of people who are perfectly obedient."[55] Indeed Arendt merely expressed a prevalent opinion when she bracketed Stalinism and National Socialism as totalitarian, but insisted on the sharp distinction between Nazism and Italian Fascism.[56] Nonetheless, Ernst Nolte wrote what remains his soundest and most striking book on the affinity of National Socialism and of Mussolini's movement as variants of fascism. In this regard Nolte has remained something of an outsider. A specter tends to haunt many of the liberals as well as conservatives in German academia; it is the "theory" of fascism.

Karl Dietrich Bracher, whose pioneering analyses of the collapse of Weimar and the rise of Nazism relied on the totalitarian paradigm so persuasive in the 1950s, has remained especially suspicious of "fascism" as a conceptual tool. Evidently uneasy with both sides, he has kept a low profile in the *Historikerstreit*—except to argue that Nolte along with the left was responsible for an unfortunate reliance on the concept of fascism.[57] In his major comment, Bracher treated the controversy as a recent symptom of the ambiguities (*Doppelbödigkeit*) inherent in the history of the Federal Republic. West Germany in effect had constantly to struggle against a sort of structural schizophrenia. It was one of two German states, the heir of two failed regimes, the arena for two generations with differing memories: "The present dispute concerns not only the orientation and meaning of our own epoch, but simultaneously the interpretation of a totalitarian 'past,' which is not easy to historicize but does not simply pass away despite its temporal distance."[58] Given these burdens, Bonn faced the recurrent danger of a relapse into ideological thinking with its contempt for constitutional procedures. The peace movement and antinuclear demonstrators offered empty formulas that hovered "in the borderland between democracy and dictatorship." Political responses such as these threatened to become "pseudo-religious concepts of salvation" that might incubate future totalitarian ideologies." Bracher cited offenders on the left but argued that the distinction between left and right made little difference for the grand simplifiers of history—as the late 1960s had already demonstrated "when we critics of an all-too-general concept of fascism were opposed by a front from Nolte via Habermas to the extraparliamentary opposition."[59]

Why was Nolte's view of fascism so distressing to Bracher? Nolte's *Three Faces of Fascism*, his first major work of history, the product of an outsider to the profession that won him a university position, remains his most brilliant book. Nolte surveyed three avatars of fascism: the right-wing Action Française, a legacy of nineteenth-century counterrevolution, emerged as a protofascism; the Italian movement and regime constituted the classic synthesis; and National Socialism completed the cycle as a fascism radicalized by its anti-Semitism. The movements allegedly exemplified a dialectical progression: Italian Fascism instituted as a regime the presuppositions of Action Française but also negated its intellectualism. Nazism likewise perfected, but was antithetical to, the traits of Italian Fascism, and tacked back toward Action Française by virtue of its anti-Semitism. Nolte's argumentation was also Hegelian in that fascist theory and practice allegedly formed each other. The movements not only actualized the ideas of the leaders; the experience also formed the ideology: practice was premise.

Significantly, Nolte did not seek to explain fascist success in the historian's conventional way, by filling in sequential development. Instead he sought to fit a series of increasingly adequate definitions to the movements as they unfolded. The usual effort to establish causal chains was replaced by an asymptotic search to define the fascist minimum. For Nolte historical phenomena have entelechies toward which they tend more or less imperfectly. To define was to explain; indeed he has continued to rely on this "essentialism" in his recent articles. To declare the gulag to be "a logical and factual precedent" of Nazi terror is Nolte's equivalent of a causal statement.

Despite this essentialist approach, Nolte rightly insisted on the historical specificity of fascism. As a doctrine and movement it was the product of a particular political epoch: the era of world wars (including its imperialist prologue), of the crisis of liberalism, and of the Bolshevik revolution. At the same time fascism incorporated a more general impulse. It was a reaction against the modern process of emancipation and a radical denial of the liberal society that nurtured it.[60]

Only in retrospect have the darker implications of Nolte's complex argument emerged. Granted that as early as 1963 Nolte suggested that the perplexities of modern man to which fascism attested required "sympathy." However, he also insisted that fascism had committed a crime "which is beyond comparison with anything the world has ever seen—even including Stalin's reign of terror against his own people and his own party."[61] He still believes that despite the gulag, the Soviet Union was closer to Western development than National Socialism.[62] But Nolte has retreated from his clear indictment of Nazism, taking refuge in a grand scheme that interprets Marxian socialism and fascism as revolts against the liberal and industrial world. In the original work, fascism had been most comprehensively defined (hence, by Nolte's lights, explained) as a reaction to political and economic processes of "transcendence," which had been embodied successively in liberalism, socialism, and the Russian Revolution. In ordinary language, transcendence referred to the left's characteristic aspiration to liberate men and women from the hierarchies in which tradition had embedded them. It meant emancipating an unfettered human nature from the constraints on consciousness and practical life imposed by poverty, class, or national community. In turn, this radical project called forth the conservative effort to reroot man in a hierarchical political community, anchored in historical time and specific territory. Fascism in effect was a radical form of the conservative program. But over the last decades Nolte has changed his emphasis. Fascism is less a reaction to socialism. Marxism and fascism both appear as reactions to the process of transcendence, which itself looks less like emancipation than Weber's disenchantment of the world. "The industrial revolution was the first phenomenal form of the abstraction of life, which is basically practical transcendence." Marx's interpretation of this transcendence as the capitalist mode of production was intended to demonstrate the inevitability of the transformation of the abstraction of life into the concreteness of individuals who have become universal.[63] The parallels go further: Leninism is to Marxism, in effect, as fascism was to conservatism: "Marxism discovered in Leninism its inversion [*Verkehrung*] but at the same time was thereby brought closer to its truth."[64] It can hardly be surprising that threats of extermination and race hatred are deeply rooted in the process of transcendence and the ideological reactions of left as well as right. Capitalism embodied its own threat of class annihilation and generated the fear of liquidation that Marx would later brandish against the bourgeoisie. "A prescription obviously fulfills its purpose only when it destroys the disease and thereby restores health." (Again the flawed teleological analogue.) From technological unemployment to Auschwitz: fascism, in effect, becomes only a terrible counterprophylactic.[65] Is not the logic confirmed when Marx and Engels' occasional visions of international racial struggles are cited, not to mention Marx's ugly asides on Jewish physiognomy (Ferdinand Lassalle as a Jewish nigger)?[66] This excursus echoes the tentative treatment—once again the pseudointerrogative—of Israel as an inverted fascist state, which made its way into Nolte's 1976 book, *Germany and the Cold War*.[67]

No wonder that a common-sense political scientist such as Bracher was unhappy with these ruminations. Bracher stressed the institutional causes of democratic breakdown, not the similarities of idea systems. By the late 1960s he was concerned with the rise of the rightist National Democratic Party (NPD) and was unwilling to agree with Nolte that fascism was only a malaise of the interwar period. He wanted to educate Germans about their own civic vulnerability; hence the title of his survey of Nazism, *Die deutsche Diktatur* (*The German Dictatorship*): no question of an international fascism there.[68] Nor was Bracher alone in his discomfort with "fascism" as an ideal type. The theory of fascism became the ideological trope of the university left toward the end of the 1960s. As the student movement demanded an intellectual reckoning with the generation of their fathers (one that the 1945 changes had largely omitted to undertake), it was "fascism-theory" that served as a crude ideology. National Socialism was interpreted, in line with interwar Marxist analysis, as a reaction of capitalism in crisis. The reductionism was suggested by the title of one popular book: *Formen bürgerlicher Herrschaft. Liberalismus-Faschismus* (Forms of bourgeois rule: liberalism-fascism).[69] The subtler works of fascism-theory drew on "Bonapartist" explanations proposed by the dissident left under Weimar. Bonapartism (first suggested by Marx's analysis in *The Eighteenth Brumaire of Louis Napoleon*) argued that a class stalemate allowed the state to escape domination by a ruling elite and to emerge with autonomous power as a dictatorial apparatus. The Bonapartist or fascist state imposed a dictatorship upon all classes precisely in the bourgeoisie's own interests, which it could not guarantee under a liberal regime because of the bourgeoisie's own internal class divisions or weakness vis-à-vis other classes. The cruder works of fascism-theory did not accept the heterodox Bonapartist analysis, already condemned between the wars. They tended to recapitulate East German scholars' "Stamokap" (state monopoly capitalism) analysis, which attributed the Nazi seizure to the machinations of a narrow financial and industrial elite.[70]

The theory of fascism was not just an intellectual exercise. It often justified a serious assault on the intellectual independence of university scholars.[71] It was easy to proceed from denouncing ideas to denouncing professors: Nolte was scarred in such conflicts, and even scholars sympathetic to the left, Habermas himself and Iring Fetscher, were led to criticize the assaults on liberty of thought. At left-wing centers, such as Frankfurt or the Otto Suhr Institute at the Free University of Berlin, moderate professors sometimes felt they had to certify successful examination results for students who had mastered only the crudest Leninist formulas. Reform legislation (the so-called *Drittelparität*: in effect a voting by academic estate) stipulated a student and secretarial as well as professorial voice in faculty selection until the Federal Constitutional Court declared that the right to nominate professors accrued only to other professors. As in the United States, the radical wave soon dissipated. The unreconcilable groups were already in the Extraparliamentary Opposition (APO); a handful were attracted by terrorism. The achievements of the Social Democratic government after 1969 brought others back to mainstream politics. But as in Paris, and to a degree in the United States, the revolt deeply scarred many professors. And if any one cluster of ideas typified the ascendancy of the radicals it was the theory of fascism—no longer just a typology to guide research, but apparently the left's ideological wedge that had to be resisted.

Anglo-American historians have also been uneasy about the concept of fascism, and certainly have rejected Bonapartist or other Marxist approaches to fascism-theory.[72] But the rejection has gone too far. Despite all the variations among fascist experiences, the historian of interwar Europe is confronted with a cluster of political movements and then regimes, each glorifying the combat experience as a source of moral legitimacy, given to paramilitary uniforms and formations, elevating a single leader, fiercely hostile to Marxian parties and trade-union movements, contemptuous of liberalism and parliamentary governments, violent in rhetoric and in action. Not to allow a common term for that characteristic historical formation seems excessively nominalist.

In Germany the opponents of fascism theory have emphasized a particular argument. For if there was any one demonstration that fascism was not a legitimate generic concept, critics reasoned, it was the fact that anti-Semitism was fundamental to the Nazis and almost extraneous to the Italian Fascists. The radical anti-Semitism that characterized National Socialism clearly demonstrated that no affinity could link Italian Fascism and Nazism; hence no neo-Marxist notion had a real foundation. The implications of this insistence on the centrality of anti-Semitism were not always clear. To many onlookers it appeared just admirable and entirely unproblematic. Leading German interpreters were facing up, it appeared, to the German disease, confronting it and resisting the evasions characteristic of an earlier generation. If only the East Germans would do likewise. But there was more to it. By insisting on this centrality, German historians were also emphasizing the anti-Marxian thrust of their interpretations. At a time when the Springer-Verlag and Franz Josef Strauss were the greatest champions of Israel, and the German left was itself indulging in ugly anti-Israeli, indeed anti-Semitic, rhetoric, the historiography of Nazi specificity seemed a healthy response to these trends. But might the emphasis on Nazi anti-Semitism not harbor its own apologetic thrust?

This is a difficult issue to raise, laden with sensitivities, subject to misinterpretation. But at the major conference held in the cavernous Reichstag building to mark the fiftieth anniversary of the Nazi seizure of power, the alignments were revealing. There Walter Hofer and other opponents of fascism-theory again insisted that anti-Semitism had been the hallmark of Nazism. And in the major closing address, the neoconservative (though once SPD-affiliated) philosopher, Hermann Lübbe argued that the period from the end of the war through the 1950s, so often condemned for its unwillingness to face up to Nazi crimes, had actually been an era of silent self-examination. There had been no repression of the past. "This partial silence was the social-psychological and politically necessary medium for the transformation of our postwar population into the citizenry of the Federal Republic." The very effort to reintegrate former Nazis, Lübbe argued provocatively, was intended to facilitate a democratic consensus for the new Bonn republic. Given the fact that so many adults had been caught up by Nazism, a moralistic purge or exclusion would only have sown continuing rancor. Hence the students of the late 1960s, who claimed to be the first decisively to repudiate National Socialism, were in fact fleeing the civic responsibility of the West German community and denying responsibility for the German past. The argument with fascism, Lübbe charged, became transformed into a method for delegitimizing the Federal Republic.[73] The speech was provocative. The journalist Carola Stern paraphrased the message: "Everything would have turned out well if it hadn't been for the left."[74] And Hermann Rudolph responded that Lübbe's version of the past must lead to a falsely dichotomized image of postwar history. Lübbe contrasted the supposedly profound thinking through of Nazism with the student rebellion's strident theses of 1968. But, Rudolph objected, Lübbe's view undervalued the change of consciousness that actually took place from the mid-1950s through the 1960s and produced a second formative period of the Federal Republic. As for Lübbe's claim that the unwillingness to purge Nazi offenders represented a conscious effort to integrate them as democratic citizens without their regrettable past—how could "subjects" exist without their past? No new "identity," Rudolph tartly suggested, could be created through a dose of historical oblivion.[75]

Lübbe gave offense; but did Bracher feel so differently when he later wrote that the university conflicts of the 1960s had "politicized and often . . . objectionably distorted" historical controversies?[76] Thus two years before Bitburg the debate at the fiftieth-anniversary conference placed on the agenda key themes of the historians' controversy: above all the conservatives' insistence that the left's analysis of fascism (implicitly Marxist, always citing Horkheimer's vague proscription: "Any one who wants to stay quiet about fascism shouldn't talk about capitalism") was implicitly subversive; that it precluded finally working through the past, and that it destroyed the possibilities for identity.[77] But there was a key difference. At the Reichstag conference, leading historians insisted upon the Third Reich's anti-Jewish policies precisely to discredit the left's theory of fascism.[78] By the time of the *Historikerstreit*, the specificity of the Jewish issue had been subordinated. To be sure, the Jews were one group of victims . . . among others. Rightly understood, the kulaks in Russia, liquidated as a class, or the Wehrmacht conscripts, slain in defense of their homeland against Allied plans for partition, were all victims. Since the fear of fascism—that is, of fascism as an ideal type that calls capitalism into question—no longer prevails, emphasizing Nazi anti-Semitism is no longer necessary. The conservatives, even the historians of the *juste milieu*, no longer need to fear and condemn a left that was disturbingly open to anti-Semitic currents.

The outside observer is thus led to a painful question. Was the insistence on the centrality of anti-Semitism, which seemed so admirable a facing-up to the German past, in part at least just a strategy for dealing with the radical left? Was anti-Antisemitism instrumentalized for political purposes? The question bears on politics as well as on historiography. Grateful as Israelis are for whatever understanding their beleaguered position finds in European intellectual circles, which are too often prepared to equate policies regarding the West Bank with "Auschwitz," is the support from Springer or Strauss entirely free from German domestic political motivation?

The Dangers of Historicization

Another hard question intrudes: Is there any responsibility on the historians' left for these new tendencies? A new controversy has erupted about the implications of "historicization." Nolte has claimed "historicization" as his objective.[79] Is the approach—unclear though it may be—irremediably tainted by his results? Was it not Martin Broszat (as Joachim Fest reminded readers) who set the agenda in 1985 with his plea for a historicization of National Socialism?[80] As Dan Diner asks in his introduction to a recent collection of essays on this subject, "Must the project of historicization of National Socialism necessarily lead to the positions that Nolte's name now stands for?"[81]

Broszat and Hans Mommsen would certainly reject this imputation, but the Israeli historian Saul Friedländer, who respects their work in most ways, shares some of Fest's judgments. Friedländer believes that

Broszat's "historicization"—which he sees as emphasizing the long-term modernization processes that continued through the Nazi regime (such as the development of the welfare state, the evolution of women's status, and the leveling of social elites)—too easily leads to an apologetic "historicism." It loses sight of the regime's fundamental criminality insofar as it discusses long-term developments in the role of women, or economic policies, that allows no moral condemnation. It pleads for the historian to drop his critical "distance" from the regime. It asks, finally, that the historian treat the epoch 1933–1945 as one era among others. "Writing about Nazism," Friedländer protests, "is something entirely different from writing a history of France in the sixteenth century." Historicization, he believes, does suggest that the Third Reich should be written about as if it were as remote as sixteenth-century France.[82] (He leaves unanswered whether four centuries after the Third Reich we shall be allowed to write about it as if it were so remote.) Dan Diner suggests the dilemma more forcefully: ultimately (as Christa Wolf's epigraph suggests, and as Nolte explicitly denies), Auschwitz is not understandable:

> Auschwitz is a no-man's-land of the mind, a black box of explanation; it sucks in all historiographic attempts at interpretation, is a vacuum taking meaning from outside history. Only *ex negativo*, only through the constant attempt to understand why it cannot be understood, can we measure what sort of occurrence this breach of civilization really was. As the most extreme of extreme cases, and thus as the absolute measure of history, this event is hardly historicizable. Seriously meant efforts at historicization have so far ended in a prioris of historical theory. Efforts at historicization undertaken with other intentions, which relativize or level out the event, necessarily end in an apology. This too is a lesson of the *Historikerstreit*.[83]

I agree—Auschwitz remains incomprehensible. But Broszat is asking for historicization of the Third Reich as a whole and not just of Auschwitz. Auschwitz remains one aspect of the regime, indelibly associated with it, but not the total experience for most Germans. Historicization, it seems to me, is an effort not to understand Auschwitz, but to understand a regime in which Auschwitz and a lived normality (even if only as a species of false consciousness) could coexist. It endeavors to get at the simultaneity of banality and apocalypse, or, as Peukert says, "barbarism and the everyday."[84] For Friedländer, Diner, and others, however, such an effort to understand must exculpate. The "everyday" aspects of the Third Reich possess the same moral and historical significance as Commandant Rudolf Höss's garden outside the enclosures of the crematoria.

But must the effort at "historicization" end in apology? I think it more precise to say that it must risk apology but need not lead to it. Unfortunately the term *historicization* is fuzzy; it underestimates earlier efforts to understand the regime in historical context; it leads to the truism (exploited by Nolte's defense) that the historian must historicize. Critics are correct when they sense that the methodology of "historicization" involves a reviewed *Historismus*, hostage to subjectivity. It seeks to go beyond the "structural" history, built upon political science models, that characterized Bracher's work. It strives for a recreation of *mentalités* under Nazism. The key hermeneutical category has become another unfortunate term: that of *Resistenz*, a concept advanced in the collective project directed by Broszat concerning Bavaria under Nazism.[85] *Resistenz* was intended to describe a mixture of acceptance and rejection below the threshold of outright opposition. It has come to include activities as diverse, say, as church attendance, asking for higher pay, or sarcasm about the local Nazi leader. The term is criticized here not to blame the populace for not having placed their freedom and lives at risk. Rather, *Resistenz* misleadingly suggests an expression of outright dissent that would have been subjectively more consistent and objectively more effective than was in fact the case. The term, moreover, implies a psychological consistency to the groups applied. Should a good Catholic conservative, angered, say, by efforts to remove crucifixes from schools but happy to think that Communist riffraff deserve what they get, be characterized by his *Resistenz*?

Suppose, however, the term *Resistenz* were replaced with a more neutral description such as "selective disapproval." Would the project of "historicization" seems less offensive? To be fair, Broszat's plea is not just for a new hermeneutical approach to Nazism. This might indeed mean succumbing to a new historicism with its tendency implicitly to justify the past: *tout comprendre c'est tout pardonner*. But Broszat's historicization involves more than just emphathic understanding. It relies on treating the Third Reich as one epoch among others and thus following the long-term trends that run continuously through all recent eras. He cites welfare policies as a key example: Nazi projects in this sphere can be judged as part of a long-term development of social insurance; they are not stamped by genocidal policies.[86] Of course, there are dangers: the recent historical investigations of eugenics already suggest that genocidal policies will soon be interpreted by those who wish to dissolve the specificity of the Jewish issue as just an escalation of the earlier eugenic thinking that characterized many Western societies. There will always be a *danger* of apologia. But, despite the concern of Diner and Friedländer, it is not clear how such a danger can be eliminated from the historical enterprise. The critical historian must always attack the texts one by one.

Broszat's demand for historicization followed his earlier exposition of the notion of Nazi "polycracy." His influential analysis of the Third Reich emphasized not the totalitarian authority of the regime, but the contending centers of power. It stressed confusion and administrative rivalry among the agencies Hitler successively established and whose claims he barely adjudicated.[87] In this reconstruction of Nazi rule political outcomes followed much less as a result of ideology than in the classical view of totalitarianism. The conflicting sources of authority, moreover, allowed oases of relative freedom, interstices where control was not absolute. For this reason, the emphasis on polycracy encouraged the concept of *Resistenz*. National Socialists often backed down in power confrontations. They might lock up Communists, but they shied away from confrontation with the church, hesitating to remove crucifixes from Bavarian schoolrooms and halting the euthanasia program when clergy and relatives protested (or at least postponing it until the outbreak of war diverted attention to violence abroad). The war also demonstrated that if foreign leaders—even of countries occupied by the Germans—resisted, the Nazis left its Jews relatively undisturbed (if only, it was believed, for a while). In short, Nazi rule depended upon voluntary compliance. The history of *Resistenz* thus became the history of the possibilities for noncompliance. It was logical, therefore, that the historian of polycracy should direct a major project that explored the spotty impact of Nazism on the local level in Bavaria. It also made sense that the historiography of everyday life, with its stress on the possibility for *Resistenz*, became an important research field. The recent flurry of *Alltagsgeschichte* and of administrative case studies builds on a decade-long dissolution of the traditional picture of a Hitler-dominated regime with unlimited power flowing out from the center. Tim Mason has linked several parallel debates concerning the character of the Third Reich. The arguments concern the nature of power (centralized or polycratic) and of control (totalitarian or fragmented), the role of ideology (fundamental to outcomes or secondary), the impulse provided by Hitler (all-important or episodic)—and in each case the scholarly disputes tend to separate those whom Mason terms "intentionalists" from those described as "functionalist."[88]

Mason's brilliantly intuitive characterization has seemed specially appropriate for the debates concerning the history of the Final Solution. The intentionalists stress the centrality of anti-Semitic ideology; they interpret the Holocaust as requiring centralized orders, insist that these explicitly emanated from Hitler, and stress that they logically fulfilled long-nurtured aspirations. The functionalists elaborate "the twisted road to Auschwitz." They stress the rivalry among contending agencies, the escalation of killing from the local level, the debates among second-echelon officials of how to solve the Jewish problem once forced emigration was excluded.[89] The arguments have aroused deep passions, often among those whose clear rejection of National Socialist sympathy has never been in question. Saul Friedländer, a clear intentionalist, finds Hans Mommsen's functionalism deeply disturbing, much as he finds the related "historicization" upsetting. In Friedländer's view, both efforts are similar. They dissolve specific guilt for the horrors of Nazism. Responsibility for an unspeakable crime becomes diffuse and elusive. Not so, the functionalists respond. In fact they assign responsibility to the whole Nazi apparatus of genocide and do not confine it to a "singular" Hitler who can serve as alibi for the others. Since this is an argument concerning which approach more undermines historical responsibility, it is hard to resolve on objective grounds. Nonetheless, despite the concerns of Friedländer, it has not been the intentionalists who have protested the new revisionism. Hildebrand, who insists on the absolute centrality of Hitler, has repeatedly spoken out in defense of Nolte, whereas the functionalist Hans Mommsen has been a major opponent of the neoconservative historiography. Or, as Friedländer might suggest, was it only because the functionalists had originally opened the Pandora's box of "historicization" that they finally sought so hard to close it?

As in so many historiographic disputes, the issues are overdrawn. Hildebrand and other intentionalists ask whether the regime was conceivable without the drive, force, and charisma of a Hitler. But to recognize Hitler as having played a vital role, to see his single-minded mania as crucial to the extermination policy, does not invalidate a functionalist view. Functionalism concerns the way the regime operated; it is not a statement about the sources of legitimacy. Hitler represented the *fons et origo* of ideological legitimacy, not necessarily the ultimate legislator. Of course he was essential to the criminal energy expended: Himmler and Heydrich might have organized murder more efficiently, but they would not have legitimated it. The horror of the results is not diminished by a functionalist analysis of the Final Solution. On the other hand, Broszat's agenda of historicization has entailed some curious arguments. What is the relevance of pointing out that the Third Reich carried through policies that democratic regimes also adopted, that—to take the often-cited welfare case—the German Labor Front envisaged a social insurance scheme similar to the Beveridge Plan?[90] Why should this be surprising? A modern labor market imposes structural demands even on governments that have murderous agendas. The argument seems beside the point and unlikely to advance historical understanding. No critic of Nazism denies the normal range of policy: officials of the Third Reich exploited Keynesian-type deficit finance; of course hospitals functioned; von Karajan and Fürtwängler produced music; the post office delivered mail. Similarities in postal service do not usually justify comparison of regimes. What are morally significant are the few institutions that were murderous, not the many normal aspects of running a society.

This does not mean that technical policies and controversies within the regime during the years 1933–1945 cannot be considered, say, as part of a different history. The evaluative stance must depend on what question the historian is posing. If the motivating inquiry is the nature of the Nazi regime as a historical or political phenomenon in general, then to cite the multiple aspects of normal life as an offset to the extraordinary apparatus of terror is to trivialize. If the motivating inquiry is the long-term role of the state in the labor market or the evolution of family policy, then the appropriate developments of 1933 to 1945 can be treated as a chapter in a longer and less morally charged history.[91] Likewise, it is appropriate to explore the decision-making processes within the regime not only as a result of ideology but also as a particular species (unattractive, to be sure) of bureaucratic politics. In the work to which the historicizers of the left keep referring, the wartime opposition of the Finance Ministry or Labor Ministry to the German Labor Front's ambitious plans for old-age and sickness insurance followed lines of intragovernmental rivalry found in most modern state bureaucracies.[92] At the same time, bureaucratic conflicts over social policy may indeed illuminate Nazi decision making more generally and thus cast light on the initiation of the Final Solution. Certainly if the scholar sets out to write the history of the regime or of National Socialism or of the German nation in the same period, then these "normal" bureaucratic aspects cannot be simply offset against the murderous ones. Maybe God draws bottom lines; historians need only record the entries in the ledger.

Thinking through the relationship of bureaucratic politics to ideology reveals one of the difficulties of Mason's functionalism. The problem is not that genocidal decisions were implemented and escalated at lower levels. It is that bureaucratic momentum can be murderous only within certain contexts. It is important to understand that Hitler might not have envisaged Auschwitz when he dictated *Mein Kampf* at Landsberg prison in 1924 or became chancellor in 1933. (What his "fantasies" allowed is another question.) But it is also important to recall that whereas in most societies bureaucratic momentum can lead to thoughtless policies and heartache, only where the central legitimating norms have been perverted and made criminal can the average functionary's zeal lead to genocide.

The haunting questions about the history of the Final Solution—that is, the perpetrators' history, not necessarily the victims'—are not, strictly speaking, historical questions. They are questions that arise with specific reference to the past but could also concern the present. The problem of ethical coherence remains a philosophical one. The psychologist and moralist as well as the historian must deal with the issue of how men and women can be apparently normal and yet killers. Sartre, for instance, insisted that one could not regard anti-Semitism as a black spot in an otherwise decent personality: instead, anti-Semitism had to be understood as a pervasive character disorder. It did not allow the anti-Semite to be considered otherwise normal.[93] Satisfying as it may be to insist on a coherent moral identity, Sartre's position may not be correct. In the case of the art historian who is also a spy, or the murderer who is also a family man, dog lover, and contributor to charity—how do we seek, perhaps not so much identity,[94] as moral coherence? Does the historian presuppose that underlying radically different behaviors there is a unified moral self?[95] Further investigation of killers may postulate some psychopathic identity, some radical lack of human sympathy that characterizes an entire biography. It may also be the case that the moral self is a fragmented self, and that an intuitive commitment to the sanctity of life, at least for those outside our immediate circle of family and friends, does not exist.

The positing of moral coherence for an epochal event presents at least the same order of difficulty. It might be asked, why should the historian agonize over such nonhistorical questions? She or he need only tell it as it was. The problem is that "as it was" implies a moral stance; historians just cannot avoid having judgments implicated in the marrow of existential and causal statements. "As it was" implies at the least that it was not something else—hence that explicit or implicit choices were made, thus that responsibility needs to be assessed. Herein lies one reason why the historian cannot avoid analogy. The only way the moral dimension can be addressed is through comparison with similar or less similar situations. The method for assessing responsibility is jurisprudential, that is, by comparison of cases and possible precedents. The historian does not so much tell it as it was as offer analogues to the way it might be now.

The centrality of analogue is further determined by the fact that even while history studies classes of events it also traces individual processes of development, unique in their cause and course. To recapitulate this old saw of historicism is not to diminish its validity. It remains an important truth, although it is not the whole truth. But insofar as they are unique, historical phenomena are never fully accounted for by reference to other events. The singularity of historical events must remain to a degree ineffable. That certainly holds for Auschwitz, but it also holds for ordinary politics and society. Insofar as the historian studies what is unique, he cannot directly communicate it. He can re-present it only by plausible analogies.

Historical analysis involves causal explanation (causal in that the forces bringing an event to pass are accounted for) only to a degree. Historical explanation has another dimension as well. It implies making an event plausible as a lived experience. Does this mean just reasserting the old Diltheyan program of psychological *Verstehen*, or, with less reliance in irrationalism, the historical idealism of a Croce or Collingwood? The answer is no, because the enterprise is less direct and feasible than they foresaw. It is precisely the extremes of twentieth-century history taken up in these chapters that make the intuitionist or idealist project unfeasible. Explanation—in the sense of making an event plausible or understandable—can be approximate at best. For most of us there can never be a psychological merging of historian and protagonist. Even the limited degree of illumination that can be reached depends upon finding imperfect analogues for the experience described.

Comparison helps to establish typologies—"fascism," "genocide," "totalitarianism"—which, in turn, serve the historian as matrices of analogy. Comparative history, rightly understood, is not a branch of history; all history is condemned to comparison. The analogies allow comprehension of past developments that can never be exactly like something else, but can be understood only insofar as they are somewhat like something else. (In Robert Musil's novel, *The Man without Qualities*, the title for Part I, "The Like of It Now Happens," might well serve as the general heading for any work of history.) In this respect history diverges from the social sciences, even from historical sociology. The social scientist envisages the typology not merely as an evocative analogue, but as the real objective of knowledge. For the historian *quâ* historian, such generalization can classify the past, but can never "explain" it in the senses described above. The historian's task is to draw the right analogues from the quiver of experience—or, expressed more technically, asymptotically to fit successive typologies or analogies as if they were regressions. For events such as the Final Solution, the analogies may fall woefully short. Not for the last time in this connection do Walter Benjamin's fragmentary theses seems the most appropriate insight into a historiography adequate for Nazism: "To articulate the past historically does not mean to learn 'how it really was.' It means to seize memory as it flashes brightly in a moment of danger."[96]

4

German History as Case History

Accurate scholarship can
Unearth the whole offence
From Luther until now
That has driven a culture mad,
Find what occurred at Linz,
What huge imago made
A psychopathic god . . .

> —*W. H. Auden,*
> *"September 1, 1939"*

AUDEN, WHO WROTE THESE LINES as war broke out in
Europe, was slighting the capacity of "accurate scholarship" really to
deepen understanding of Germany's aberration. Indeed the Nazi experience does test the limits of what history can "explain." In one sense
history can account for every phenomenon retrospectively by citing an
earlier event. In another sense the historian can never adequately "explain." No cause seems intuitively sufficient to account for the brutal
effects of 1933–1945. Auden's word *psychopathic* accurately suggests the
departure from normal behavior: historians are at a loss, as are psychol-
ogists who are called in to diagnose the mild-mannered mass murderer.
Prediction before the fact was impossible; the case history is purely a
retrospective tool. Nonetheless, once the diagnostician tries to make
sense of the case history, he or she must revert to comparison. Abnor-
mal behavior implies a norm.

A Separate Path?

Perhaps the most comprehensive single case history was Karl Dietrich
Bracher's *Die deutsche Diktatur* (*The German Dictatorship*), which
twenty years ago surveyed the origins and history of the Third Reich.[1]
Appearing at the end of the 1960s, it reflected the author's preoccupation with the current emergence of the neo-Nazi NPD, which the

author treated in an epilogue. As the title indicates, Bracher emphasized his country's particular vulnerability to authoritarianism, not the general phenomenon of fascism (which, he charged in the recent controversy, had been vastly overblown, not least because of Nolte's early influence).[2] The concept of totalitarianism was of greater value. Although *Die deutsche Diktatur* relied on it less, Bracher's early focused studies had drawn heavily on the idea. Those still-invaluable works— *Die Auflösung der Weimarer Republik* (The dissolution of the Weimar Republic) and *Die Nationalsozialistische Machtergreifung* (The National Socialist seizure of power)—testified to the influence of "American" social science in the 1950s.[3] More precisely, they reflected a once-German sociology, divested in transatlantic exile of its dialectic or decisionism and reimported to the country of origin. Monumental summation though it was, Bracher's sort of historical analysis no longer motivates. It does not "historicize," as Broszat and Mommsen demand. It seems clinical, remote from the lived experience of the Germans.[4] It is to what actually happened as macroeconomic theory is to the worker who gets laid off. The case-history approach, moreover, implies characterological defects, in this case long-term divergence from the "normal" Western powers. It suggests that all that needs to be explained is "the whole offence /From Luther until now."

In fact the historians' controversy exploded at a moment when the whole notion of German history as a case history was under attack— and not merely by a conservative, such as Michael Stürmer, who resents the implications that the country must be viewed continually as a patient in therapy.[5] There has been a far more widespread turning away from German history as case history. This is probably just as well. The case history is devoted to explaining an outcome known by the historian; it must impose a catastrophic entelechy. It presupposes pathology. Certainly, given Leni Riefenstahl's adoring crowds awaiting their Führer, or Goebbels' and Hitler's harangues denouncing a world of diabolical foes—England, the Jews, Bolshevism—the notion of national pathology came easily. The behavior *was* deviant, by the standards that had been accepted in Germany as well as in neighboring countries. The problem with the case history is not that it falsely diagnoses the patient (can we really dispense with a notion of deviant behavior?), but that for national societies, at least, it is too crude a tool. It reduces the history of the subject to one of latent illness, when the whole complexity of sociopolitical behavior needs to be comprehended, even, finally, if only to understand the illness. To go beyond a mere chronicle, any historian must pose questions about the past. But the questions will limit the possible answers. They need continued broadening and revision, and not only because there have now been almost forty years of good postwar German history to set against the twelve bad years. Kohl, Dregger, and even the American ambassador may urge an upbeat approach; that is not the issue. The historiographic problems abide; one poses new questions to get more complete answers than the case-history allowed. History as deviance takes us only so far.

On the other hand, even historians who wish to put the Third Reich in perspective, so to speak, do not deny that German national politics often turned out badly. Unification came late, parliamentary government was stillborn or ineffective, rhetoric and behavior oscillated between the overweening and the servile. The judgments are obviously comparative, but how did the historian account for the series of unfortunate divergences from the Western norm? The prevailing postwar case history contrasted the failures of German revolutions or the weakness of liberalism with the "successful" Anglo-American and even "successful" French outcomes. It ascribed the failures to the insufficient social and political assertiveness of the German bourgeoisie. Some of the conservative historians have resurrected a countermodel. But theirs is a case history, too. The conservative historians tend to attribute German difficulties to adverse geopolitical circumstances. Put simplistically, one diagnosis sees Germany as a victim of its archaic class structure; the other, of its neighbors.

The concept of bourgeois failure often underlies the paradigm of flawed national development referred to as the German *Sonderweg*. *Sonderweg* means special or separate path, with a clear implication of historical deviance. Originally the concept had favorable connotations. During the period of the French Revolution, German writers congratulated themselves that their country had been spared Latin excess. No revolution was needed in Germany, since the new Prussian civil code or Kantian philosophy brought the benefits of legal universalism. During World War I Thomas Mann contrasted a profound German culture with a superficial European civilization—the one deep, meaningful, full of soul; the other literary, witty, prone to superficial chatter. "What we call 'civilization,' and what calls itself civilization, is nothing more than this victorious advance, this propagation of the politicized and literarized middle-class spirit, its colonization of the inhabited areas of the globe. The *imperialism of civilization* is the last form of the

Roman idea of unification against which Germany is 'protesting' . . . she has never had a more terrible battle to wage than against this one."[6] Britain was perhaps more problematic. German conservatives had admired its nineteenth-century stability and envied its empire. It was a mixture of smugness and insecurity that led German commentators to contrast *Helden* with *Händler*, heroes with tradesmen. The natural wealth of the United States might attract immigrants, but the country was wild, disorganized, and crassly materialistic. Germany had not surrendered to mass democracy or political party corruption; its bureaucrats rendered a selfless service.

The idea of German divergence from the West also served historians critical of the country's development. Somewhere Germany had gone wrong. For some, the deviant path started with the fragmented Reich of the Middle Ages. Others condemned Luther's vehement rejection of Rome as the turning point. A more plausible point of divergence lies in the seventeenth century, when British parliamentary elites prevailed over the Stuarts, while the Prussian towns and provincial estates were browbeaten and subordinated by the Great Elector. Then, in the late eighteenth and nineteenth centuries, while France and Britain progressively broadened democratic electoral participation in national politics, Prussia and Germany secured only constitutional compromises that preserved the political role of an East Elbian landed elite and a powerful monarchy. Intellectual historians similarly argued that the German philosophers had confined concepts of freedom to the realm of ideas alone, seeing politics as a less important arena. Enlightenment liberalism in Germany viewed the universal applicability of law as the decisive achievement, overlooking the issue of who made law and what public procedures it stipulated. Procedural fairness substituted for democratic power.

In short, Germans had undergone no liberal revolution as had Britain, the American colonies, and France. A timid, tardily emerging bourgeoisie sold out to feudal power and prestige. The lower middle class of artisans and tradesmen—so Marx and Engels explained the failure of 1848—briefly flirted with radicalism, only to take fright before the proletariat and revert to reaction: "Humble and crouchingly submissive under a powerful feudal or monarchical Government, it turns to the side of Liberalism when the middle class is in the ascendant; it becomes seized with violent democratic fits as soon as the middle class has secured its own supremacy, but falls back into the abject despondency of fear as soon as the class below itself, the proletariat, attempts an independent movement."[7] Max Weber's major intellectual project could be described as the history of bourgeois modernization. Belated though it was in Germany, it had to be carried through precisely for nationalist reasons: "It is dangerous and ultimately irreconcilable with national interests for an economically declining class to retain political domination in its hands. But it is even more dangerous if classes that are moved by the prospect of economic power, and therefore by the expectation of political rule, are politically unripe for state leadership."[8]

During World War I Thorstein Veblen similarly argued that Germany had borrowed Britain's advanced technological achievements without having had the time to internalize the values of workmanship and democracy that such an industrial system had nurtured among the English.[9] This concept of a lag between economic and political modernization continued to mark influential historical interpretations, including Eckart Kehr's innovative studies during the Weimar era,[10] and the work published by Alexander Gerschenkron and Hans Rosenberg during their Berkeley emigration.[11] Similar views dominated other American studies, devoted to demonstrating where Germans had repeatedly failed to liberalize, or pursued variants of conservative thought that praised wholeness, organic nationalism, spiritual commitment, and a subordination of critical reason.[12] By the 1960s such concepts were reimported into Germany and served as a major intellectual source for contemporary historians such as Jürgen Kocka, Hans-Ulrich Wehler, and Heinrich August Winkler. Ralf Dahrendorf also assimilated them into his influential liberal critique of conservatives and corporatist social-democrats in *Society and Democracy in Germany*.[13]

By the late 1960s the paradigm of flawed modernization had apparently come to dominate Germany historiography.[14] According to the scenario, economic development had raced ahead (although an allegedly premodern reliance on cartels and protectionism marred the record), but archaic political elements persisted. With Japan and Germany chiefly in mind, Barrington Moore proposed that in societies undergoing modernization from above—that is, in countries where enlightened oligarchs of the old ruling groups had rationalized their political control and promoted industrial development—a susceptibility to later fascism was likely.[15] For Winkler, the status anxieties of a lower middle class and the yearning for a stable estatist society had a crippling effect on democracy.[16] Jürgen Kocka compared the fascist trajectory of Germany's white-collar employees with the healthier political career of America's equivalent group. He also examined how the powerful image of the old Prussian bureaucracy inhibited the formation of modern industrial, meritocratic hierarchies.[17] In all this work, the implicit model of desirable development was Britain or the United States. The historiography testified to a progressive international cooperation. Its practitioners drew on earlier German social theory as retempered in the United States and looked admiringly to the French social history program of the journal *Annales,* or to applied econometrics. History would forge ahead as a social science.[18] Many historians retain this conviction, and in some ways it underlies Habermas's own appeal to a community of Western progressive and liberal values. Among such a constituency, the *Sonderweg* must naturally appear a flawed path, one that postwar Germany finally had to overcome.

Today this historical paradigm is in great disarray—challenged originally by historians from the country that was supposedly the model of desirable political development. Ralf Dahrendorf asked in effect: Why wasn't Germany England? In fact it was not so different, Geoff Eley and David Blackbourn have responded.[19] It was no accident that at the end of the 1970s two British historians should challenge the idea that Germany was a Britain manqué. A generation of British economic decline prompted widespread soul-searching as to what sources of economic vitality the Federal Republic possessed that Britain no longer controlled. Was it not true, asked historians and journalists alike, that the British middle class had aped the values of Britain's aristocracy, building great houses in the country and choosing finance or the civil service over industrial entrepreneurship?[20] Whereas the amalgam of aristocracy and business elite had once been credited with facilitating the triumph of British liberal democracy, now the same fusion was blamed for an industrial climacteric dating from the 1870s. British commentators stood the old Veblen-Weber critique on its head. The earlier critics of Germany had lamented the "feudalization" of the German bourgeoisie and its resulting political timidity; the diagnoses of the 1970s blamed gentrification of the British bourgeoisie for economic timidity. It was only a matter of time before such a revision led to the conclusion that in important respects Germany had been no less bourgeois than Britain.

Blackbourn and Eley's work found a ready audience among German conservatives, who were happy to have their own criticism confirmed by outsiders. Conversely, those criticized felt somewhat betrayed by sophistic spokesmen from the Western societies that they had held up as a historical model to emulate.[21] In retrospect, however, it is easy to see how vulnerable the *Sonderweg* paradigm had become. The approach had achieved a historiographic ascendancy in the wake of the bitter controversy over Fritz Fischer's 1961 interpretation of German aims before and during World War I. Fischer's unsparing critique of German annexationist goals had fed into a broad attack on the defensive assumptions of the historians who reemerged in Germany after 1945. Fischer's work argued that 1914 German policy had remained in the grip of industrial and agrarian elites. His harsh indictment of statesmen, earlier depicted as unwilling participants in the war, sharply contrasted with the consoling view that Germany had behaved little differently from her adversaries. Fischer maintained in effect that German aspirations in World War I were of a piece with Nazi goals after 1933. The thesis undermined the comforting, sometimes complacent or apologetic notion that Germany had been seized by "demonic" forces in 1933 or had suffered (so opponents derisively termed the approach) a factory accident (*Betriebsunfall*).[22] In the wake of the Fischer controversy, given the ascendant left-wing culture of the universities, and the spirit of 1968, the critical historians who stressed long-term German peculiarities captured the historiographic high ground.

It was above all on the terrain of the Second Empire (1871–1918) that the conservative historians were routed.[23] Gerhard Ritter and others, some, like Hans Rothfels, returning from exile, had studied in the pre-Hitler faculties at the feet of historians who themselves were formed before World War I. They had treasured the Bismarckian nation-state as the culmination of German development. With its rich university establishment it was remembered as a happy fusion of power and culture. Only unwillingly did this older generation concede (as did Ritter, for instance) that this sunny era was shadowed by excessive militarism and truculence.[24] But their criticism had been largely confined to the petulant William II and the steamy politics and ambitious military circles of his court. In the 1960s and early 1970s the Second Empire was finally stripped of any remaining refulgence. Its bourgeoisie aspired to feudal values; special interests undermined needed fiscal reform; its civil servants could govern only by mobilizing a constant anti-Catholic, then anti-Socialist propaganda, or by encouraging imperialist ventures abroad. Its vaunted universities turned out to be hostile to intellectual independence; a narrow conformity hampered artists and playwrights.

In retrospect, this bleak picture of the Second Empire demanded too rigid a perspective:[25] How could German industrial hierarchies have been so burdened by premodern legacies at a time when the economy grew so vigorously and pioneered so many technologies? How could the professors have been so conformist at the very moment they were helping to create modern sociology, physics, mathematics, and art history? How could the civic culture of Germany have been so atrophied when parties and the press debated so vigorously and mobilized so many voters? Could working-class participation in politics really be dismissed as merely "negative integration," to contrast with the genuine integration of the British proletariat? How did one tell the difference between authentic and spurious integration—especially at a time when labor had a powerful party in Germany and was barely organizing one in Britain? Any why, if the British working class had been so triumphantly integrated, has it apparently remained more refractory, persistently proletarian, and separate from the rest of society?[26]

Moreover, some of the Kaiserreich's historical critics themselves undermined the notion of Germany's special defects by reviving the concept of "organized capitalism" originally proposed by the Social Democratic theorist Rudolf Hilferding. Organized capitalism was a typology of political and economic development according to which an early era of market-oriented liberal capitalism (say, up to 1870 or 1880) had been superseded in the late nineteenth century by a dense amalgam of political and economic measures. These included protective tariffs, governmental welfare policies, and the rapid formation of cartels and labor unions.[27] Organized capitalism suggested a meshing of state and economy that foreshadowed the welfare state and macroeconomic management of post-1945 Europe. But the heuristic claims of the concept were transnational. It proposed a general stage of capitalist development, not an exclusive German trajectory, even if the case was largely modeled on German evidence. Organized capitalism necessarily undermined the *Sonderweg* emphasis in which many of the same historians had already invested.

Other intellectual issues were also bound to accumulate. Did not foreign-policy decision making have more autonomy than Eckart Kehr's "primacy of foreign policy" (and, by extension, the works of Fischer or even Wehler) allowed?[28] Had not the eager mobilization of social science models—modernization, construction of ideal types, theories of fascism—undermined the specifically historiographic effort to "understand" what historical actors meant by their activity? Most fundamental: Was there really one Western norm from which Germany diverged? Could the international alignment of 1939–1941—the democracies against National Socialist Germany—durably serve as the basis for the social theory of the postwar era? Were not French and American developments each as different from Britain's and from each other's as Germany's was from them? After all, the interpreters of American civilization in the 1940s and 1950s had emphasized the unique legacies of the United States in contrast to those of Europe as a whole. Postwar commentators on France who were disillusioned with the "stalemate society" of the Fourth Republic revived Alexis de Tocqueville's contrasts of French republican failures with America's democratic success.[29] In effect they asked, "Why wasn't France America?" at the same time that Dahrendorf asked, "Why wasn't Germany England?" As of the 1950s and 1960s an implicit teleology of modernization had made America and Britain appear the fitting fulfillments of social and political development. France and Germany played the role of deviants, although Germany's deviance had more disastrous consequences. Only a generation of French and West German successes, British decline, and American floundering from Vietnam through Watergate and beyond caused the premises of these models to be questioned. Upon scrutiny every nation had its own exceptionalism.

Abandoning the *Sonderweg* paradigm, moreover, accounted more satisfactorily for historical phenomena outside Germany as well as within. On the one side: Britain, historians recalled, remained persistently governed by an aristocracy deep into the nineteenth century. Arno Mayer's claim that a European old order that "was thoroughly preindustrial and prebourgeois" maintained itself until 1914 may be overstated, but it certainly shows Britain (and, less plausibly, France) to be as socially conservative as Germany.[30] On the other side: abandoning the *Sonderweg* as a starting point let historians do justice to the strengths of German civic life. The facile notion that Germans had no self-governing tradition crumbled as historians reemphasized a tissue of occupational associations, municipal self-government, and economic organization. Germany was hardly a feudal society bereft of urban institutions.[31]

Not surprisingly, the new assessment of Germany shifted its chronological focus. The principal terrain for reevaluating the nineteenth century was no longer the Second Empire of 1871–1918, but the century before unification. Historians reassessed the self-governing

towns, the reform efforts of the late Holy Roman Empire, the enthusiasts of the French Revolution, and the new entrepreneurial, professional, and bureaucratic cadres of the Napoleonic and Biedermeier
eras. They stressed the social and legal flux of the early nineteenth
century: signs of crisis that certainly revealed regimes were narrow and
archaic but also testified to economic and political ferment.[32] Even as
French historians stressed the role of "sociability" in providing the
networks of republican politics in the early nineteenth century, Germans explored the mushroom growth of *Vereine:* associations based
upon local patriotism, agricultural improvement, or local economic
development; shooting clubs; or circles of newspaper subscribers. In
effect, conservative historians could reap the harvest of this research to
undermine the former model of German political backwardness.
Thomas Nipperdey's recent synthesis of German history from Napoleon to Bismarck destroyed the old Biedermeier clichés of a militarist
Prussia, a sleepy south, and a timid bourgeoisie to depict a society
engaged in lively political debate.[33] The result included hard knocks for
liberalism but a regime certainly "capable of development"—hardly
the perpetually handicapped *Sonderweg.* Nineteenth-century Germany
had a history and not merely a case history.[34]

Differences or Deviance?

Is there any persuasive power left to the *Sonderweg?* If every nation has
its own *Sonderweg,* deviant behavior is a meaningless concept. Still, as
Jürgen Kocka has pointed out, among those countries with which
Germans chose to compare themselves, Germany alone chose an authoritarian path.[35] The Germans picked their own relevant universe of
comparable countries—and diverged significantly. But even if the historian seeks to jettison the case-history approach, is there no valid
model of German national development that explains the vulnerability
to authoritarianism? Was Nazism, then, merely the contingent product
of immediate political factors? Is German national identity to be pronounced unproblematic? Alternatively, was National Socialism an ail-
ment of capitalism in crisis that happened to strike the country that had
lost World War I and had been subjected to a humiliating peace treaty?

   It seems clear that the *Sonderweg* concept as originally formulated
can no longer serve. To adduce a stunted bourgeoisie or a middle class
overawed by Junkers and military prestige will no longer adequately
account for the annexationist fervor of 1914 or the vulnerability of

Weimar democracy. Many historians will still object: Surely the Germany of 1914 relied more than other countries on military solutions, whether Bismarck's wars of unification or heavy-handed diplomatic pressure in the years before the outbreak of war. It took greater pride in military splendor, had its elites more attuned to drums and trumpets than inveterately civilian Britain. But even in this respect the comparison is less clear-cut than often remembered. If militarism seemed endemic within Germany—"Kennst Du das Land, wo die Kannonen blühen?" so Erich Kästner parodied Goethe in the 1920s—Englishmen outside their island exercised a military and racialist domination throughout an empire extending from Ireland in the west to the Raj and Capetown and Hong Kong. Germany, it might be countered, was "authoritarian" and stratified. And yet Britain's class society was as profoundly elitist as Germany's. There was more velvet glove and less iron hand, but no bared arm. It is hard to find indices of German stratification and even of class arrogance for which Britain lacked equivalents.

By 1914 most European states shared concepts of individual rights. They argued on manhood suffrage; they limited their monarchs' reveries about autocracy. A diehard Junker, Oldenburg-Januschau, might fume that the German emperor should be able to take ten soldiers and shut the Reichstag, but this was recognized as anachronistic posturing. The emperors as well as the elected officials of Eastern and Central Europe found it necessary to live with a dissenting press and party organization. This does not mean societies were uniformly democratic. Major reservoirs of abitrary power persisted in factories and on the land. Vast domains of landlord rule supported by debt peonage, harsh vagrancy laws, and political clientelism precluded meaningful democratization in the Italian Mezzogiorno, Andalusia, Russia and Rumania, rural Hungary, eastern Germany—and the American South. But outside these regions political competition and dissent were usually vigorous. Indeed these huge game preserves of landlord power provided an important basis for the flowering of liberal culture in the late nineteenth century. Magyar magnates, British Liberals and Conservatives, Southern Democrats in the United States Senate, lawyers from Palermo, could develop parliamentary debate into an art form reminiscent of Burckhardt's renaissance state. Still, was there no difference between Britain and Germany? No structural proclivity, so to speak, toward authoritarian or military decision making in the Reich, but not in Great Britain? And if not, why not?

As Marc Bloch insisted fifty years ago, comparison involves establishing differences as well as similarities.[36] Moving beyond the case-history approach should not preclude trying to understand real distinctiveness. The fact that German bourgeois achievements were long underrated does not mean that political life in Berlin was equivalent to that in London or Paris. Bureaucrats, the court, parliaments, and parties played different roles. Inherited titles conferred prestige everywhere, but the power they brought varied from country to country. Despite the battering that the *Sonderweg* thesis has undergone, despite the correct insistence that Germans enjoyed a vigorous civic life, political organization, and public debate, the countries were run differently. Paul Kennedy has updated the argument forcefully: "Whatever the area selected—controls by the representative over the executive, prerogatives of the monarch, role of the army, management of the economy, freedom of the press, supervision of the educational system—the German position was more authoritarian and state-directed."[37]

Kennedy's summary, however, slights the fact that the British elites neither desired nor required so assertive a state apparatus. The political conflicts of the seventeenth and eighteenth centuries ended by confirming that the British upper classes would govern their national society for their own benefit. Analogous crises in Germany, especially in Prussia, had a different outcome. Urban patriciates and rural notables were overawed. They remained influential at the local level but were constrained to enroll as civil servants or army officers if they wished to play a national political role. The bargain was made attractive by affixing noble titles to state service and letting landlords have increased power over their local peasants and peasant lands. Subsequent chances to redress power relationships were not really exploited: hence the "failures" of liberalism in 1815, 1848, and 1862. As of the early twentieth century, the German parliament played less crucial a role, could not limit discretionary royal authority, and certainly emanated no executive power of its own. Political analysts believed the difference lay in the constitutional prohibition on Prussian/German cabinet officials' sitting in the Reichstag (hence belonging to a party coalition), but this was only one of several distinctions.

Perhaps the salient difference between the German regime and the others lay in the role of parties.[38] Britain and the United States were essentially party states, a commonplace fact but one that continually impressed intelligent observers.[39] No constitutional provisions sanctioned parties. Nevertheless, these associations designed to canvass for power, to speak for those in broad agreement on policies to be advanced, and to reward with office those who wished to compete became the crucial institution for governance under conditions of general male suffrage. It was no accident that political sociologists such as Max Weber, Robert Michels, and Moisei Ostrogorsky spotlighted the rule of parties from the 1890s on. In Britain and America national parties were cohesively organized before the state took on expanded administrative roles in the latter nineteenth and twentieth centuries. Indeed they emerged as a force for coherent governance precisely because independent, executive power was set back in Britain and temporarily annulled in the United States. This was never the case in Germany. There, parties developed in the shadow of a prestigious executive and a strong bureaucracy. Certainly party delegations in the Reichstag had to be appeased to pass a budget and conduct policy (this was no easy matter), but policy initiatives derived largely from civil servants.[40]

German parties were certainly strong in terms of organization. They were ideologically coherent, they had important links with interest groups and newspapers, and their basic array survived the upheaval of 1918, if not of 1933 and 1945. But the historian must distinguish dimensions of strength: if cohesiveness was high, the passion to govern was low. When the parties inherited sovereign power in the debacle of November 1918, they were unprepared to exercise it. German party leaders had not wanted to rule per se. They wanted to be consulted, certainly sought policies favorable to their economic interests, and (especially in the case of the Catholics) insisted on recognition from government ministers that their support was indispensable. Success was measured by standing within the party organization, not domination of a national agenda. Parties served as transmission belts. Parliament confronted an executive that in theory was independent of the parties, even if they could make life difficult. The result, as Max Weber noted ruefully during World War I, was merely negative. England could be rightly termed a democratic state (*ein Volksstaat*); "whereas a parliament of the ruled that can exert only a negative politics with respect to a ruling bureaucracy represents the plaything of an authoritarian state."[41] In England, access to government remained crucial. Parties aspired to decision-making power; their representatives constituted the executive. So, too, in France. If not permanent parties, major parliamentary coalitions demanded decisive power. The great clashes of the pre-1914 Third Republic involved issues laden with implications as to who ruled—the church or the republic—and whose values would be hegemonic.

Another distinction potentially handicapped German parliamentarism. Its capacity to live with a majority of the left without a civil war or an authoritarian coup remained untested before the revolution of 1918. In Britain and France governing coalitions replaced each other according to electoral outcomes. Had the Labour Party or French Socialists emerged with decisive blocs of delegates before World War I, they probably would have been admitted to a share of cabinet power. In Germany electoral results did not mandate different coalitions. And the prospect of a majority dependent upon Social Democratic delegates appeared more frightening and might have triggered some sort of authoritarian coup. Nonsocialists accepted SPD power as a lesser evil in the revolution of 1918, but many of them preferred an authoritarian political solution rather than permit the party to play a leading role after 1930. The capacity of the German political system to allow for peaceful alternation of coalitions was precarious.

Stressing these impediments to democratization does not require endorsing a German *Sonderweg*. History sometimes repeats its opportunities. Setbacks are not always permanent. Parties and parliament would probably have acquired more power (if only by default) had World War I not suspended "normal" political conditions.[42] Granted, every move toward "opening"—the effort to quash the Kaiser after the *Daily Telegraph* interview, the reformist electoral victories in the elections of 1912—provoked a conservative backlash. Nonetheless, over the long term, a new political equilibrium that conceded more influence to a parliamentary majority and did not rely upon quarantining the SPD was certainly one plausible scenario.[43] The *Sonderweg* approach, however, allows little scope for the transformative impact of what might be termed "normal crises." Every apparent reform becomes at best a pseudo-reform that only stabilizes the old elites.

The *Sonderweg* thesis, moreover, purports to explain political outcomes according to societal factors, and societal factors of a special sort. It implies that the flaws in German politics resulted from some deficiency in the society or underlying culture. Granted that German institutions differed from those in other Western countries, granted that they placed liberal-democratic outcomes under a greater handicap—did they differ because of proximate factors or did they differ because of "deeper" reasons? It is the search for allegedly more profound (or "structural") causes that distinguishes the analyses of Marx and Engels, Weber and Veblen, and their recent heirs. The structural difficulties, moreover, are of a particular kind. The societal factors that allegedly have weighed so fatefully on German politics are the residues of an earlier, prebourgeois era.

The concept of the *Sonderweg* implies a theory of belated development. Other societies, which are viewed as normative, shed their feudal past through one form of bourgeois revolution or another. Not so the Germans. According to the scenario, the remnants of a premodern society of estates or *Stände* remained embedded in semimodernized form. Archaic guilds remained until the 1850s, then crystallized in public-law corporations, thus inhibiting the rise of a modern citizenry and producing petit-bourgeois chauvinists obsessed with status, as fictionally exemplified by Heinrich Mann's *Untertan*. The bourgeoisie won reserve officer status in the army by virtue of their education and internalized the rigid outlook of that antidemocratic caste. The East Elbian Junkers preserved outmoded rights of justice over the peasantry until 1872 and informal jurisdiction thereafter. In 1849 they extracted a skewed suffrage that enhanced their political preponderance in Prussia; and in 1878 they extracted a protectionist tariff that allowed them to remain on the land as feudal agrarian capitalists. The bureaucracy, with its dependence on the monarch and its life tenure of secure office, discouraged more meritocratic hierarchies. "Not economic reasons are responsible for the political immaturity of the German bourgeoisie," declared Weber in his celebrated inaugural lecture of 1892. "The reason lies in its unpolitical past . . . And the serious question for the political future is whether it isn't now too late to catch up."[44] In effect, the caterpillar of the old regime went into the cocoon of nineteenth-century social transformation and emerged . . . a fatter and more rapacious caterpillar.

What critics of the *Sonderweg* idea have objected to is the notion that a "backward" societal substructure inevitably led German politics to turn out so miserably.[45] On the one hand, they argue, when German politics turned out badly it did so because of deficiencies at the level of politics alone: miscalculation, arrogance, hostility to compromise, narrow economic goals. A major piece of evidence in this regard is the new interpretation of the Weimar electoral returns: the voting results suggest that Nazism was a broad political protest, not the work of a frightened lower middle class.[46] Second, the critics question the indices of backwardness. Too many of Germany's urban dwellers formed political associations, organized, sought votes, read newspapers. Too many Junkers were deeply involved with banks and industries. Too few shopkeepers and small independent businessmen persisted to be a decisive influnce on the grass-roots upheaval against the Weimar Republic. And to argue from the negative case, too many British shopkeepers had the same petit-bourgeois, often chauvinist mentality that identified with imperial success and kowtowed to social superiors. Why should the behavior in England known as "deference politics," which supposedly helped entrench parliamentary liberalism, be condemned as a prop of the *Obrigkeitsstaat* (authoritarian state) in Germany? The liberal societies were hardly free of premodern legacies (and at all levels of society). Each polity rested upon a cumulative sedimentation of social structures. Insofar as political patterns corresponded to social organization, they did not reflect any one level of social or economic development. Thus each nation's politics involved organizational forms, conflicts, rivalries, and outcomes that transcended any one-to-one determination by those elements.

Geography as Destiny?

If we renounce the *Sonderweg* thesis, with its implications of archaic or "backward" politics, can no generalizing explanation of political differences be found? Some conservatives have refurbished a rival historical paradigm, one first proposed in the late nineteenth century. This is the quasi-determinism, not of social structures, but of geographic situation. Michael Stürmer has proposed that German historical identity has emerged from the nation's central position in Europe with exposed frontiers to east and west. Reading Hagen Schulze, one is tempted to conclude: *Man ist wo er ist:*

> What is different about the Germans? Their inability to find a historical image that allows for national identity and self-consciousness over the long run has a host of causes, but they all lead back to one final reason: Germany's position in Europe. Throughout the centuries Germany has been Europe's No-Man's land, a legion of Germanies, *les Allemagnes,* as the French say, a host of large and small territorial states between the Meuse and Memel, Adige and Belt, in which German is generally spoken . . . There is no natural midpoint: no country has had so many capital cities in its history as Germany, from Aachen to Goslar, Nuremberg, Prague, Vienna, Frankfurt, to Bonn. The country flows apart; it has no natural frontiers; its lines of communication, moreover, are chopped up by mountains and rivers.[47]

Not only does Germany have no central organization, no coherent boundaries; it also has jealous and powerful neighbors to east and west. France faced only one powerful adversary at a time: first Spain, then Germany; Russia faced only Germany—Germany lived supposedly in constant menace of a two-front war once she managed to contest France's determination to keep her fragmented and powerless. It is in Stürmer's phrase *Land der Mitte*.[48] The exposed geography, moreover, is the alleged source of German political difficulties: *"Die Lage Deutschlands—conditio Germaniae* . . . the place of German history, in the center of Europe, was always its primary condition. In the center of Europe lies the German question, lie the chances and limits of German freedom, self-determination and sovereignty, first in old Europe, then in the era of nationalism, and even still, where we stand, beyond the national state."[49] In effect, Stürmer and Schulze have dusted off Sir John Seeley's axiom of the 1880s: the liberty a country can allow itself is in inverse proportion to the pressure on its borders. After twenty years of *Primat der Innenpolitik*, the *Primat der Aussenpolitik* has returned.

The image is not entirely fictitious. The great historical epics on which Germans grew up (at least until 1945) involved Frederick of Prussia in his continuing wars, dashing off to beat the French at Rossbach, rushing east to defeat the Austrians at Leuthen, then briefly prevailing over the Russians at Zorndorf, thereafter to be harried on two fronts and saved by the providential death of the tsarina in 1762. (Goebbels and Hitler consoled themselves with the supposed parallel when Roosevelt had his stroke three weeks before the end of the war.) The ambitions, annexations, and preemptive strikes by which Fritz got himself into these situations were usually less dwelt upon. Of course, Bismarck, too, remained acutely aware of the two-front danger; he neutralized his potential enemies, only to see his successors rather lightheartedly allow a Franco-Russian rapprochement. Nor was the "land of the middle" merely a geopolitical and strategic constraint. It also influenced political thinking. Generations of socialists on the left dreamed of bridging French rationalism and Russian peasant socialism. Radicals of the right warmed to soulful Russian autocracy. Slavophile distaste for Western frivolousness appealed to German cultural conservatives.[50] The idea of Germany as an ideological and geographic bridge between East and West hovered before the nationalist, reactionary political critics of the Wilhelmine Empire; the National

Bolsheviks of Weimar; and briefly even before such early adherents of the CDU as Jakob Kaiser until the Cold War foreclosed these reveries. The temptations to bridge the two camps still hovers among the neutralist-minded of the SPD. Peter Bender, who denies that a political realization of *Mitteleuropa* is possible, still yearns for Germany to play some role between East and West. *Mitteleuropa,* he writes, is now at best a community of constraint among partitioned peoples, but it could become a community of interests to overcome the consequences of division.[51]

Mitteleuropa, Stürmer would quickly object as a believer in NATO, is not the only implication to draw from the idea of the *Land der Mitte.* The latter is suggested as a historical paradigm, not as a visionary policy. But does geographic position determine historical outcomes? Poland, also a nation without natural boundaries, caught between powerful neighbors, expanded for two centuries, then was partitioned at the end of the 1700s, while Germany was largely unified over the next century. Geography alone cannot explain their different fates. Historians ascribe Polish disintegration to social structure and political institutions: a stratified landed society, with a jealous and broad nobility unwilling to accept effective central authority. *Primat der polnischen Innenpolitik?* Consider the inverse relationship: Geography has been called on the explain why England, blessed by its island security, not requiring a standing army with its tendency to reinforce the executive vis-à-vis parliament, could afford to be liberal. But then what of seagirt Japan, whose nineteenth- and twentieth-century political patterns bear so many striking resemblances to Germany: modernization from above, the need to assimilate a military aristocracy, hothouse industrialization, a weak parliament, a borrowed Bismarckian constitution, a reliance on militarism, bullying behavior in foreign policy, and a disastrous expansionism? Geographic parameters do not suffice.

Historical speculators from Hegel through Spengler to George Kennan have ascribed regime types to geographic factors. The conservatives have attacked the primacy of domestic policy to reassert the apologetics of geographic determinism. But although the advocates of the *Primat der Innenpolitik* one-sidedly stressed expansionism as a reflection of elitist politics at home, still there was something to the argument. There is no point in replacing the *Sonderweg* with the *Land der Mitte,* which insufficiently specifies particular historical outcomes. Although it has become fashionable to insist, rightly, that politics is a vital part of collective life in its own right, to be fought for in its own terms[52]—a sphere of activity mobilizing citizens through the passion to rule or to resist rule—politics can also be about societal interests.

The reaction against the *Sonderweg* has come to involve a reaction against models of class determination, a hostility to the Marxian relationship of base to superstructure. More broadly it constitutes part of the grand penance for the 1960s, of the dissatisfaction with neo-Marxism, of the subsequent enthusiasm for hermeneutics and subjectivity, the fascination with memory, and the supersession of modernism. Certainly, social science in the last decades has proposed useful alternatives to simplistic models of socioeconomic causation. But it has also suggested models or approaches that in the final analysis account for too little. Consider three alternatives, each initially revealing, but each ultimately elusive in explanatory power.

1. Cultural anthropology, important in its reminder that systems of values and discourse impose a logic of their own, ends by claiming that politics is hardly other than a form of ritual carried on for its own sake. *Homo politicus* becomes *homo ludens*. In Germany the champions of anthropologically informed history at the Max Planck Institute in Göttingen are its major advocates, although it informs an active school of researchers into the history of everyday life.[53] Since oral history has been taken up with enthusiasm, these methods have been used to approach the National Socialist experience from the grass roots. The result has yielded a far more differentiated picture of how ordinary citizens made their small compromises or found interstices that allowed them, if not to resist, at least to stay aloof.[54]

But there is a danger, brought out during the debate over the 1985 film *Heimat. Heimat,* conceived by its director, Edgar Reitz, as a counterstatement to the American television series *Holocaust,* traced family lives in a small Palatinate village from the 1920s to the postwar period. The twelve-hour film marvelously evoked the succession of generations and the gradual loss of rural isolation. It exploited and itself epitomized the apparent yearning to recover historical roots, not in high politics but in childhood communities. For the villagers in the film the Nazi regime appears as a transitional and marginal presence, tempting them to opportunism, but muffled and remote. As the director claimed, for many rural Germans this distant quality was authentic: his task was to show the apolitical fabric of their hometown life. Again the problem arises of "identification" with some historical actors and not with others: Reitz's villagers are a bucolic counterpart to Hillgruber's Wehrmacht. From their perspective, the realm of political domination can be dismissed as ultimately unimportant for everyday life.[55] But does not the artist or the historian have to maintain a simultaneity of viewpoints? Historical ethnography tempts the historian to abandon his detachment and to become a folklorist. *Alltagsgeschichte* begins by showing how partially or how subtly power works. It can end by having power and domination disappear into an ether of popular culture.

2. Political sociology, with its belated insistence on the "relative autonomy of the state," a discovery that could seem remarkable only for those who had read Hans Rosenberg on Prussia without reading Otto Hintze, tends to reify a vague bureaucratic agency or dissolve in abstractions.[56] As historians and political sociologists lose faith in neo-Marxist explanation, they have tended to cite state priorities and bureaucracies as self-sufficient causal elements in history. The champions of state autonomy have arrived at their formulations largely by way of the neo-Marxist model of "Bonapartism." This analysis, attributable originally to Marx's analysis of Louis Napoleon's success in *The Eighteenth Brumaire,* suggested that a stalemate between rising and declining classes gave the state a decisive political role it might not otherwise have. By way of Nicos Poulantzas' work it characterized David Abraham's analysis of the crisis of Weimar.[57] Pressed into the service of a conservative viewpoint, it seems to have influenced Michael Stürmer's analysis of the Bismarckian regime as "Caesarist," that is, as one that sought to bypass classes and interests and seek a plebiscitarian mobilization of the masses for the purpose of power politics.[58] Increasingly the social scientists advancing the model of state autonomy have dropped the ideas of social stalemate, emphasizing only the resources and objectives of the state, sounding like prodigal sons and daughters of the German historicist tradition. Once again the realm of the political is granted an autonomous status. Political activity becomes self-justifying; however, the practitioners of politics are not an aristocracy born to rule or a group of intellectuals intoxicated by discourse. Instead they are entrenched spokesmen for continuing bureaucracies, identifying with Leviathan. In this respect the emphasis on state economy is akin to the third alternative, the most recent model proffered by German historians.

3. Neo-Machiavellianism (more precisely, perhaps, a Clausewitzian revival) stresses politics as force and rule. Nipperdey starts his history by recalling how Napoleon transformed Germany by virtue of con-

quest: "Only someone who has become ideologically blind to power and focuses exclusively on social movements and 'internal' policy can underestimate this factor."[59] But the issue is not whether Bielefeld's historians, say, ignore force and power. The fact is that power itself, and even military outcomes, must be understood in a broader context. Why was Germany so vulnerable to the French revolutionary armies from the outset? If the historian will not take into account the differing levels of ideological and social mobilization or the costs of social stratification, military contingency can also prove an insufficient explanation. Perhaps it is time to "bring society back in."

The larger point is that no single historical paradigm deserves canonical status. Models of exceptionalism frequently tempt the historian or political scientist. Tocqueville provided one for France, when he proposed that a long history of governmental centralization, under monarchy and revolution alike, reduced local self-reliance and condemned the revolutionary experiments of 1789 and 1848 to despotic outcomes. Frederick Jackson Turner offered the frontier thesis as the key to American history, allegedly shaped by the availability of free land. In line with the celebratory mode of American studies in the 1940s and 1950s, Louis Hartz proposed another: the absence of a feudal past.[60] Each version has posited a critical variable. These can often be persuasive, but they are only partial. After Vietnam the once-reassuring idea of an American *Sonderweg* has also lost credibility. But if such paradigms of national history must reluctantly be left behind, on what historical basis can we ground a sense of national identity? Ultimately, according to many of the German historians, intellectuals, and politicians, identity is what their historical quest is about. History has been conscripted for orientation, but if history lacks a coherent pattern, what orientation can it provide? Is it not appropriate to ask whether the German historians and their public are asking too much from history?

5

A Usable Past?
Museums, Memory, and Identity

In 1596 Matteo Ricci taught the Chinese how to build a memory palace . . . To everything that we wish to remember, wrote Ricci, we should give an image, and to every one of these images we should assign a position where it can repose peacefully until we are ready to reclaim it by an act of memory. Since this entire memory system can work only if the images stay in the assigned positions and if we can instantly remember where we stored them, obviously it would seem easiest to rely on real locations which we know so well that we cannot ever forget them. But that would be a mistake, thought Ricci . . .

—*Jonathan Spence*

In the Museum of German History

Matteo Ricci's palace was not planned as a real building, but as a fictive structure of the mind; only imagined pavilions were flexible enough to accommodate the growing inventory of an active memory. Almost 400 years later Chancellor Kohl decided to give the Germans a memory palace, indeed two of them, but of real buildings and artifacts. The young citizens of the Federal Republic were to have a sense of "whence we come, who we are as Germans, where we stand, and where we are going."[1] The difficult question, however, was what should be remembered and how these memories ought to be related. Even as the "revisionist" controversy embroiled German historians, they plunged into a related debate concerning the government's plans for its history museums: the House of History (Haus der Geschichte) in Bonn, which would present the four-decade progress of the Federal Republic; and the German Historical Museum (Deutsches Historisches Museum) in Berlin, adjacent to the monumental Reichstag building (now used for exhibits and congresses), which would house the memorabilia of the German national territories since their origins. These plans have aroused strong feelings.[2]

Although the lines of division were not identical, the debate over the museums could be seen as one aspect of the historians' controversy. From Joachim Fest's embittered viewpoint, the museum controversy merely prolonged "the cleavage that runs through historical scholarship and divides it into two camps . . . The theory of a right-wing conspiracy, with which Nolte, Hillgruber, Stürmer, and Hildebrand are crudely connected, the defamatory accusations, and the extension of the conflict to the Historical Museum" all were the work of those who, "put simply, want to preserve and exploit Hitler and National Socialism as a sort of antimyth."[3] But this is too simple a diagnosis. True, critics on the left fear the museum will exploit history to revive a conventional sense of nationality, a clichéd and assuaging picture of the German past.[4] Nonetheless, some of the historians who have been highly critical of the "right" in the historians' controversy staunchly defend the mission of the museum. To be sure, they have stressed the need for "critical," thematic exhibits of social history—exhibits recalling hierarchy or oppression, militarism, prejudice, and genocide; halls devoted to the history of everyday life—rather than a linear presentation of conventional political development.

Consequently there have been two orders of debate. The internal discussion among the historians entrusted with the planning of a museum is reflected in the compromise formulations of the official *Konzeption*. That Concept in turn has been subject to a strident public critique from the more fundamental skeptics, several already engaged in the historians' controversy. No matter how it may be organized, for some critics any sort of museum is problematic in its own right. It has become a project identified with the Kohl government; it will claim massive funds; it is freighted with ideological aspirations that are fuzzy and confused at best, reactionary at worst, and perhaps impossible to realize in any case. It raises new questions about the relation of image, text, and public education. It has become a surrogate for that "identity" so frequently invoked and so rarely specified.

Museums are fashionable in the 1980s. The accumulation of fortunes and of a skewed affluence, the rise of a postmodern style that relies on historicizing pastiche, and perhaps the faltering of grand reformist projects for the future have led to a refulgent inventorying of culture.[5] New wealth in Japan or California drives art prices to vertiginous heights. The interest in ethnic origins encourages cultural reconstruction, revives old guidebooks, resurrects "old towns" (German cities now have their *Altstadt*) and neighborhoods, restores factories, churches, synagogues. Western societies have been living through an era of self-archaeologization.

West Germans have been in the forefront of museum enthusiasm. Over 50 million visitors traipsed through the country's museums in 1981, an average of about one visit per person. Two hundred twenty-seven new museums opened in the 1960s, almost 300 in the 1970s, and the 1980s have witnessed what has been termed a euphoria of museum organization (*Gründungseuphorie*).[6] Would any other country have devoted the degree of public discussion the West Germans have to plans for a collection of historical artifacts? The French furor, first over the Pompidou Center, erected in the late 1960s, and most recently over the new Musée d'Orsay, also placed museums at the center of public debate. In large measure, however, the French debate concerned the aesthetic value of the art to be housed, and the new approaches to exhibiting it. The stuff to be displayed was not really in question. The objects existed; there was a recognized subject for each museum, whether contemporary or nineteenth-century art. What should actually go into a history museum, especially a German history museum, is far more problematic. Part of the German debate has been a dispute over whether there can even be a coherent museum, that is, whether a unified visible presentation of a problematic history is possible at all. The museum has come to represent not merely a pedagogical project, but a contested allegory of German national identity.

Some of the difficulty lies in the lack of suitable models for the planned undertaking. West German historical exhibits have enjoyed encouraging success. The modest "Questions for German History," originally set up in the Reichstag building in 1971, followed by the 1981 Prussian exhibit, testified to what Michael Stürmer has emphasized as a thirst for history.[7] Encompassing historical museums, however, have remained problematic enterprises. The German National Museum in Nuremberg, consolidated in the last century, was organized around art and cultural artifacts and did not aspire to present historical development as a whole. As part of the leftist legacy of the late 1960s, organizers of the new Historical Museum in Frankfurt instituted a frankly Marxian and didactic exhibit. But, according to one of the originators of the current Berlin concept, Frankfurt was precisely the model that must be contested. It sought to inculcate "an unambiguous left-oriented history: partisan and also frequently false and, moreover, full of bizarre discontinuities." From a "temple of art" the museum had become a "place of learning."⁸ In Frankfurt, moreover, the heavy-handed historical texts became the spine of the museum while the nonliterary exhibits served only as alleged documentation. Shortly after Frankfurt opened, the Bonn government, responding to the wishes of then president Gustav Heinemann—a Protestant pastor who had broken with the Christian Democrats over West German rearmament and was associated with a tradition of nonsocialist dissent—dedicated an exhibition in the Baden town of Rastatt to the history of German resistance. Rastatt is a site associated with the democratic revolutionaries of 1848 and 1849. The museum was intended to celebrate the theme of rebellion and the history of the common man, which Heinemann felt East Germany was seeking to monopolize and the West Germans needed to integrate into their own historical legacy. The Rastatt exhibit followed the history of dissent from supposed medieval peasant uprisings to the Peasants' War of 1525, through the German Jacobins of the 1790s and the defeated revolutionary Forty-eighters, to the Revolution of 1918, and finally to the beginnings of the Federal Republic.

The East German version of this progression also hovers as one sort of model, if primarily a negative one. The Museum for German History, after all, is housed in the elegant baroque Prussian Zeughaus (Arsenal) on Unter den Linden. By recent Western standards, the exhibits appear a bit homespun and down-at-heel, but the theme is perfectly coherent. German society unfolds through the ages, revealing how the peasant community, the feudal manor, the absolutist state, and the industrial factory arose successively out of the material and technological forces of production, but then congealed as reactionary and constraining. German history appears as a chain of liberating transitions and counterrevolutionary setbacks. Models of the Prussian manor under feudalism, uniforms of the ascendant bourgeois-national Prussia, even one case devoted to the American War of Independence among other bourgeois revolutions, lead the visitor along the dialectical path of progress. Exhibits on Junkers or industrialists illustrate the forces of political reaction seeking to turn the clock back. But the museum does not rely on text alone. Exhibits of weaponry, ship models, and cameras entice the always technologically curious German audience. Newspapers and posters evoke the "fascist" success after 1930, which along with Hitler's war takes its place as the most recent counterrevolutionary setback to working-class advances. The defeat of the fascists (never Germans) by Soviet liberators and the inauguration of the German Democratic Republic provide the culmination not only of the museum, but evidently of the course of German history itself. Certainly, to maintain such a consistent concept requires significant omissions. Somehow German national participation in the events of the Third Reich fades: fascism serves as a capitalist demiurge in its stead. Concentration camps are evoked almost exclusively as centers for persecuting political dissenters: Auschwitz, Treblinka, and the other extermination centers are hardly cited: Jewish victims seem an embarrassment. The non-Communist Resistance perishes with a very low profile, while Communist Party leader Ernst Thälmann achieves apotheosis. Granted, the exhibit is itself the product of a historical materialism that reigned in the East Germany of the 1950s and 1960s. It has not been updated to reflect the more sophisticated diversity allowed by current East German historiography. Nevertheless, it still represents one alternative for a German history museum: a linear and coherent sense of reaction and progress—the dialectic in glass cases.

One other model available to the German planning committee was the Smithsonian's Museum of American History in Washington. Here is an anarchic opposite to the axial concept that prevails among the East Berlin exhibits. In the Zeughaus one follows a careful progression of arrows toward modernity; on the Mall exhibits can be entered in almost any sequence. Linear chronology does not govern. The Washington visitor enters a great hall in which a massive swinging Foucault pendulum (what is the connection with American history?) progressively knocks down pegs that indicate the earth's diurnal rotation. With the exception of a dense exhibit on family life in the generation after the American Revolution, there is no readily apparent developmental concept. The most linear exhibit is devoted to the inaugural gowns of the First Ladies—retrograde in its implications about women, but immensely popular. There are exhibits of major technological innovations: steam engines, farm implements, printing, cameras, textiles. The great political or social struggles of American history are interspersed among the artifacts of material culture. The sequence on labor introduces such negative aspects as antiunion repression. Likewise the exhibits on ethnic minorities include regalia of the Ku Klux Klan. But the dominant impression conveyed is clearly the redemption of the nation through technology and the machine. The nineteenth-century moment is dominant. Nor is this surprising, since the heart of the collection was the overflow from the old Smithsonian collection. In effect, the Museum of American History inherited an attic full of wonderful bric-a-brac that its curators sought to order.

This is a museum that may touch on history; but it is hardly a museum *of* history. (Indeed, it is likely that the Smithsonian's Air and Space Museum has exerted greater influence on the West German plans, not as a historical exhibit, but as a skillful combination of artifacts and a striking organization of exhibition space.)

Still, despite its undisciplined exuberance of gorgeous locomotives, the art deco glitz of a reconstructed Translux, the succession of costumes, the bounty of campaign buttons, the Museum of American History has one feature in common with the more disciplined but far less opulent DDR museum. There, too, the technological exhibits occasionally break loose from the constraining didactic framework. They claim the visitor by their own fascination and not just by their role in class struggles. Their intentions may be opposed, but the collections on the Mall and on Unter den Linden both presuppose that material and technological forces underlie historical change. These impulses are conflictual, sometimes constraining, ultimately collective in the East Berlin version; energetic, liberal, compatible with small-town values according to the Washington exhibits—but in each case progressive.

What the West Germans have sought is a history museum in which collective political and social development will remain more central a thread than in Washington, but less unilinear in its unfolding than in East Berlin. The origins of the project go back a decade. In 1979 President Walter Scheel, who had served first as the Free Democratic Party foreign minister during Willy Brandt's *Ostpolitik* initiatives, visited the Munich Institut für Zeitgeschichte—a respected research center on German history of the Nazi and post-Nazi era—and suggested the possibility of a permanent exhibit on German history. The hope was to engage a broader public with the positive as well as the negative legacies of German history. Berlin authorities had discussed the idea of a historical exhibit since 1978. The surprising success of the 1981 Prussian exhibit encouraged them to look for an encore, while the new Kohl government, with its claims to represent a shift in political values, *die Wende,* also had a historical agenda. By 1982 two projects were envisaged: a House of History in Bonn that would allow the small capital city to have its own exhibit on the history of the Federal Republic, and a forum or museum for German history in Berlin. The Kohl government officially proposed the Bonn House of History in October 1982. This proposal mobilized less active an opposition than did the 1984 Berlin project. It was less grandiose a concept, and Bonn certainly did not have the left-wing cultural constituency that enlivens the former capital of the Reich. The Bonn House of History was designed "to strengthen that historical self-awareness on the one hand, and on the other, to anchor it in the framework of the national and international relations and connections in which the Federal Republic exists and which determine our political life in the strongest way."[9] The same aspiration to anchor a West German historical consciousness also motivated the original supporters of the Berlin project. According to Hans Mommsen, the initiative for a museum of German history in Berlin originated with the publisher Wolf Jobst Siedler. (Siedler is deeply conservative, but equally independent. He issued Hillgruber's most controversial essays but also sharply criticized Ernst Nolte's recent volume, *Der europäische Bürgerkrieg*, when shown it in manuscript.) The suggestion was embodied in a memorandum to the Berlin Senate by Michael Stürmer, Hagen Schulze, Hartmut Boockmann, and Eberhard Jäckel, historians of differing political orientation. Boockmann himself reports that Richard von Weiszäcker, then serving as mayor, solicited the project.[10] The senator for cultural affairs (roughly a minister for culture for West Berlin) envisaged a more modest Forum für Geschichte und Gegenwart (Forum for History and Contemporary Affairs) in the unexploited exhibition space of the Martin Gropius building. This conception, however, was trumped by a second government proposal in May 1983, for the grander German Historical Museum. On the occasion of the thirty-fifth German Historical Congress in Berlin in October 1984, the chancellor announced that the government planned to give Berlin a history museum for its 750th anniversary in 1987. The idea of the Forum for History and Contemporary Affairs, which its predominantly Social Democratic advocates felt would allow a more community-oriented series of exhibits, seminars, or workshops in oral history, yielded to the grand national museum, somewhat as if a project for an experimental theater had been elevated into a plan for a state opera.

Kohl envisaged the museum as a "national mission of European stature,"[11] but the idea awoke misgivings among the opposition Social Democrats, who already felt themselves excluded from the planning for the House of History in Bonn. In May 1985, SPD members of the Berlin House of Representatives organized their own "working group for a museum of history and culture" to retain some influence over the planning. Hans Mommsen effectively drafted their critiques and counterproposal: "The task of the SPD, which has been consulted

neither formally nor informally about the decisions recently taken by
Bonn . . . consists in preparing conceptual initiatives in the expectation
of offering the governing parties the possibility of resuming substantive cooperation, and to do their utmost to keep the planned enterprise
from becoming just a costly heap as a monument to the conservative
trend."[12] Mommsen's memorandum claimed that the Forum idea corresponded far better to the actual German situation. A full-blown
museum would evoke a Wilhelmine nationalism, and was an archaic
concept: "The cultivated, elitist [*bildungsbürgerliche*] notion of a
museum, which was the reflex of nation-state formation, cannot be
credibly imitated in the twentieth century." Initiative passed, however,
to the Committee of Experts summoned by the federal minister of
urban planning and construction in Bonn. The experts included historians and political scientists; publisher Siedler; a few museum directors; and, as chairman, the president of the Stiftung Preussischer Kulturbesitz, the agency responsible for administering the major art
collections bequeathed from pre-1945 Germany. The delegates proposed by the original Berlin working committee were deemed too
fractious, but after some negotiations the government Committee of
Experts was enlarged and asked to work out a Concept by March 1986.
The SPD working group in Berlin was not appeased. In mid-
November it published a report warning that, despite the assurances of
the experts, the planned museum might inculcate "a primarily nationalist historical image."[13]

By late March 1986, the sixteen-member Committee of Experts submitted its Concept for a "German Historical Museum" to the minister
for urban planning and construction. Released a month later, the Concept represented the labor primarily of a subcommittee of seven experts, including two of the original proposers, Hartmut Boockmann
and Michael Stürmer, and a spokesman for the moderate left, Jürgen
Kocka. Not surprisingly, the report was a painstakingly balanced document, suffused with a didactic earnestness. It incorporated both the
reformist demands for a critical approach that would prod new questions and criticism, and the conservative concern with "identity":

> The museum . . . is to stimulate argumentation, but also to offer
> possibilities for identification. Above all, the museum should help the
> citizens of our land—as Germans and Europeans, as residents of a
> region, and as members of a worldwide civilization—to become clear
> who they are, where they are coming from, where they stand, and in
> what directions they can go. For them and for visitors from other

countries the museum should provide a survey of German history in its European connections and its inner diversity—neither excusing nor accusatory, but sober, self-critical, and self-aware.[14]

What questions did the report seek to resolve? First of all, who were the Germans? Stürmer had originally proposed a museum for the nineteenth and twentieth centuries, concentrating on the creation and vicissitudes of the German nation-state. The report called for exhibits dating back to Celtic and Roman forebears but really starting with the early mention of *Deutschen* in the ninth century. What regions counted as German? Germans, so the contemporary historian and political scientist Arnulf Baring would point out in an interview critical of the project, had exerted formative influences as far afield as Sicily and Novgorod: "We have to preserve the memory that it was essentially we Germans who set the stamp on the continent, without succumbing to expansionist or imperialist longings."[15] But a new museum in West Berlin that showed Poznan, Kaliningrad, or even Vienna as German was bound to prompt outcries of revanche. The Concept thus wrestled with complexity: "It is characteristic that Germans have lived mostly in a plurality of states and that the German area of settlement was surrounded by a wreath of border and mixed zones." The museum would have to make clear that the history of Burgundy, Switzerland, the Netherlands, and Austria belonged to the history of the Holy Roman Empire or was connected with it. But no implication must follow that this connectedness was to be revived: the absence of sharply delineated ethnic borders "will be made visible as a source of tensions and conflicts as much as of cultural richness, productive symbioses, and complex emanations." Perhaps inevitably the Concept was clearer about what had to be avoided than what might be included. Agreed: the Federal Republic had no single historical image; as a pluralist society it encouraged competing historical models. "The Museum therefore must not attempt to transmit *one* message . . . It has to remain capable of change and development—without, of course, escaping into amorphous arbitrariness, without renouncing choices and judgments. [Admittedly] these challenges remain in a tension, which, however, can be largely overcome in the concrete work of setting up the museum."[16]

The committee devoted its major effort to translating historical ideas into physical configurations. The Berlin Social Democrats had advocated temporary exhibits that would address evolving public concerns rather than an immediate and definitive effort to organize German history. The *Konzeption* made some concessions to the need for temporary exhibition space and conceded that the locally favored Martin Gropius building would serve while the museum was under construction and might be exploited later for spillover exhibitions. But the experts clearly emphasized a major permanent core for the museum. Within its walls, though, the report envisaged two different approaches: a thematic one likely to appeal to social historians and a chronological one that presumably reassured the traditionalists. The report called for 35,000 square meters of exhibition and reception space (about seven football fields) and warned that the 250 million marks initially budgeted would be insufficient. The Pompidou Center in Paris, they pointed out, had cost five times as much and offered about three times as much total usable space. The physical aspects of the museum received loving attention, although final plans were to wait for an architectural competition. Still, the committee could not resist specifying the design tasks. Visitors would enter the exhibits via an orientation atrium that would feature a large relief map of Central Europe either beneath a walk-around gallery, directly underfoot, or on the walls, and onto which the shifting settlement patterns of the Germans could be projected. In a smaller foyer, visitors would be instructed about the value of the artifacts as sources. Thus prepared, they would pass into halls devoted to chronological epochs: early peoples, Carolingian and high Middle Ages, late Middle Ages, early modern (the Reformation apparently to occur between them), the nineteenth century to the revolutions ending World War I, the Weimar Republic, and the Third Reich.

Concerned lest the chronological halls overemphasize traditional national development, Kocka and the social historians emphasized the "in-depth" exhibits (*Vertiefungsräume*) that would take up related developments in social, economic, and cultural history or could emphasize comparative developments. The in-depth hall for 1933, the report proposed, would explore the world economic crisis and differing national reactions. It would also examine the interwar challenges to liberal democracy: Stalinism, Italian fascism, dictatorships in other countries, and successful liberal-democratic responses. The in-depth hall for 1945 would look at the war as a global phenomenon and ask whether 1945 meant the end of a German *Sonderweg*. Such exhibits stipulated demanding and valiant pedagogical efforts. Nonetheless, the report did not suggest that the in-depth exhibits would be significantly different from the presentation of alternative interpretations envisaged for the chronological exhibition halls. If there was to be a chance for really new approaches it would have to be in the six major "thematic spaces," which could explore such continuing human concerns as peace and war, work and leisure, gender relations, religion and society, sickness and health, and Jews in Germany—the last to trace the history of early prejudice, emancipation, and genocide.

Perhaps a committee dominated by historians is not the optimal forum in which to generate a concept for a museum. Might it not have been better to start with a frank acceptance of the likely clientele: busloads of contemporary German schoolchildren, like their American counterparts rambunctious, impatient, unlikely to linger over the issue of whether a confederation would have been a viable alternative to Bismarck's empire; or sightseers tired from trekking the long Berlin stretches from the Tiergarten and zoo to the Victory Column, to the Reichstag and the Wall . . . to the museum? A sharp-tongued critic expressed his concern that "myriads of subventioned Berlin tourists and visiting groups of Bonn parliamentary delegates will file by the sacred cows of the German past in both museums, their gaze more or less amazed, more or less dulled, more or less weary."[17] Granted that history should be about old and new themes, politics and power, work and hierarchy, love and gender and family, might it not have been better to organize the exhibits more centrally around key themes of German life over the centuries: for example, the seven centuries of guilds or the wealth and role of city-states and urban culture, of bureaucratic and military authority, of piety and inwardness, of adolescent rebellion and romantic counterculture, and, finally, of Germanic expansionist dreams and periodic ethnic intolerance? Instead the committee's report tended to read like the subheadings of one of the German handbooks of history adapted and readapted since the nineteenth century. The defenders of the work attributed this impression to the haste that was required. It may well, however, have been due to the fact that committee members were highly aware of the conflicts they must overcome, but did not consider how much they really shared. The problematic assumption that identity was historical identity and that temporal sequence was the privileged form of conveying a national culture united their work—and perhaps limited the originality of the outcome.

When the committee indulged its imagination, it was to fantasize more about architecture than about culture:

> Around a central space, which has as its theme a historical nodal point or the explanation in depth of the selected historical problem, other rooms can be arranged, which are devoted to comparisons, flashbacks or flashforwards, the presentation of controversial points of view or the connections with non-German history. The architectonic form might be conceived of as a "serpentine," "spiral," "honeycomb," or as a system including "cellar/ground floor/second floor/attic," or as a "tower."[18]

Most historians must content themselves with planning ideal curricula and syllabi. The committee, however, could allow itself to envisage a spatial analogue of "Western Civ" (in its Germanic incarnation) on the banks of the Spree, its in-depth spaces, epoch halls, and theme rooms to confront the massive hulk of the gutted Reichstag. One might almost imagine the spirit of Albert Speer hovering over these collective reveries, regretting that he had been fated to replan Berlin for an earlier client and could not be reincarnated, now purged and postmodern, as architect for a thousand years of Reich history.

Criticism of the museum project has come from those on the left of the historians' controversy, not from the right. If conservatives were unhappy about the concessions to social history and pluralism and critical reflection, they did not offer a counterproject. Kocka's victories for thematic exhibitions did not reassure all his Social Democratic likeminded colleagues. Even some of his friends privately warned that the neoconservatives will turn this project to their own purposes no matter how stoutly he has defended his theoretical ideas in the overall planning. Some have been scathing. Why put up a museum near the Reichstag building, Arnulf Baring asked in his Der Spiegel interview, when the Reichstag building had long since become merely a museum? As a symbol of failure—of the proclamation of the Weimar Republic in 1918, the site of the Reichstag fire in 1933, of a Russian soldier waving the Red flag of conquest at the end of April 1945—the Reichstag was clearly, Baring urged, the most fitting house of German history. If there had to be a new museum, better a provisional tentlike structure that could be adapted over time. The idea of dividing the museums discredited the entire project. West Berlin was being vouchsafed the exhibits of national failure, while Bonn's House of History was degenerating into a billboard space claimed by all sorts of interest groups. Indeed, the entire project testified to a certain failure of nerve. "Optimistic eras, like the social-liberal epoch until 1974, look forward, believe in social-technological projects, in large-scale reforms. Today no one believes in this any more . . . the times are retrospective."[19]

Was it just politics that motivated the dissent? "The conflict over the Historical Museum, this much is clear," charged a commentator in the *Frankfurter Allgemeine Zeitung*, "is not primarily a question of research, not a struggle between spokemen for enlightenment versus obscurantists. It concerns politics, not scholarship; questions of power are involved, not questions of knowledge."[20] This is half true. Certainly there was a division along party lines; the most outspoken academic opponent, Hans Mommsen, drafted the Berlin SPD's critique of the Bonn planning procedure. On July 2, 1986, the "Art and Culture" working group of the SPD parliamentary party sponsored a public hearing in Bonn that developed into a daylong exchange of accusations and defenses. Jürgen Habermas, opening with an attack on neoconservative revisionism similar to the one that was to appear in *Die Zeit* a week later, concluded that it would be better to cancel the museum if it might end up supporting such neoconservative trends. Mommsen charged the Committee of Experts with being far too conservative, and he spared only the exhibits on the Middle Ages from criticism. Senator Franke of Bremen accused Richard Löwenthal of naïveté for his collaboration, while a Berlin delegate charged Kocka with opportunism. Löwenthal and Kocka responded with vigor. Löwenthal, who as a youth had participated in anti-Nazi politics in Berlin, emigrated to London, then returned, eventually to become an intellectual spokesman for the moderates in the SPD, stressed his own hostility to neoconservative revisionism. But the museum, he asserted, would counteract these tendencies. It could reinforce a valid historical awareness, which postwar German youth regrettably lacked. Kocka insisted that the themes of economic and social history emphasized in the plan would preclude any dangerous nationalism, if the government adhered to its recommendations.[21]

The critics were not reassured. Mommsen disclaimed any personal criticism of Kocka but continued to criticize the plan for its incoherence and its traditionalism. The chronological exhibits were outdated in their periodization and interpretations and overpowered the thematic exhibits.[22] He was particularly harsh on the *Konzeption's* suggestions for treating the collapse of the Weimar Republic and reproached the committee for stressing the impact of the Great Depression as the implicit explanation for the rise of Nazism. Neglecting the role of the army and the parties meant presenting "a traditional interpretation of the Weimar Republic" that slighted the results of recent research. The related "in-depth exhibition," he charged, also precluded new questions and courted the illusion that a noncontroversial selection of material might be possible. Just a portion of the funds planned for Berlin, if placed in the hands of local and regional historical museums, would do more to encourage a historical sense and employ out-of-work historians than

> a mammoth project that sticks a museum (which has to rely, moreover, on papier-maché and plastic because the artifacts of the past are no longer recoverable) right on the very site, symbolically enough, of political decision making of the shattered German national state. Bonn's self-presentation of the living West German half-state would thus be counterposed to a monument to the dead national state comparable to fascist types of representational structures. It's hard to believe that this will help solve the problems of our present and future.[23]

Mommsen's critique was unsparing but also, in light of the sketchiness of the committee's Concept, too demanding. Perhaps it reflected the fact that his own often-brilliant, sometimes-unconventional assessments of Weimar and the Third Reich were not incorporated in the concept for the museum. It was easy sport to make fun of the committee's allocation of 1,200 square meters for the first medieval hall versus 1,600 for the early modern era and 800 for Weimar. It was also easy to discern traditional approaches behind the suggested exhibits. Some of the alleged incoherence arose clearly enough from the necessity to accommodate differing views. Stürmer would get his concept of the "land of the middle"; Kocka's influence was perhaps most apparent in the report's recommendation that social inequality and hierarchy be highlighted as recurrent themes in the chronological rooms. Nonetheless, Kocka's participation and Mommsen's concern reflected the shared conviction that the public use of history is important, that the elusive commonality of being German can be clarified through the representation of the past.

The museum story is not yet finished. In the fall of 1986 the conservative Hanns Martin Schleyer Foundation (named for the industry spokesman slain by terrorists) and the Social Democratic Party's Friedrich Ebert Foundation both sponsored meetings in the Reichstag building. At the Schleyer discussions, Michael Stürmer charged that the campaign against the museum was a defamatory show trial. At the Ebert conclave, Freimut Duve, who had organized the SPD hearings in Bonn the previous July, reproached the historians who had worked with the government for having sacrificed their independence.[24] At the German Historical Congress in Trier in October 1986, the cultural historian Hermann Glaser attacked the hasty inauguration of the project and charged that "our transaction with history takes on a cosmetic character." Other commentators, such as Christian Meier, questioned the necessity of such a massive project.[25] Museum directors felt they had been largely ignored in the planning. How was such a grand museum to be constructed when no collection had yet been assembled? Was the result to be a "reading museum or a house where history could be discovered and experienced?" asked Mrs. Pohl-Wever, the director of the Bremen State Museum.[26] At the end of 1986 there were still many misgivings.

What sort of history was to emerge from the museum? What sort of identity? How central must the Third Reich be? Christian Meier argued that after Auschwitz all was changed, and he proposed building the museum around a central space devoted to the history of the National Socialist regime, World War II, and the destruction of the Jews. From this center different hallways could lead the visitor forward or backward in time.[27] The Holocaust and the Jewish issue must remain a difficult challenge. For the experts who drafted the *Konzeption,* the story of the Jews in Germany must be treated as part of a long and troubled history; they envisaged a separate exhibit for the history of the Jewish communities, their nineteenth-century Emancipation, and their persecutions. Still, the whole point of the museum, certainly for the conservatives, was to stress that the Third Reich's Final Solution was not the culmination of German history. When divested of its current exculpatory or political intent, this view is sustainable. Christian Meier's vision is unlikely to do justice to German history. It would also distort Jewish history. And it would certainly provoke a reaction that defeated any pedagogical purpose. Nonetheless, it is unclear that the dispassionate treatment of the Jewish issue envisaged in the *Konzeption* really conveyed the momentous atrociousness of events. As one reporter commented, committee members decided it was best to place this genocidal crime on the same level as other, more explicable Nazi measures, when in fact Germany—so she cited Hannah Arendt—had shattered the moral structure of the Western world.[28]

Despite misgivings the project had to go forward. The Berlin plans labored under a pressing deadline: the 750th anniversary of the city, competitively commemorated in East and West. The architectural proposals also aroused misgivings—the competition for the placement of the museum led to defections from the jury and the withholding of a first prize. The second- and third-place projects were accepted as bases of further discussion, and the Senate decided on the building site.[29] Hesitations had to be overcome by October 1987, when Chancellor Kohl arrived for a formal groundbreaking. The process was one of consensus through weariness.

For Chancellor Kohl and his advisers the Berlin museum has incorporated contradictory attitudes. On the one hand, their stance is reverential: history is a continuing presence that endows the Germans with national consciousness and orientation. At the same time, the museum represents a claim to master the past. The Germans will package and subdue their history by suitably arranging its relics. But even a museological mastery of the past remains a false conception. As the Bochum historian Jörn Rüsen said at the forum sponsored by the Ebert Foundation, the question was not what history could teach us, but what we wanted to learn.[30] No one can master the past; one can only interrogate it. This task does not exclude trying to ask about identity. Hartmut Boockmann correctly responded to critics from the left that the notion of historical identity was not to be condemned outright. How else, except through awareness of "identity," could a museum help later generations ever feel a sense of involvement with the crimes of their ancestors during the Third Reich? Again, the question must be what concept of identity is at stake: a passive infusion by some mystical history, or an active commitment. Identity is the result of accepting responsibility, a point Habermas implied in November 1986.[31] How does a museum help in that civic task for an audience that often believes it had the "grace of late birth"? Ultimately by presenting its visitors historical choices, not just *faits accomplis*.[32]

National identity, or identification, has become a threatening concept to the left in the German debates.[33] Perhaps the museum presents some remote dangers. Did the museum planners envisage the effects on visitors as they entered the proposed atrium with its large relief map of Central Europe and watched the projected laser-beam settlement patterns touch down on Memel or the Masurian lakes, where 100 years ago German farmers controlled the land and 700 years ago Teutonic knights bashed Slavic skulls? Would these visitors learn that geography meant fate, that Germans had been hemmed in by clever or rapacious neighbors, or even that geography meant challenge and Germans were destined to spill out to the Narew and the Vistula? Most probably they would just sense the vanished remoteness of those earlier eras, hopeful at best of seeing Masuria someday as campers, not conquerors. (The more realistic concern was that visiting Poles or Czechs might claim a revanchist agenda.) National identity can hardly be instilled by a two-hour tour through the corridors of the Early Modern Room or a comparison of different countries' reactions to the Great Depression. In any case, identity is layered. It draws one to region and town and, perhaps for the young, to a wider Europe. We know that nationhood still claims a primal loyalty; the Olympics and the fates of hostages confirm that still-basic reaction. But intellectually our empathy can grow. We can recover the spiritual homelands of the Enlightenment, of Western constitutionalism, as Habermas claimed, perhaps even feel the claims of a threatened human species.[34] Identity itself is not the problem, but the limitations placed on identity.

Some major problems must be overcome if the German historical museums are to be a success. The first difficulty—the opposition's distrust of the museum as a conservative ideological project—will probably be mitigated by the passage of time. Whether for valid or partisan reasons, the planning process rankled the SPD. As Freimut Duve declared with admitted polemical intent at the 1986 Römerberg discussions: "to open an Autobahn no longer counted for very much . . . but to open a German museum to crown the administration of a German chancellor aroused appropriate distrust."[35] Nonetheless, by late 1987 partisan distrust was beginning to fade. Some historians such as Christian Meier were still skeptical of the project, disappointed with its conventional linear presentation of a national narrative, but accepted it as a *fait accompli*. The high costs suggested that the museum would be completed only in stages. The initial phase, which would consist of a temporary exhibition much as the SPD had urged, would probably last several years.

A second difficulty could arise from the plan for *two* museums. The one impression that neither side in the dispute should wish to create is that German history ceased in 1945. To be sure, the West Berlin museum will take its exhibits beyond the fall of the Third Reich to the present day. Nonetheless, the impression remains that it is still predominantly a *schwarz-weiss-rot* museum, tracing the rise and excesses of the German national state, consigning Bonn's allocated 1,200 square meters to the status of epilogue. For conservatives, the danger of two museums is that the Berlin collection might convey the impression that all history before 1933 was a prologue to the Third Reich. The left could worry that the Bonn House of History would confirm that the pre-1945 past has ceased to be a concern. Since the politics of public projects in the Federal Republic demanded two museums, it is important that each museum's exhibits throw as many bridges as possible across 1945.

A final problem will remain in any case. This is the inherent difficulty of presenting history through centrally sited exhibits. Ultimately a museum, as the spokesmen for these institutions have emphasized, is not a book. Its visitors do not have the time to read and reread. The museum must instruct crowds; it must exert a fascination and give pleasure even if some displays should evoke sorrow and pain. How permanent exhibits can accommodate the continual revision of historical consciousness will remain a difficult problem. In art museums paintings can be easily rehung. Natural history museums arrange exhibits around relationships based upon physical structures or common environments. But it is one thing to set up an exhibit around, say, arthropods or small mammals (the visitor does not have to evaluate a moral component), and quite another to present such difficult themes as Bismarck's wars or the appeals of National Socialism. For Jürgen Kocka, a decided advocate, the success or failure of the project would depend less upon the formal Concept that he helped to draft than upon the quality of the new director, and he found the curator chosen by the summer of 1987, Christof Stölzel, imaginative and flexible.

Some nations *are* virtual museums; in Britain, for example, continuity and quaintness remain cultivated, often with an implicit political agenda. But West Germany has hardly been a museum. Its state had to be recreated, its cities rebuilt, its values transformed, its society opened up along more meritocratic lines than before 1945. Hence perhaps the longing for a museum as a sanctuary for continuity unavailable in public life. The museum is problematic, however, because it does not seem likely to meet the expectations it first aroused. By October 1987, when Chancellor Kohl came to Berlin to break ground, skeptics seemed resigned, and advocates less certain and more moderate. The museum might well fail to encourage the sense of national identity once anticipated by the conservatives, but it could also fail to prod the active questioning of the past allegedly sought by the left. It no longer appears the hothouse for public discourse that it promised to be initially. In this sense, too, the museum project is an allegory of the more general limitations on civic life. The questioning must depend on the visitors, as on citizens. For a generation Germans have talked of mastering the past. To place it on exhibit, to reify memory through corridors of chronology, represents some sort of mastering of the past. But this suggests that the goal may have been misspecified, to be realized only as the past passes into glass cases. Adorno's concept of "working through" the past remains a more constructive specification, at the same time more demanding but in its forswearing of definitive results more feasible.[36] The historians' controversy is a reminder that there are spurious as well as genuine ways to work through the past. Which mode the museum will offer has yet to be determined.

History as Identity

Thomas Nipperdey wittily reversed Ranke's famous dictum that "Every epoch is related directly to God" when, arguing for an open agenda, he replied to Habermas that "All German history is related indirectly to Hitler. And to the Federal Republic."[37] Only God can reveal whether Ranke is right. Nipperdey is certainly right, although some aspects of German history are related more directly than others to Hitler or to the Federal Republic. The historians' controversy is over which aspects. But is also raises a further issue: not merely which version of the past is valid, but what historical themes are legitimate or worthy of study. This issue becomes all the more acute once history is appealed to as a source of identity: each dimension of identity— whether in terms of nation or class, or as West European or Central European, as heir to Western rationalism or Christianity—accords preeminence to particular themes, sometimes even to methodologies. The chancellor's speeches, the museum debate, other exhibitions, radio and television interviews—all have focused on "German" identity as problematic. To specify national identity through history has traditionally involved turning to the great narratives of high politics. In this respect the current dispute resembles controversies that have divided historians since the famous *Methodenstreit* at the end of the nineteenth century. The issue has repeatedly been what range of activity constitutes history's privileged or specific subject matter. Ranke never said that all people were equally significant. Whose history counts?

The question is fraught with political implications. Just as Prussia long had a three-class suffrage that weighted the votes of its wealthy citizens more heavily than its poorer ones, in effect it had a three-class historiography. The history and struggle of nation-states were accorded most significance, a hierarchical evaluation still affirmed by Andreas Hillgruber: "Despite the significance of all long-term developments, the great differences between the great world powers have basically determined the course of general history even in the nineteenth and twentieth centuries."[38] A history of local communities, prepolitical peasantry, or tribal units might intrigue, but it did not enjoy the centrality and prestige of the national agglomerations. The history that examined recent class alignments and conflict was usually the province of left-wing dissidents, discounted as historiography even as its protagonists were discounted at the ballot box.[39] In this respect, as Eckart Kehr noted in the 1920s, social history was deemed tantamount to socialist history.[40]

For the remarkable Prusso-German historians from Ranke through Meinecke, the creation and maintenance of the nation-state was the big story of the nineteenth century. That epochal struggle, in Meinecke's view as he outlined it in his famous 1907 volume *Weltbürgertum und Nationalstaat (Cosmopolitanism and the National State)*, required the progressive subordination of residual universalist sympathies. For Meinecke, the path to German nationhood was best understood as an evolution of consciousness, specifically as an emancipation from a limiting cosmopolitanism. Germans had had to understand that the nation was an individual entity, with immanent obligations for its own survival and prosperity.[41] They had had to learn how to constitute a state among states: Prussia was the instrument of this process, and Ranke's history and Bismarck's statesmanship had been major contributions. True enough, Ranke's history had a universalistic component. However, "unlike Humboldt, Fichte, Schiller, and Novalis, he did not elevate the German nation as such to a universal, spiritual nation representative of all mankind. His consciousness and the consciousness of his time were too realistic and concrete for that."[42] By the time he got to Ranke and Bismarck, Meinecke felt that the work of liberation from an inhibiting universalism was complete.

Meinecke's historicism presupposed that the nation was analogous to the individual, its highest law one of self-development. Cosmopolitanism and fraternity were noble ideals, but the conflict between the ethical imperatives of the individual nation and humanity as a whole was ultimately unbridgeable. Nations were not members of a peaceful community: they were collective entities molded by struggle through time. Insofar as they existed in a plurality, they did so as potentially warring states, an insight already formulated by Hegel, and later formalized by Carl Schmitt as the essence of "the political."[43] This viewpoint had a methodological corollary. Just as a universalistic ethical framework had to be left behind, so a historiography whose sympathies, judgments, and approaches were rooted in a cosmopolitan vision was also inferior. History was reaffirmed as an individualizing study; its characteristic method was the intuitive penetration of individual agents. It was inappropriate to seek general causal laws in history, just as it was inappropriate to seek overarching moral obligations governing the conduct of nation-states.

Meinecke was enough of a moderate to modify his confident expression of Prusso-German historicism. He dissented from the pan-German historians during World War I and increasingly worried that national individualism, expressed by ideas of "reasons of state," had grown disproportionally. At the same time, he did not ascribe the development to Germans alone; his new work stressed the growth of the concept from the Renaissance through Frederick the Great. The *Idee der Staatsräson* was less innocently defiant of transnational norms than the slightly supercilious *Cosmopolitanism* of almost two decades earlier. After World War II, the old historian felt that even more of the Enlightenment spirit had to be recovered.[44] Nor was he the only one. The aging Gerhard Ritter, celebrator of a conservative nationalism, saw the shadow side of a Prussian military tradition he had not recognized earlier.[45] But at the same time, setting the dominant tone for the profession as a whole until the 1960s, they ascribed the "German catastrophe" to broader, Western trends—the rise of nationalism, socialism, the atomization produced by mass society—cultural bacilli, in effect, that happened to find post-Versailles Germany a particularly vulnerable host. National Socialism sometimes appeared just the end result of the French Revolution; the authentic Prussian tradition had found its final expression in the German Resistance. It was against this conservative reading of the epoch between the French Revolution and World War I that the historians of the *Sonderweg* mobilized in the 1960s.

They also contested the historicist methodology on which the Prussian historical tradition was based. It is remarkable in retrospect that Meinecke's work of 1907 appeared so exciting and innovative. To be sure, its effort to find the premises of political history in the world of ideas broke with the focus on political narrative alone. But in comparison with, say, the collective mentalities that the French would explore under Lucien Febvre between the wars, or the beginnings of social history, Meinecke's intellectual history seems far less innovative today. Part of the reason it could be welcomed as so fresh and exciting was that it revivified political history and the historicist tradition after one of the most bruising controversies racking German historiography. This was the conflict surrounding the work of Karl Lamprecht, a social historian often mistaken in his methods and rather primitive in his typologies. From the early 1890s, Lamprecht offended by his brusque challenge; he championed a history of society as a whole, not a one-sided emphasis on politics. By shifting focus from national ideas, by looking at other artifacts of community, such as place-names, settlements, and alleged stages of cultural development, Lamprecht posited an anthropological notion of community that was infrapolitical. He reasserted that history should seek general laws of social development; and he rejected the privileged status of individual nations. It was the journal Meinecke edited, the redoubtable *Historische Zeitschrift*—still today the major academic organ for the conservatives—that opened its pages to the bitter attacks upon his alleged pseudo-positivism. And it was Meinecke's study, in a sense, that provided a model by which the historicist, individualizing approach could triumphantly renew itself.[46]

Still, Lamprecht's program implied an important alternative. Its origins lay with Johann Gottlieb Herder, who had in a sense invented German nationalism, but as an expression of ethnic and linguistic community that might be counterposed to French cultural models. Herder's early *Another Philosophy of History* (*Auch eine Philosophie der geschichte*, 1774) along with subsequent work could be construed as a charter of anthropological consciousness. The program of Herder, then of Lamprecht, accommodated a nonconflictual ethnicity. The Rankean agenda, and Meinecke's canonization of it as the Prusso-German tradition, presupposed that there could be no political nation without international struggle, without abandoning the cosmopolitan transnational norms of an earlier period. The Lamprecht controversy was bitter because, as a conflict over historical method, it was also an implicit argument about the formation of the German Reich. It involved a critique of the Prussian program, of the Berlin university establishment nurtured by the Hohenzollern state—of what Meinecke praised as the fusion of power and culture.

Under radically changed conditions this amalgam of power and culture appeals to the conservative historians today. For Stürmer, the Western alliance is the cadre of power; but to play a role within NATO the country must have an unproblematic sense of its history. This requires not merely coming to terms with the National Socialist past but also understanding that in postwar Europe there were no historical alternatives to the Bonn republic. The Federal Republic is a fatherland by default. Certainly it is logically consistent that Habermas's Germany be West Germany; for the allegiance to which he appeals is the constitutional community of the West (even if Habermas feels uncomfortable with the military alliance that is also an expression of Western solidarity). But how does Stürmer's sort of West German nationalism come to terms with the DDR? If pressed to elaborate their views, historians such as Stürmer probably would argue along the lines that Meinecke did when justifying Bismarck's *Kleindeutschland*—the Prussian-led state that excluded German Austria—as an ingenious acceptance of national compromise: a trade-off of nostalgic yearning for real existence and vitality in the international arena. Does this mean full acceptance of two states—the practical implication of Social Democratic *Ostpolitik* to which critics objected? Or does it mean the theoretical claim of an overarching German national community, the claim that even Brandt and his successors have never renounced? Today's West German social liberals find it easier to say outright that for any foreseeable future there will always be two German nations, but German conservatives must ultimately view the German Democratic Republic as an appendage—a community of countrymen temporarily outside a real German nation-state. The conservative search for national identity implicitly resumes the theory upon which West Germany was made a nation in 1949. Delegates to the constitutional convention and parliamentary leaders through the 1950s could not accept that the creation of the Federal Republic meant the enduring exclusion of East Germany. The somewhat sophistic and desperate argument (probably not desired or believed by Adenauer, and not even accepted by SPD leader Kurt Schumacher) was that West Germany would be a "magnet"; ultimately it would attract the eastern zone to complete the nation. West Germany was like Italy in 1866—lacking Rome and Venice, Trieste and Trent, but clearly the nation and supposedly likely to recover these remaining provinces in a finite interval. The Federal Republic of 1949 might lack Berlin and Leipzig and Dresden, but—so the founders' myth insisted—they were likely to be recovered soon.

There was little choice for West German residents in 1949: they could have either a rump territory without autonomy or a rump state with progressively increasing autonomy. But to justify choosing the latter political leaders had to pretend the rump would be completed. There may in fact have been chances for reunification and autonomy later, in 1952—or earlier, in 1947—but that constitutes another debate. In any case, conservative historians such as Stürmer have bitterly denied that such opportunities ever arose.[47]

Stürmer evidently distrusts the vague longings for a wider community that sometimes seems to underlie West Germans' concern about the fate of East Germans. Indeed it is hard to ascertain how important these longings might be. On the one hand, West German citizens entertain no concepts for substantive German reunification. There exists a refreshing lack of concern with the Reich. Stürmer's compatriots lack Stürmer's anxiety about identity. On the other hand, this saneness can still coexist with a regret for a wider German community and concern about the other side of the Wall. That is why two states of mind coexist in West Germany: the free and easy sense of belonging to the West, for which the cadre of national community is clearly the Federal Republic; and, on the other hand, a residual potential for nostalgic reunion. Both moods can exist: West Germany is the nation in the indicative, Germany the homeland in the subjunctive. There is no tangible thrust for reunification: there is no reason to point with anxiety toward disloyalty to the West. But there is always the possibility of other concerns. To be a West German is to have not a latent political agenda, but a potential political agenda: "The German question has put on weight in thirty years," Peter Schneider has written with metaphoric accuracy, "and you can't claim that Germans west of the Elbe fret over it very much . . . A more realistic inference is that most Germans west of the Elbe have long since reconciled themselves to partition. In their separation pangs they resemble a lover grieving not so much for his loved one, as for the strong emotion he once felt. In Germany, it seems, time doesn't heal wounds; it kills the sensation of pain."[48]

The community of conservative historians, I believe, hopes to transform this generally nonproblematic acceptance of West German identity into a more historically redolent one. In effect, it wants to convert West Germans' quotidian at-homeness within what amounts to a national economy (like a latter-day Customs Union) into a historically freighted loyalty. It seeks to make Konrad Adenauer as gripping a figure as Boris Becker—precisely to inoculate against any potential attractiveness of an all-German community. In the Weimar era those leaders, such as Thomas Mann and Meinecke himself, who came to support the new German republic as the best choice available, even if it did not compel emotional loyalties, were called *Vernunftrepublikaner,* republicans by virtue of reason. All citizens of the Bonn republic are in one sense *Vernunftrepublikaner*—and herein lies the difficulty for those seeking a German historical identity. How can history be used to orchestrate an emotionally fulfilling national loyalty if that loyalty must be to a West German state alone? To continue the musical metaphor: Habermas's score is clearly Mozartian. Stürmer may prefer Beethoven—but may he not finally end up with Wagner instead?

This is not to say that a West German historical identity cannot be validly encouraged. Between the wars, Austrian national consciousness was a fragile framework of loyalties. In 1918 Austrian Socialists sought to dissolve their German Habsburg rump into a large social-democratic German-speaking nation. The Entente did not permit this early *Anschluss.* It did allow it twenty years later, when Austrian Nazis wanted to dissolve their country into a large National Socialist Reich. In between, Austrian Catholics fought to impose an autonomous national vision. They really succeeded only after World War II, when Socialists and Catholics could make a historical vocation out of their neutrality. The State Treaty of 1955 confirmed the historical validity of their country and gave it a historical role not so much as a "bridge" between East and West, but as the keystone that kept the two sides of the European arch from collapsing on each other. That passive achievement, testifying in part to the strategic nonimportance of Austria (why otherwise would the Soviets have relinquished their voice?), also provided a basis for a positive national identity.

What role exists today for a West German nation-state? Two visions of nationhood have been in most dramatic contention. One is as a member of Habermas's community of liberal democracies; the other is as a trusted constituent of Stürmer's Western alliance. Each role raises some potential inconsistencies for its advocate. Habermas sometimes seems uncomfortable because the community of liberal democracies is at the same time a military alliance. On the other hand, adherents of a traditional concept of national identity certainly accept NATO, but sometimes chafe that West Germany enjoys less autonomy than their major allies, France and Britain, not to speak of the United States. Will the demand to shed the so-called obsession with guilt be accompanied by the proposal to acquire the most compelling sacrament of sovereignty, an independent nuclear deterrent?

Still, one should not overdramatize the problems involved in constructing a usable past for the West Germans. Both Habermas and Stürmer point to the dangers inherent in the other's ideas. Nevertheless, most of the historians can live with the ambiguous status of West Germany. They find it has ample precedent. A unified German state existed only from 1871 to 1945, and even then it excluded large numbers of German-speakers. The historians' situation also has historiographic precedent: the most sensitive of their academic forebears always felt the tension between national individuation and broader, transnational trends of development. In this respect the historian who could probably serve as the most relevant predecessor was Otto Hintze, the meticulous student of the Prussian bureaucratic state, who after World War I enlarged his concerns from careful studies of mercantile policies to wide-ranging essays on the origins of Western parliamentarianism. This he sought in the feudal state, with its "estates" or "orders" that counterbalanced despotic tendencies. Germany shared in this Western development along with England and France; it thus had a Western and a liberal historical vocation. Concurrently Hintze sought to mediate between methodologies, to cling to the historicist emphasis on unique developments, but simultaneously to apply the insights of Weber's ideal-type procedures in order to make comparisons and generalizations. He endeavored to reconcile the two approaches by studying comparative processes, such as feudal estates and the origins of constitutionalism, as transnational, but still singular historical formations.[49]

Hintze was no liberal. Eckart Kehr recognized that Germany's defeat in 1918 transformed Hintze from a "proud, honest, unrhetorical, unobjectionable imperialist" into "almost a Social Democrat."[50] In part because of this transition, in part because of his effort to adapt Weberian methods, he has appealed not to Stürmer or Hillgruber, but to the Bielefeld historians, Kocka and Wehler. In effect they have recapitulated Hintze's deepening involvement with Weber, but whereas the old Prussian historian came to the great Weberian themes, such as bureaucratization, rationalization, and forms of domination, from the right, Kocka and Wehler have come from the left. In Wehler's massive new history of German society—the major current West German work that forms a pendant to Nipperdey's volume—the earlier concern with the primacy of domestic policy has significantly evolved. Wehler explicitly organizes the work around three autonomous axes or dimensions of development, which he takes from Weber: economy, political rule, and culture. He declines to follow the Hegelian or Marx-

ist contrast between state and civil society, in which transformations in
the latter realm drive both spheres onward. Yet the debt to Marx
reemerges in Wehler's fourth domain of analysis, that of "social inequality," which is conceptualized as the most pervasive result of the
interaction among the three axes.[51] Indeed if inequality emerges in
some way from the three Weberian dimensions, it still remains the
"main question of every historical social research, every analysis of
stratification, every social history . . . its weight in politics can hardly be
overestimated."[52] All history at least includes the history of class conflict. But Marx no longer dominates the firmament.

What the German historical community as a whole might well take
from Hintze is his hard-won insight that German history must be
understood as part of a larger European development; likewise, that
any serious approach to historical study must be open to social-
scientific methods. Whereas a one-sided *Historismus* early in the century depicted Germany as victor, a one-sided neohistoricism now
threatens to present Germany as victim. If there is to be a positive, and
not merely a passive, historical identity forged for the Federal Republic, then it must be as a component of a transnational system of
values.

In fact all parties in the debate presuppose that necessity. It was
endorsed, for example, in the Concept for the German Historical
Museum, discussed above. But the disputants diverge over what system of values should form the basis for a Germany-in-Europe. As
Habermas has written in his third major statement concerned with the
controversy: "It is not the affiliation of the Federal Republic to the
West that is at issue, but the question set by the neoconservatives,
whether the option for the West must not effectively be anchored in a
renewed national self-consciousness."[53] In other words, what sort of
Western option? The Western alliance of traditional nation-states, at
ease with their own history (the option of Stürmer and the conservatives)? The Western community of liberal values (Habermas's community of postconventional identity)? The Western instauration of welfare states put into place after 1945 under the impetus of organized
labor and social democracy (the option of what might loosely be called
the Social Democratic historians)? Although each option envisages a
Western framework, each presupposes a different version of German
national identity.

To be sure, I am not extending the spectrum of views to a more
extreme West German right, which nurtures an anti-Western national-

ism in *Nation Europa,* links up with the National Democratic Party of the 1960s, looks to mentors such as Armin Mohler, the apologist for Weimar's conservative revolutionaries and editor of *Criticon,* and evokes nostalgia for nineteenth-century poets and painters or for Holy Roman emperors in its small glossy magazine, *Mut.* The youthful adherents of the movement denounce American colonization of the Federal Republic, while its academic leadership, such as the historian Helmut Diwald at Erlangen or political scientists Bernard Willms, Wolfgang Seiffert, and Gerd-Klaus Kaltenbrunner, produce nationalist tracts and apologetic history. Yet the themes taken up by the far right can make a more mainstream career for themselves: Hillgruber's *Zweierlei Untergang* makes some of them presentable with footnotes, while the current pervasive concern with identity may have been launched with the 1978 book of rightest Henning Eichberg: *National Identity.*[54]

A word should be said about the German historians who cannot be included in any of the categories above, namely those of the German Democratic Republic. Through the 1970s East German official spokesmen allowed no recognition of an overarching German citizenship: a nation was defined by its social system, and two countries shared the terrain that Germany once occupied.[55] But the efforts of the Honecker regime to intensify interchanges with the Federal Republic, to annex the legacies of an older Germany, to commemorate Luther, Prussia, and, most recently, the 750th anniversary of Berlin, has encouraged a more open stance with respect to nationality and history.[56] East German historical scholarship has likewise become more elastic and refined. The spectacle of the *Historikerstreit* across the frontier prompted some predictable "Stamokap" responses to alleged West German reactionary tendencies.[57] The harder the ideological line, the easier to criticize any debate about national identity in the West. But this stance is clearly outmoded. East German historians have undertaken a range of studies largely freed from narrow ideological determinism.[58] The relationship of national achievements to social organization has become genuinely problematic once again: biographies of Frederick the Great and Bismarck no longer reflect predictable class categories.[59] Likewise, a more positive interpretation of Nietzsche becomes an indication of whether DDR intellectuals can push ahead with historical reassessment.[60] Indeed two sorts of pressure must continue to push East German historians toward reexamination of their national past: on the one hand, the rapprochement with the Federal Republic; on the other, the painful confrontation of earlier taboos that is occurring throughout Eastern Europe—including the Poles' reconsideration of earlier anti-Semitism and the Russians' halting rehabilitation of Stalin's victims such as Bukharin. Throughout the societies with a burdened past, the question "Who are we?" has emerged in the form "What have we denied?"

MEMORY CERTAINLY IS a prerequisite of identity, which rests on an awareness of continuity through time. The hunger for memory has been a remarkable cultural feature of the last decade. It underlies the interest in *Alltagsgeschichte,* the compulsion to think through the painful episodes of the past, the media presentations, and the museums. Indeed memory has become not just the portal to the past, but a subject of contemplation in its own right, to be analyzed as well as evoked. Memory, as in Saul Friedländer's affecting memoir, mingles private and public spheres.[61] Like some Verdian aria of renunciation set against a backdrop of war or rebellion, it conflates vast historical occurrences with the most interior consciousness. For some, memory can overwhelm and depress; for others, less scarred perhaps, it becomes addictive, akin to the melancholy of the Romantic era. Why this self-reflective longing has emerged with such force at this juncture is not at all clear. Is it because the social reformist projects of the previous generation have exhausted themselves, or just because the forces that hold memory at a distance have finally weakened, half a lifetime after the traumas evoked? In any case, although memory lies at the base of a given identity, history cannot be reduced to memory, nor can identity be specified in terms of history alone. Part of the difficulty with the German discussion has been an unreflective belief that identity is reducible to history, or that whatever one can know of identity is to be captured exclusively by the historian's craft. Sometimes for conservatives the term *identity* evokes the notion of wholeness that was the slogan for the "conservative revolutionaries" of the Weimar era. Neither Stürmer nor Nolte shares the nostalgia of these earlier destructive reactionaries. Again, Bonn is not Weimar. Still, the theme of incompleteness, of fragmentation (now historical as much as geographic), of destructive divisions that must be overcome ("obsession with guilt"), echoes earlier yearnings.[62]

Some writers have objected to the concern with identity. Historians, so Karl Dietrich Bracher and others have suggested, should not be in the identity business.[63] Jürgen Kocka has argued that "the principle of identity diametrically contradicts the principles of scientific history, of historical research," which should aspire more to the dissolution than to the construction of identity.[64] Writers on the left have posed "emancipation" as the goal of historical writing—an end to which Habermas and Wehler would subscribe.[65] On the other hand, even Habermas has become preoccupied with finding a usable concept of national identity. He, too, has conceded that historical narrative alone provides a community with the collective self-awareness it needs for future-oriented action.[66] The same premise informs the Kohl government's notion of tapping history like some spigot of German self-awareness. History is needed not only to guide policy, Hagen Schulze has written, but also to tell Germans who they are:

> It is about what the German nation-state is, and the answer to this question can emerge only from history. Only because there was a particular German nation-state from 1871 to 1945 can we say today what this German nation-state is and what it is not. The advantage of history for the present consists, in this case, in creating clarity about identity . . . If anyone is asked to inform us who he is, it is not enough for him to provide data about his present existence . . . Our identity is explained sufficiently only when our history is known: we are what we have become.[67]

Historians naturally find such an assumption flattering. It is, however, full of problems. Not that nations are not what they have become, but that they are not merely what they have become. The concept of personal identity presupposes an individual consciousness which is psychologically integrated in some way and which will cease with death. At best national identity remains an analogue.[68] The analogous element involves duration in time. In both cases memory (or a history) seems to constitute much of identity, such that individual or collective personality need not be created anew every instant. In that sense we are what we have become. But to state that a nation is nothing more than what it has become suggests that identity is like some sediment deposited by history. It implies that German identity in 1987 consists, say, of German identity from any previous point, plus whatever elements have been laid down since. German identity in 1987 would thus equal the German identity of 1945 plus the impact of changes wrought since 1945. By extension, German identity in 1945 could be taken to be that of 1933 plus the impact of intervening changes. The point is that the observer of a national culture must presuppose some initial or underlying characteristics. Any meaningful concept of a national identity must posit a subsisting component, which requires description in terms of nonhistorical variables. We need to know history, therefore, to understand identity; but history will not suffice. If it did, countries would move in worn grooves, and trajectories of development would be predictable. German history, above all, teaches that national behavior has scope for unexpected veerings and craziness, atrocious (and corrective) possibilities beyond what historical knowledge can prepare us for. To which the historian cited above might object that if we had a fuller knowledge we would be less surprised. Granted, but the knowledge can never be exhaustive.

Unfortunately, in the current debate many historians have apparently taken it for granted that national identity means no more or less than the product of national history. At any rate, they have not explicitly asked about how else identity might be construed. This is curious to an American reader. For almost all discussions of American identity revolve around the question of the American character or personality. They usually remain answers to Crèvecoeur's question, "Who is this American, this new Man?"[69] Why should so abstract an inquiry matter? Of course, if identity consists only of the accumulated silt of national experience, it can in theory be discoverable by sufficient historical dredging. But if identity implies some subsisting character that operates on giving conditions and must be understood by nonhistorical disciplines as well, expectations for history must be disappointed.[70]

Jürgen Habermas did force discussion of identity at two instances during the controversy, especially in his plea for constitutional patriotism and postconventional identity.[71] But the nature of national identity he suggested seemed insufficiently compelling even to many of his friends. It was unconvincing as a psychological description of what was involved and unable to guarantee minimal loyalties. With such objections in mind, Habermas recently returned to the theme in an address to a Danish audience. He cited historical consciousness as the "medium" for national self-consciousness. "To form a collective identity and carry it along, the cultural and linguistic interdependencies of life must be renewed in a way that gives them meaning."[72] Two components went into that historical effort: the first was the narrative construction of a meaningful past—and in this respect Habermas's formulation evoked Stürmer's concept. At the same time, however, the critical historian had to resist the socially integrative function demanded by the nation-state.[73] Overall, critical historical study did not lend itself to the production of identity—unless it were what Habermas has termed throughout a postconventional identity, a rational subscription to the liberal political community of the West.

Habermas (correctly) did not content himself with this facile correlation between an evocative, community-oriented (*sinnstiftende*) historiography and old-style national identity on the one hand, and a critical history and a postconventional identity on the other. Evidently prodded by the recent critics of his 1986 formulations, he has tried to incorporate two components into postconventional identity. Even postconventional identity involves more than constitutional patriotism. It must invoke some sense of community bond that goes beyond rational adherence to normative propositions. "Every identity which provides the basis for belonging to a collective [group] and which underlies the many situations in which the members can emphatically say 'we' must appear to remain as something unquestioned and beyond [critical] reflection."[74] Post-traditional identity apparently still rests upon some sort of loyalty as traditionally understood. It tugs at the heart as well as at the mind.

But how does Habermas justify this position? No doubt with his Danish audience in mind, he has proposed the model of Kierkegaard's radical sense of moral choice in *Either/Or*. Kierkegaard's choice is more than just a rational affirmation; like Augustine's conversion, it involves a commitment that transforms the self, that recasts identity and reconstructs its history. Like post-traditional identity, with its decision for a community of liberal values, Kierkegaard's new self would have found no spiritual home in the conventional nation-state. Nonetheless, Kierkegaard's moral inwardness did not preclude social and civic commitment. Similarly, postnationalist identity requires recognition of interdependence and community. At this point, Habermas returns to amplify and implicitly defend the concept of *Lebensform* that he invoked in his second contribution to *Die Zeit*.[75] There he argued that the enduring "forms of life" or communities (nation, family, and so on) in which Germans were born and nurtured mandated a sense of historical responsibility for the National Socialist past. How, he was asked, was this almost Burkean allegiance to an intergenerational historical community compatible with the austere rationalist foundation of constitutional patriotism? The response in the Danish address seems to be that even post-traditional identity must remain grounded in a whole range of traditional loyalties, but that this network of cultural loyalties had diverged from the nexus of nation-state politics:

As part of this development identification with one's own forms of life and traditions is overlaid with a patriotism that has become more abstract, that relates no longer to the concrete whole of a nation, but to abstract procedures and principles . . . To be sure, the commitment of constitutional patriotism to these principles must nourish itself on compatible cultural legacies. Even now the life form that is shaped by national legacies has a privileged status, even if it is only one in a hierarchy of life forms, each with a different range of claims.[76]

Does this position successfully overcome what seems to be an initial incompatibility between the loyalties of the head and the habits of the heart—between a commitment to transnational, liberal values and the collective identity generated by traditional communities? Only the latter sort of identity, apparently, justifies the demand that contemporary Germans accept a national responsibility for Nazi crimes. Would it not be simpler to accept that insofar as a West German state serves as repository and guarantor of the liberal values Habermas cherishes, its existence must be understood as a historical product; hence that it entails its citizens' acceptance of responsibility for a national past? Habermas seems so fearful that national identity must be reactionary or aggressive that he cannot accept that a nation-state also provides the framework for responsibility and reform. Consequently he simultaneously invokes infrapolitical loyalties to family, professions, and hometown communities, and supranational allegiance to a community of Western values. Somehow the condition of being German is to be divided between *Heimat* and *Verfassung*, between two levels of commitment, at once emotional and rationalist. But can the emotional hold of Habermas's "life forms" be confined to so instrumental a role? Can these communities really be appealed to only as a sort of pastureland on which constitutional patriotism is nurtured? Such an approach may ultimately provide frailer guarantees against the deformations of nationalism than would coming to terms with the multiple loyalties and potential embedded in the nation-state.

This is not to deny that Habermas's argument remains rich and intriguing. It has been more thoroughly worked through than any of the others generated by the controversy. It applies the duality of social order—as lifeworld and as instrumental association—emphasized in *The Theory of Communicative Action*. It would also be unjust to tax Habermas as utopian, since he adduces public-opinion data suggesting that some postconventional identification is gaining ground in West Germany. Not the least appealing aspect to an American liberal has been Habermas's gradual renunciation of dialectical syntheses for neo-Kantian antinomies.[77] In the face of neoconservative ideas (perhaps even since the earlier confrontation with the student left) and the postmodern distrust of progressive politics, he has strengthened his liberal commitment. He envisages the historians' controversy as—indeed has helped to make it—part of a major debate concerning the political culture of the Federal Republic.

In his Danish address Habermas asks whether the integration of the Federal Republic in the West really meant a new beginning, or just the most opportune way to preserve traditional national values. The Bundesrepublik rested on a double antitotalitarian consensus—simultaneous opposition to fascism and to communism. The consensus embodied a centrist political compromise at the same time. But the erosion of that compromise consensus forces citizens of the Federal Republic to ponder whether their integration in the Western community was merely "adaptation" or a "new orientation rooted in conviction and based upon principle."[78] From this perspective, the historical work of Hillgruber, Nolte, and Stürmer arose as a sort of conservative fall-back strategy. During the decades of antitotalitarian consensus, Habermas argues, anticommunism remained as an operative political principle. Antifascism, however, came to be little more than a ritual formula. It rallied no coalitions, excluded no options. But this shelving of antifascism required the historians as accomplices: they had to leave the Nazi era unexamined. Their compliance broke down in the 1960s. Once it did, and the conservatives were no longer able to exclude the National Socialist period from troubling historical scrutiny, no longer able to focus political attention on the dangers allegedly emanating from the left, they sought instead to normalize the Nazi period, to dissolve its arresting, problematic legacy.[79]

More explicitly than the other participants in this debate, Habermas has posed the problems that most of the historians on both sides have taken for granted: How in fact is history constitutive of collective identity? Must not analytic history, with its need for critical questioning of the past, always stand in some degree of tension to national identity? Is identity an appropriate goal for the social sciences, or is it a deluded objective? Might it not be that only a historiography relying on atmospherics, a meretricious effort to create mood and "feel," sometimes by stylistic elegance, sometimes by the piling up of picturesque details that suggest intimate familiarity, will seem to provide a sense of identity?

Identity may in fact be a spurious goal for the historian. If a grasp of
one's social values, collective aspirations, and formative national experiences is required for civic reasons, historical narrative is only one tool
among many. The analysis of myth, kinship, market exchanges, language, and art may not yield the same psychological sense of identity,
but it will help constitute an ordered awareness of values and social
structures. To understand these structural relations, the social scientist
rightly uses history as but one among several approaches. History may
remain in tension with these other, social-scientific methods, which
build on its research but seek to overcome its concern with the particular. It is worth recalling Claude Lévi-Strauss's harsh evaluation of
Sartre's claims on behalf of history in the *Critique of Dialectical Reason*.
History, the anthropologist insists, provides only a pseudo-sense of
identity: "It suffices therefore for history to move away from us in time
or for us to move away from it in thought, for it to cease to be
internalizable and to lose its intelligibility, a spurious intelligibility
attaching to a temporary internality."[80] Historiography remains
trapped in its own partialness and a Western sense of intelligibility.

> Sartre is not the only contemporary philosopher to have valued his-
> tory above the other human sciences and formed an almost mystical
> conception of it. The anthropologist respects history, but he does not
> accord it a special value . . . I believe the ultimate goal of the social
> sciences is not to constitute, but to dissolve man. The pre-eminent
> value of anthropology is that it represents the first step in a procedure
> which involves others. Ethnographic analysis tries to arrive at in-
> variants beyond the empirical diversity of human societies.[81]

Lévi-Strauss distrusts historicism and aspires to apply scientific
knowledge from outside the community under study. In effect, he
argues that even Max Weber's ideal-type methodology is too subjective
and too culture-bound. Can the historian reconstitute collective identities that are less dependent upon *Erlebnis* and subjectivity? The answer is probably not—at least not as a historian. "National character"
models, for instance, may presuppose historical conditions, but they
rely on social-psychological or anthropological variables to suggest
historical outcomes. In any case, many of these are distrusted, since
they were applied—especially to Germans—far too facilely. Germans
allegedly loved authority; they were psychologically afraid of autonomy, uneasy about status . . . generalizations that explain nothing in
particular because they purport to explain every outcome, including

contradictory ones. Nonetheless, if we need to specify a collective identity, it must include patterns of culture that are not necessarily historical.

Structured Decisionism

Let me propose some of the traits that any discussion of German identity must take into account. These do not form a historical paradigm, for they remain atemporal. What is crucial for understanding German values and institutions is a sort of structured "decisionism," which is highly rational and desperate at the same time. Desperate, in that decisionism refers to the imposing of political will, the final going beyond rational argument and the careful weighing of alternatives. German social theorists of the right (Schmitt) and the left (Kirchheimer, Habermas) repeatedly return to the nature of such decisions.

It was not just the circumstance of a Danish audience that made it appropriate for Habermas to return to Kierkegaard's decisionism for an analogy of civic commitment. Nor is it fortuitous that he also distrusts decisionist philosophies, which, he fears, glorify the nonrational and romantic. Almost twenty years ago, Habermas condemned the student left for its political romanticism; he logically distrusts the Nietzschean appeals taken up by postmodernist writers. Finally, he has remained uneasier than the historians about the legacy of Max Weber; for Weber himself typified the ambiguities of decisionism: on the one hand he remained the champion of rationalization; on the other he continually regretted the disenchantment of the world and sought to recapture an earlier vitalism. Weber's social scientist must orient his research on the basis of such a prerational decision. Weber's good political systems provide scope for political figures who are capable of decisive leadership. Such systems also allow for a direct plebiscitary component that compels an otherwise passive citizenry to exercise its will. From his 1892 inaugural lecture, tinged by regret that after Bismarck no great decisions may remain, through his methodological insistence on subjectivity, to his 1920 "Politics as a Vocation," decisionist nostalgia remains pervasive.[82] Nor is Habermas immune to this undertone that he finds so disturbing in Weber. Even in his Sonning Prize address, Habermas cannot escape positing a decisionist element to postconventional identity—the tribute that reason pays to the prerational!

Nor is it thinkers alone who manifest this decisionist preoccupation.

Bismarck's politics, in 1862, 1866, 1870, 1878, and 1887, were based on the willingness to wager on the force of personality or on war. His contempt for the liberals derived from the fact that parliament was shielded from that life-or-death wager. Conversely, Bethmann Hollweg's politics can be described in terms of decisionist despair, as the 1914 chancellor surrendered to the feeling of being helpless before the pressures leading to war. Bethmann's was decisionism by default. And Hitler's political style need only be mentioned.

But if decisionist wagers are characteristic of German politics, so too is the effort to minimize the need for them. The German approach to social choice is to narrow the scope for decision to the greatest degree possible. The result is a contrast between the domains of institutional life that are subject to pervasive rules and the residual gaps in which the rules yield to an almost despairing test of conflicting wills. In labor negotiations, for example, highly structured bargaining procedures keep the conflicting parties at the negotiating table and require several formal votes before workers can resort to a strike. But if mediation fails, the dispute arouses far greater political uneasiness than it would in other Western nations. A real test of social cohesion seems under way to adversaries and observers alike. In political conflicts, too, one observes diligent efforts to narrow the grounds of dispute—followed by profound crisis if the final differences cannot be bridged. German history is littered with the debris of efforts at concertation. The most famous was the breakdown of the last parliamentary government of the Weimar Republic in 1930, when disagreement over the last quarter percent of social-insurance contributions could not be overcome. Politics and economics develop in a rhythm of bureaucratic order punctuated by decisionist crisis.

Similar patterns of discontinuity mark personal growth and relationships. Years ago, Erik Erikson pointed out that whereas German childhood and adulthood were both highly structured, indeed constraining, stages of life, adolescence was conceded to be a time of intense inwardness and sentimental excess, far more than in other societies.[83] To be sure, the postwar internationalization of American mores has changed the German family. Nonetheless, literary portrayals, the testimony of youth groups, autobiographies, all suggest that a constraining society is counteracted either by the romantic cultivation of solitude or by intense bonding—whether among couples, classmates, or party comrades. And although this contrast has become less marked since 1945, the continuum of sociability that marks Latin societies hardly exists.

Hence the domains of normative behavior on the one side, of surrender to will and subjectivity on the other, have remained sharply separated, hardly intermingled as in the United States.

Such a division of the world leads ultimately to a desperate view of social rationality. No matter how much of life and civil society remains organized and normative, the human sciences remain ransom to subjectivity. Political life rests upon *Willkür* (arbitrary choice) as well as upon *Wahlen* (elections). Carl Schmitt (seconded on the left by his student Otto Kirchheimer) argued that the Weimar constitution, indeed liberalism in general, avoided establishing a locus for political decision, because it would not concede that the essence of politics was conflict.[84] Schmitt remains more influential than his fundamentally authoritarian views would lead one to believe. He exerts the fascination of the unyielding counterrevolutionary that de Maistre and Maurras also radiated.[85] As Habermas recently pointed out, Schmitt appeals to those who in the Catholic tradition would question "the legitimacy, or the autonomy, of the modern era." But, as Habermas recognizes, his influence is wider—not the least of his appeals is to the irrational left in the Federal Republic and Italy "who fill the gap left by the non-existent Marxist theory of democracy with Schmitt's fascist critique of democracy." Schmitt thus remains a fascinating adversary. He is the fundamental opponent of "the medium of discussion that is public and guided by argument" and thus of Habermas's own system. Schmitt has become the fashionable reference point for a radical conservative chic.[86] So, too, has Clausewitz, whose discussion of war painstakingly reviews all the constraints upon strategy and tactics but finally insists upon the battle itself as the moment of decision. It is no accident that war was Schmitt's underlying paradigm for politics. For other thinkers, too, whatever the field of activity, the structure of interpretation is similar. The contrast remains ubiquitous between reason and will, persuasion and force, analysis and subjectivity, purposive transactions and emotional cathexis, deliberation and decision. Any adequate description of German peculiarity must take into account this syndrome of structured decisionism.

Nonetheless, historians lean on such concepts of national style at their peril. It is not that algorithms of national identity are determinist in the sense, say, that an economic interpretation of history might be determinist. It is rather that such models are overdetermining; they can be invoked to account for any possible outcome of events, whereas the historian must explain why one outcome alone prevailed and others did not. This does not mean that notions of national identity do not add to insight. But they shift the search for explanation into an aesthetic dimension. The analytical historian works with different tools, and history as a discipline in which successive researchers test the accounts of their predecessors must ultimately disappoint those who seek this sort of intuition. In this respect the German historians have claimed too much for their craft. They might usefully recall Walter Benjamin's suggestions of how fragmentary historical knowledge remains. In *The Origin of German Tragic Drama* Benjamin explored the baroque theater's evocation of history as the backdrop for an allegory of ubiquitous crumbling and decay.[87] Later, after being buffeted by the events of the 1930s, Benjamin described the "angel of history" facing backward into the past but blown into the future by the wind of progress, watching the debris accumulate as he was driven away from it.[88] For the historian, too, a steady gaze at the wreckage is vocation enough.

Epilogue
Whose Holocaust? Whose History?

Unmastered Pasts

The historians' controversy is a chapter in German history and historiography, but not in Germany's alone. It is also part of a more encompassing eruption of the past, a confrontation with earlier traumas that has gripped many societies. West Germans have shared a broader, significant intrusion of history. This intrusion is twofold. On a theoretical level, it involves a debate over the adequacy of historiography. How should historians respond to the claims of memory and identity? What are the limits of the historical craft? Is every human evil comprehensible? How appropriate is analogy for understanding? These are traditionally vexing questions, now posed with renewed urgency.

The intrusion of history is not just theoretical. It is also the legacy of being an accomplice or a victim, or just an onlooker. In each case, history entails the uncomfortable presence of earlier unresolved roles. The West Germans have just debated more polemically questions that have arisen among all those who have undertaken to interrogate the repression carried out by their national communities. Historiography at this level faces a challenge because it confronts a difficult past, based on shared pain: *sunt lacrimae rerum.* The demand arises finally to explain the inhumanity wrought over a generation ago, which, given the guilt it evoked, could be "worked through" only partially in the immediate postwar period. This pain is a property not only of the Germans but also of their collaborators, their onlookers, and their victims. The historians' controversy is like a blocked analysis: a story is not yet fully uncovered; transference and catharsis are not yet possible.

Former perpetrators and victims—preeminently, though not exclusively, Germans and Jews—have been locked into a special relationship. No matter what material or other public debts are paid, confessional memory is demanded as the only valid reparation. And as a claim upon official memory, the victim's anguish comes to be seen as a valuable possession. Other peoples also want the status of victimhood. But this effort to benefit from history has disadvantages. Nietzsche feared that history could interfere with life: "I actually believe that we are suffering from a destructive historical fever and should at least recognize what we are suffering from." The "unhistorical" as well as the "historical" was necessary for the health of an individual, for a people and a culture.[1] Can there be too much memory?

By most measures the postwar history of Western Europe has been a success story. It has brought the dismantling of dictatorships and the founding of resilient democracies, the expansion of welfare, the diffusion of prosperity and education, the attenuation of earlier class conflicts, the extension of a public and professional role to women. But postwar history has also been a history of forgetting: forgetting fascism, Nazism, and collaboration. As a *New York Times* reporter stressed during the controversy, "Europe's apparent amnesia about the war is largely a willed phenomenon. Europeans old enough to remember those years have not forgotten the past, but often remember it all too well, and they deeply resent being reminded of it."[2]

But amnesia is only part of the problem. Advocates of memory cannot have just the memories they want. Memory, even Habermas's "reflective memory," is complex. Like "historicization," it can be used, not to confront the past, but to complicate it. The demand for a more subtle historiography can itself serve as an effective strategy of evasion, "revision," or normalization. Consider briefly the case of Italy, the homeland, after all, of fascism and an Axis partner in the war. Although a massive Resistance movement arose after the Germans reduced Mussolini's government to an occupied collaborationist state in 1943, passive acceptance largely prevailed before the war. Once the regime fell, the left's polarized image of fascism and resistance dominated historiography. Even after the split between Christian Democrats and Communists in 1947, evocation of the Resistance helped to unite both avowed and unavowed political coalitions into the 1970s. But the heroic contrasts that earlier rallied the left no longer seem persuasive. In the Taviani brothers' 1982 film *The Night of the Shooting Stars* (*La notte di San Lorenzo*), the once-heroic combats of the Resistance have been reduced to a brutal fight between frightened peasants. And if the Resistance is undermined, the Fascist regime likewise seems harder to reject outright. Even the Communists have sanctioned a far more complex interpretation of developments under Fascism. Historians of the left have recognized that the Fascists could successfully build a state, not merely upon repression, but on cooptation of working-class organization, infiltration of mass culture, and patronage of modernizing technology. The left certainly dissented when conservative interpreters emphasized "consensus" as the leading theme of Fascist rule in the 1930s. Nevertheless, their own research suggested that consensus could not simply be denied.[3] Nor could some forms of economic modernization. But to focus on economic advance meant implicit apologia, as was the case for the large exhibit on the interwar Italian economy held in the Colosseum in 1984. Streamlined airplanes and elegant racing cars, posters of svelte and fashionable couples on ocean cruises, projects for modern architecture were exploited to convey an ambiance of art deco modernity, what might be called (from the earlier term for the cinema of the period) white-telephone Fascism.[4] If memory comes, it now arrives with ambiguities.

The historian Henry Rousso has traced four phases in French society's confrontation of the memory of Vichy: a decade of incomplete mourning from war's end to the mid-1950s; a Gaullist insistence on France as a country of Resisters united behind the general; a "return of the repressed," signaled by Marcel Ophuls's film *Le chagrin et la pitié* (*The Sorrow and the Pity*); and, finally, since 1974 an episode of "obsession," marked on the one hand by the awaking of Jewish memory and on the other by anti-Semitic revivals.[5] In this most recent period *L'Express* published the insistence of the aged Darquier de Pellepoix, former Vichy commissioner for Jewish affairs, that the Final Solution never took place, but was a Jewish lie; and the courts had to test the truth of Robert Faurisson's "dissertation," which also argued the Holocaust was a myth. In France, notes Rousso, borrowing the term from Pascal Ory, a *mode retro* of the 1970s tried to conjure up the lived experience of Vichy, including a fascination with its inversion of values and even its anti-Semitic *chic*.[6] This is a phenomenon Saul Friedländer has referred to as Nazi kitsch, the fascination that elements of the Nazi style exert on those who would "master it": a pornography of violence (fused with banality) that its would-be describers end up revoking.[7] (In effect, some of Ernst Nolte's hypothetical comparisons of Israel's policy—or the policies of Jewish leaders—with those of Hitler convey a similar *frisson* and appeal to a similar *mode retro*.)

No such aestheticization of fascism varnishes Austrian developments. The dismay expressed by Jewish organizations and foreign spokesmen at the 1987 election of Kurt Waldheim as state president unleashed an ugly reaction. At the least, Waldheim falsified his wartime military service, even if he was not cognizant of murderous violations of the laws of war. But Austria had largely avoided any painful debate about its Nazi past. The Second Republic benefited from the Allied decision to consider the country as the first victim of Hitler's Germany; the enthusiasm of many Austrians for the *Anschluss* was overlooked. Postwar denazification measures came to be seen as part of a battle between the Austrian parties and the Allied occupiers, to be removed as soon as the country regained its sovereignty. The fact that everyone knew of some Nazi "who hadn't done too much" fed the demand for normalization, for letting bygones be bygones (what the Germans call drawing a *Schlußstrich*, or last accounting), and for "a little peace and quiet."[8] A small country was happy to overlook its past. After all, had not Austria had a Jewish chancellor, Bruno Kreisky, for almost a decade—albeit one who thought that the demand for "mastery of the past" was mere talk? The fuss raised by foreigners over Waldheim revived the unwelcome intrusions of the early postwar years. Why can't the foreigners (including the spokesmen for international Jewish agencies)—many were evidently tempted to ask—just stop scratching old wounds? Even if observers might have expected resentment and even a revived anti-Semitism from the parochial elements of postwar Austria, it must be counted as unusual to have the foreign minister circulate an official letter to his country's historians asking them to rebut the alleged calumnies of a young British colleague: "to prevent forty years of Austrian history, including the history of the Austrian resistance against Nazism and other forms of fascism, from being grotesquely distorted under the impression of a few events of the most recent period."[9]

The simple demand to recover memory, these national experiences suggest, cannot guarantee the outcome of memory. Even an edifying judicial spectacle such as the trial of Klaus Barbie cannot yield entire satisfaction. When asked which word—*la justice* or *l'oubli*—better characterized their attitude toward "the facts of 1942 to 1944," a reassuring 77 percent of French citizens surveyed chose justice, and only 19 percent believed in forgetting.[10] But Barbie, after all, was German, not French; and as a former SS officer he represented an organization that everyone recognized as brutal. Trial testimony brought out many very painful memories, but few that were "difficult" for French society. On the eve of the trial there had been concern that the Resistance would emerge diminished. The indictment specified "crimes against humanity" but was not to consider the torture or killing of Resistance combatants. Spokesmen for the defense also threatened to expose episodes of betrayal from within the Resistance. In fact, there was testimony enough of bravery and pain that the trial did not reinforce any image of a tacitly collaborationist France. In contrast to *The Sorrow and the Pity,* Frenchmen, and certainly Frenchwomen, appeared again as victims or heroes, less as accomplices.[11] The result was reassuring, but not necessarily an advance in coming to terms with the Vichy past.

The Holocaust as Asset

The hunger for memory has brought about a change in the status of victimhood. Victims used to be pitiful; their very helplessness contributed to the segregation and depersonalization that helped seal their fate. But along with other indices, the Barbie trial suggested that the status of victimhood was prized. It was painful and difficult to recall but no longer a badge of passivity and an incitement to covert contempt. This fact brings us to one of the most problematic legacies of the Holocaust. Sensitive Germans recognize that it is a continuing component of their history. Jews insist that it is a modern foundation for theirs. But if the Holocaust must be a debt for Germans, is it automatically an asset for Jews? And if it is an asset, must it be shared with other claimants to suffering? These are hard questions, but they have become painful issues in historical interpretation as well as in politics. Jews' insistence on their own victimhood, their unwillingness to be silent, has often been deemed awkward and obsessive. Still muted in America and Britain while the Final Solution was under way, Jewish insistence later helped force reexamination of what had taken place in Nazi Germany, occupied France, and elsewhere. The foundation of a Jewish national state, confirmed two decades later by the victories of the Six Day War, also sanctioned a more aggressive rethinking of a history that earlier had seemed trapped in a fatal passivity. (It also sanctioned an Israeli *Realpolitik* and could eventually legitimate an ugly "anti-Zionism" abroad). The Six Day War in effect moved the Holocaust higher on the agenda of memory, but reconsideration sometimes meant a more aggressive exploitation of the dead, a more exclusive property right in suffering.

To be sure, postwar Jewish identity depends upon the Holocaust. Whether as a goad to a more assertive role in the Diaspora or as a basis for Israeli nationhood, the crimes Jews suffered serve as a central legitimation. But a Holocaust-centered Jewishness involves new contradictions, especially outside Israel. Jewish suffering is depicted as ineffable, uncommunicable, and yet always to be proclaimed. It is intensely private, not to be diluted, but simultaneously public so that gentile society will confirm the crimes. A very particular suffering must be enshrined in public sites: Holocaust museums, memory gardens, deportation sites, dedicated not as Jewish but as civic memorials. But what is the role of a museum in a country, such as the United States, far from the site of the Holocaust? Is it to rally the people who suffered or to instruct non-Jews? Is it supposed to serve as a reminder that "it can happen here"? Or is it a statement that some special consideration is deserved? Under what circumstances can a private sorrow serve simultaneously as a public grief? And if genocide is certified as a public sorrow, then must we not accept the credentials of other particular sorrows too? An American historian of Polish ancestry argues that, with the German invasion of 1939, the Poles became the first people in Europe to experience the Holocaust and that historians have so far "chosen to interpret the tragedy in exclusivistic terms—namely as the most tragic period in the history of the Jewish Diaspora."[12] If Polish Americans claim their own "forgotten Holocaust," what recognition should they enjoy? Do Armenians and Cambodians also have a right to publicly funded holocaust museums? And do we need memorials to Seventh-Day Adventists and homosexuals for their persecution at the hands of the Third Reich?

Germany and Israel and the countries in which Nazi crimes were committed certainly present special cases. For the sake of decency Germans need—and many recognize the need—to make provision for memory. And the need is not just for anodyne admonitions (*Mahnmale*) against war and violence in general, but for specific memorials that record their society's former crimes and particular victims.[13] There is a problematic quality to those confessions that dilute the particular targeting of Jews, even if only to stress that there were other victims as well: "The thesis of the 'singularity' of the Holocaust is to be rejected," one younger historian has written, "because, wittingly or not, it hierarchizes the victims of the National Socialist machinery of destruction." Although this judgment appears in an essay that valuably insists that there was a continuum of "discriminations, selections and eradication," all of which allowed "everyday life" in the Third Reich to facilitate the Final Solution, it still presents an element of evasiveness. If historians diffuse the target, the Final Solution will become a specimen of social-

Darwinist eugenics gone wild, capitalist crisis, twentieth-century inhumanity, a sea of complicity in which everyone founders—everything but a crime committed by some Germans against many Jews.[14]

On the other hand, if it behooves Germans to stress the anti-Jewish specificity of the Holocaust, it is sometimes important for Jews to do the opposite. In Israel, of course, the Holocaust can be a public as well as a private sorrow. It certainly helps legitimate the state, even if it cannot legitimate any particular frontiers or policies. There are reportedly ten public institutions in Israel, such as musuems and research centers, specifically devoted to the Holocaust—what a liberal American Jewish magazine has called a "memory industry." This "industry" has produced what one Israeli theologian has condemned as a new Holocaust religion that refuses to credit other genocides as equally authentic: "Biafra was only hunger, Cambodia was only a civil war; the destruction of the Kurds was not systematic; death in the Gulag lacked national identification marks . . . The Holocaust is a collection of human acts which has turned into a transcendent event." But in fact, the author argues, "the Jewishness of the Holocaust (like its Germanness) is only one aspect of its horror, the most crucial aspect from our point of view but by no means exclusive." The only response must be to understand the Holocaust as a human possibility that arises from the discourse of exclusion, and not just as the basis for a new Jewish national religion. The difference between this perverted Holocaust myth and the appropriate one "is essentially political: It is the difference in the use which the living make of the memory of the dead, the present of its history."[15] It is the perverted myth that exploits the memory of an infinite horror to justify even a far less repressive behavior.

The obligations of memory thus remain asymmetrical. For Jews: to remember that although they seek legitimation of a public sorrow, their suffering was not exclusive. For Germans: to specify that the Holocaust was the Final Solution of the Jewish problem as its architects understood it. The appropriateness of each proposition depends upon who utters it.

For Jews to ask such specific acknowledgment from Germans can, it must be understood, encourage an ugly reaction (as has taken place in Austria). Was not the normalcy of the Federal Republic, the lack of edginess to West German political life, so Golo Mann asked brutally in 1960, due in part to the very absence of Jews? "What I am saying here sounds cynical and is in fact an extremely dangerous, delicate observation. But it must be made. The astonishing success of the Bonn Republic in the eyes of its own people and thus in the eyes of the outside world, the relative composure that characterizes public life in Germany today, has something to do with the fact that the German Jews have fled or were murdered."[16] No matter how easily liberal Germans reassure Bonn's Jews that they are again part of the professions or welcome at table, for many the feeling persists that a Jew is never quite at home in Germany.[17] For a while before the Palestinian issue arose, a cloying philo-Semitism was fashionable. That period of patronization is past. With the late 1970s the years of insensitive obliviousness seemed at hand: the Bundesrepublik had paid its dues to Israel;[18] its intellectuals were free to compare the Jewish state's treatment of Arabs with the Nazi treatment of Jews, who now seemed to have a lot to answer for: oppression, patriarchy, and colonialism. Of course there will always be outrages—swastika-smeared gravestones, drunken insults—but they are not the main issue. The problematic development is what Andrei Markovits has called in an essay on the Greens "the new uninvolvement" (*die neue Unbefangenheit*). By this he means a sort of *ingénu* insouciance that enables the younger generation to "work through" the Nazi past but also reassures them that it was someone else's history, a left-wing version, in sum, of Chancellor Kohl's "grace of late birth":

> The danger exists that the Greens will become an ever-more-significant part of a political culture of "the new uninvolvement," which in the public consciousness of the Federal Republic has taken hold of the complex and singular relationship between Germans and Jews, thus too of the Holocaust . . . which the German left has never really worked through . . . and henceforth, given the process of incipient "normalization" of German historical consciousness, is finally supposed to disappear from public awareness.[19]

But does not the demand for renewed German *Befangenheit,* for a sense of involvement, confirm that Nolte was somehow right: that there is an obsession with the past? This past cannot pass away. Why indeed should it be more obsessive than other pasts? Not because of the deeds themselves, but because of the complicity and shame, which precluded a full confrontation. Commentators from the right and the left have suggested that such an inability actually contributed to the stability of postwar societies. "To the degree that the manifestations of memory have revealed a society incapable of finding the thread of its history, to that degree the society progressively reaffirmed its consensus. Is the syndrome not the price of that evolution?"[20] But is this not to argue that we must build the future on forgetting the past? This seems a flawed remedy. The answer to obsession is not forgetting, but overcoming: the basis for consensus is not obscuring but repairing so far as is possible, and avoiding the categorizing of species that lay at the origin of "life unworthy of life." Thereafter let the historian insist that Auschwitz was not the end of history; it was not the entelechy of the twentieth century. It alone does not characterize our era; the movements toward emancipation that can be ranged alongside the monstrous repressions—the role of women, of racial minorities, the spread of democratic regimes—are also part of the twentieth-century record. It is possible to make a fetish of Auschwitz. Granted, the distinction between mourning, honoring, analyzing—all legitimate ends for the historian—and fetishizing is a hard one: Not the method, but the use of history establishes it. History should contribute to reconstructive effort, efforts by, as well as on behalf of, earlier victims.[21]

Postmodern Historiography

The *Historikerstreit* incorporates several conflicts. It involves a struggle over the controlling political analogies in the discourse of the Federal Republic. But it is also the German form in which what might be called postmodern historiography challenges the achievements of the last generation's social-scientific analyses. It involves a sharp attack on history as a would-be social science and a critique of any implicit theory of progress or redemption. Jürgen Habermas can be taken as the Federal Republic's preeminent spokesman for what might be called the liberal-democratic or social-democratic "metanarrative": the conviction that knowledge substantially reflects the real world, is progressive, and can change politics and society. Even a nontheoretical historian such as Andreas Hillgruber senses this when he entitles his response to Habermas *Aufklärung 1986.*[22]

Postmodern historiography, in effect, is attempting to fill a void left by the erosion of the earlier social-democratic premises of post-1960 history and politics. Fill it with history as ritual, discourse, or carnival. Sometimes the purpose has been to explore the hitherto neglected ways by which actors without formal power could nonetheless contest the hierarchies that regulated their everyday lives. In such a case the new history still presupposes a world of real power and struggle. But in some historical and anthropological reconstructions, politics loses any instrumental rationality. It no longer embodies socially purposive aspirations, whether for emancipation or for domination, and appears only as ritual or theater, the state as cinema. Whatever the new and allusive subject, the major thrust of postmodern historiography is the unmooring of politics from any unambiguous correspondence with social structure. The distinction (and presumed linkage) between state and civil society fades: both dissolve into an ether of discourse that is endowed with the causal preeminence the Marxists earlier reserved for economy and class alignment. Once language is recognized as problematic and opaque, it becomes an active agent for the postmodern historians. Similarly, memory itself becomes not a simple act of recall but a socially constitutive act. The German version of these trends is the invocation of "history," less as a record than as a problematic constituent of identity. Postmodern German historiography insists that society constructs itself through history, so Clio's task is increasingly self-reflective—not critically reflective in Habermas's terms, but self-absorbed, almost narcissistic.

The political agenda of postmodernism is indeterminate. The point is not that it need be reactionary; it can be radical. (Benjamin's theses on the philosophy of history nominally invoked historical materialism, but actually undermined, or at least radically transformed, whatever insight it might contribute.) The political result has not yet been decided. So too in the *Historikerstreit*, the result is unclear. The demand for "historicization" expresses the ambiguities. It licenses the right as well as the left. There is considerable potential for conservative interpretations. What fills the interpretative gap between social structure and cultural or political outcome can be a neo-*Historismus* that justifies the past by appealing to the good conscience of those who committed it. What can also fill the gap is a certain aestheticizing of politics—a revived distaste of mass democracy, a covert celebration of elites disguised by an appeal to folk culture and artisanship. Not by chance is Michael Stürmer fascinated by handicrafts and aesthetics and ideas of luxury, as well as authority. Not by chance does his critique of the Kaiserreich stress the incapacity of elites constructively to channel mass impulses such as democratic nationalism. In the hands of less controlled political writers, such judgments could lead to an aestheticized reaction à la Ernst Jünger. Not that the first-rate products of postmodern historiography will not be impressive. Certainly through their presentation of picturesque antiheroes and the mimetics or symbolism of conflict, they can sometimes be more revealing and more pleasurable than formulaic efforts to relate politics to class structure. And their political legitimacy is not at issue: conservatives, neoconservatives, and paleoconservatives are all entitled to their own history.

But surely, it will be protested, this is far too abstract. How, it will be asked, do revisionist accounts of Auschwitz or apologias for the German army represent any historiographic postmodernism? This is not the claim. They are not cited as postmodern works, but as products of a diffused postmodern historical sensibility. The point is that the growing acceptance of postmodern criteria for what constitutes historical knowledge has legitimated the new revisionism. The fashions of historiography have altered, but quality goods and shoddy can still both find a market. The protean concept of "historicization" expresses the change; it applies the history of *mentalités* to National Socialist Germany. History must be the story of what people thought and felt. For Nolte what Hitler did matters less than how he envisaged the world. Historicization is a sort of anti-Cartesian meditation: a phenomenology content with knowing the most banal, constraining, or downright murderous mental states.

Habermas, along with others, has tended to interpret the *Wende* too narrowly. The shift that began in the mid-1970s was not just a simple turn to neoconservatism. It followed upon a more general exhaustion of an earlier historical faith, revived with the forces of European democracy in 1945 but seemingly worn out after 1968. The institutional form of this earlier ideological bouyancy was the easy triumph of the welfare state in an era of prolonged economic growth. But this trend has been arrested. It may be that the educated public turns to history for consolation, or just for a respite from future-oriented thinking. German history offers less consolation than others, so the task is more problematic.

What sort of social and historiographic reconstruction will in turn follow the contemporary postmodern vogue is unclear. Social scientists and historians will not be able just to restore the earlier transparent sociology that presented the economy, the political system, and the cultural "lifeworld" as influencing each other in an easy and unproblematic relationship. The accumulated critiques of such diverse postmodern thinkers as Foucault, Derrida, Lyotard, and Rorty have undermined confidence in such a connection. How a post-postmodern left can define a nonsimplistic program is unclear. How it will attempt historical "understanding" is also uncertain.

To be sure, German social thought has not produced postmodern critics of the stature of the French theorists. This is not only because the Germans had a different 1968—one that was less anarchic and more intimidating, less targeted on a social order and more focused on individuals—but also because the Germans had 1933, with its devastation of an intellectual community, the effects of which are still felt; and 1933, to borrow a phrase from Nolte, was "more original" than 1940 in France. Without postmodern theorists of the stature of the French, West German postmodern critiques have tended to take the form of revivals: neo-*Historismus* (Hillgruber and Stürmer), neoconservatism, and neostructural functionalism. Niklas Luhmann is the outstanding representative of this sociological tendency, highly intelligent and the closest match for Habermas, whose search for a general social rationality he finds utopian: Luhman's social world is composed of different realms of activity (political and legal, economic, erotic), each with its own code of means–end rationality.[23] For this reason the *Historikerstreit* has not left compelling theoretical documents that will remain as significant philosophical statements, with the exception perhaps of Habermas's efforts to work out concepts of identity. But if the Bonn Republic has not produced the scintillating postmodern thinkers that Paris has since the 1960s, its intellectuals can still draw upon predecessors that lend their debates sophistication and style, such as Benjamin and Adorno. Consequently, the *Historikerstreit*, focused on an intensely German issue of responsibility, is part of a larger conflict. On one side are those for whom history, if hardly a story of progress, is still a summons to enlightenment and to the advance of reason through the analysis of violence and repression. On the other side are those for whom history bears witness to obscure drives, unavoidable suffering, and universal reversions.

This opposition would all be terribly familiar had it not been for the fact that the slogan of "historicization" has served both sides in the conflict. It is the ambiguity of that methodology—its reformist summons to see through the structures and evasions of a society; its reactionary potential to justify the most destructive anxieties—that heralds a postmodern historiography, and not merely a rerun of earlier ideological clashes. More perhaps than disputes over "narrative" or "reading" or "discourse" in Anglo-American historiography, the *Historikerstreit* poses real political alternatives. One can seek to harness a postmodern "historicization" for emancipatory purposes—fusing in effect Habermas's faith in progressive social science with Benjamin's "flash of memory in a moment of danger"; or one can employ it to conjure up what the French have called the *mode retro:* the aesthetic evocation of earlier repression in the name of historical understanding. The first alternative runs the risk of producing a simplistic and politicized historiography. The second may allow a closer approach to how it actually was justified, if not how it actually happened. The sirens of historicism sing their beautiful songs again. Are the rocks less dangerous?

Notes
Index

Notes

Introduction

1. For a useful English-language résumé of the positions see Norbert Kampe, "Normalizing the Holocaust? The Recent Historians' Debate in the Federal Republic of Germany," *Holocaust and Genocide Studies*, 2 (1987), 61–90. The major texts of the controversy, with a few afterwords, have been published after some painful negotiation as Rudolph Augstein et al., *Historikerstreit. Die Dokumentation der Kontroverse um die Einzigartigkeit der nationalsozialistischen Judenvernichtung* (Munich: Piper, 1987). An unauthorized partial collection with Marxist commentaries—Reinhard Kühnl, ed., *Vergangenheit, die nicht vergeht: Die "Historiker-Debatte." Darstellung, Dokumentation, Kritik* (Cologne: Pahl-Rugenstein, 1987)—had to be withdrawn from the market after copyright infringement suits were threatened. The Federal Republic's Foreign Ministry thought the controversy important enough to send a collection of the major texts to all its embassies and consulates on November 6, 1986; Auswärtiges Amt 012-312.28 RE 66/86. The following notes provide translations, at their first occurrence, of the titles of the articles in the controversy.

2. See Peter Bender, "Mitteleuropa—Mode, Modell oder Motiv?" *Die Neue Gesellschaft, Frankfurter Hefte*, 34 (April 1987), 297–304.

3. Peter Schneider, *The Wall Jumper*, trans. Leigh Hafrey (New York: Pantheon, 1983), p. 29.

4. As Michael Stürmer, one of the chief protagonists identified with the conservatives, wrote, if West Germany was supposed to be treated as a neurotic patient, "What would be the place for the cellar children, to which I, born in 1938, was damned? Or the place for the refugee children, like my wife?" See "Weder verdrängen noch bewältigen. Geschichte und Gegenwartsbewusstsein der Deutschen," *Schweizer Monatshefte*, 66 (September 1986), 690; also Hilmar Hoffmann, ed., *Gegen den Versuch, Vergangenheit zu verbiegen* (Frankfurt am Main: Athenäum, 1987), p. 111. See also Peter Schneider, who (born in 1940) argues that the contending historians were born in the 1920s and 1930s—and thus felt implicated as participants: Schneider, "Hitler's Shadow: On Being a Self-Conscious German," *Harper's Magazine*, September 1987, pp. 49–54. On the other hand, although members of the younger generation were silent, they were rapt spectators at the seminars and presentations on the theme.

5. Jürgen Habermas, "Vom öffentlichen Gebrauch der Historie" [On the public use of history], *Die Zeit*, November 7, 1986.

6. Dan Diner, "The Historians' Controversy—Limits to the Historization of National Socialism," *Tikkun*, 2 (1987), 78.

1. The Stakes of the Controversy

Epigraph: Hermann Rudolph, "Vom Nutzen der deutschen Geschichte" [On the use of German history], in *Anno 86* (Munich: Bertelsmann Verlag, 1986), p. 124.

1. The articles and speeches arising out of the Bitburg controversy are collected in Geoffrey H. Hartman, ed., *Bitburg in Moral and Political Perspective* (Bloomington: Indiana University Press, 1986).

2. For Dregger's letter see ibid., p. xv; see also his call for "elementary patriotism" in the budget debate of the Bundestag, September 10, 1986, cited in Martin Broszat, "Wo sich die Geister scheiden" [Where opinions divide], *Die Zeit*, October 3, 1986.

3. An additional issue was whether the "good" soldiers might not also be tainted by atrocities—not the occasional killing of prisoners or civilians out of fear and anger, but systematic killing of prisoners on order. Certainly on the Eastern Front and in Serbia, the Wehrmacht collaborated in ruthless policies; ordinary military units in Russia were systematically instructed to kill Communist Party prisoners and did not fundamentally contest directives to go beyond the codes of war. See Christian Streit, *Keine Kameraden. Die Wehrmacht und die sowjetischen Kriegsgefangene 1941–1945* (Stuttgart: Deutsche Verlags-Anstalt, 1978); Charles W. Sydnor, Jr., *Soldiers of Destruction* (Princeton: Princeton University Press, 1977); also Horst Boog et al., *Der Angriff auf die Sowjetunion: Das Deutsche Reich und der Zweiten Weltkrieg*, vol. 4 (Stuttgart and Freiburg im Breisgau: Militärgeschichtliches Forschungsamt and Deutsche Verlags-Anstalt, 1983); and Omer Bartov, *The Eastern Front, 1941–1945: German Troops and the Barbarisation of Warfare* (London: Macmillan/St. Antony's, 1985); Christopher R. Browning, "Wehrmacht Reprisal Policy and the Murder of the Male Jews in Serbia," in *Fateful Months: Essays on the Emergence of the Final Solution* (New York: Holmes & Meier, 1985), pp. 39–56. Bitburg, though, hardly raised these issues in public; those opposing the visit did so either because they rejected *any* honoring of the German military effort, or because they said the SS graves fundamentally tainted the whole cemetery.

4. Speech by Richard von Weizsäcker, May 8, 1945, in *Verhandlungen des Bundestages;* translated in Hartman, *Bitburg,* pp. 262–273.

5. Address by Helmut Kohl during the ceremony marking the fortieth anniversary of the liberation of the concentration camps, April 21, 1985; distributed in English on April 22 by the German Information Center, *Statements & Speeches, 7,* no. 11 (New York, 1985); also in Hartman, *Bitburg,* pp. 244–250.

6. Ernst Nolte, "Vergangenheit, die nicht vergehen will" [A past that will not pass away], *Frankfurter Allgemeine Zeitung* (cited hereafter as *FAZ*), June 6, 1986.

7. Speech by Richard Burt, May 23, 1986, cited by Hans Mommsen, "Suche nach der 'verlorenen Geschichte'? Bemerkungen zum historischen Selbstverständnis der Bundesrepublik" [Search for a 'Lost History'? Comments on the historical self-conceptualization of the Federal Republic], *Merkur,* 40 (1986), 864–874.

8. Thomas Nipperdey, "Unter der Herrschaft des Verdachts. Wissenschaftliche Aussagen dürfen nicht an ihrer politischen Funktion gemessen werden" [Under the rule of suspicion: Scholarly expression cannot be judged by its political function], *Die Zeit*, October 17, 1986.

9. The term was allegedly used by Günther Rühle, former drama critic of the *FAZ,* when he defended the planned performance of Rainer Fassbinder's anti-Semitic *Garbage, the City, and Death.* He later claimed to have said only, "The Jews must not be kept in a game preserve to the end of time." The reader can judge the extent of improvement. For the Fassbinder controversy see Johann N. Schmidt, *"Those Unfortunate Years": Nazism in the Public Debate of Post-War Germany* (Bloomington: Indiana University Jewish Studies Program, 1987).

10. Primo Levi, "The Memory of Offense," in Hartman, *Bitburg,* pp. 130–137.

11. The most interesting debates took place among the French. For the most ruthless position see Maurice Merleau-Ponty, *Humanism and Terror,* trans. John O'Neill (Boston: Beacon, 1969), who came close to arguing that whoever lost a political struggle could not protest the penalties that followed. To take part in a historical or political movement was to recognize that defeat was tantamount to accepting guilt. "We don't judge, we choose sides," says Henri in Simone de Beauvoir's fictional dramatization *The Mandarins,* trans. L. M. Friedman (London: Fontana, 1960), p. 144. See also Albert Camus's *The Fall,* trans. Justin O'Brien (New York: Knopf, 1958) for a later effort to think the matter through.

12. Cited by Michael Stürmer, "Was Geschichte wiegt," *FAZ,* November 26, 1986.

13. Nolte, "Vergangenheit, die nicht vergehen will": "Steckt nicht in vielen der Argumente und Fragen ein Kern des Richtigen, die gleichsam eine Mauer gegen das Verlangen nach immer fortgehender 'Auseinandersetzung' mit dem Nationalsozialismus aufrichten?"

14. To suggest, as does Joachim Fest, that the use of poison gas (the insecticide Zyklon B even more than carbon monoxide) merely reflected a barbarous efficiency obscures part of its horror. Mass execution by gas relieved the psychological pressure on SS machine-gunners (see Christopher R. Browning, "The Development and Production of the Nazi Gas Van," in *Fateful Months,* pp. 57–67). But gas also evoked a persisting fascination with delousing and killing vermin, images of which recur in German newsreels that show Polish, Russian, and Jewish prisoners being happily disinfected.

15. Hans Mommsen, "Stehen wir vor einer neuen Polarisierung des Geschichtsbildes in der Bundesrepublik?" in *Geschichte in der demokratischen Gesellschaft. Eine Dokumentation,* ed. Susanna Miller (Düsseldorf: Schwann-Bagel, 1985), pp. 71–82.

16. Mommsen, "Suche nach der 'verlorenen Geschichte'?" pp. 869–870.

17. Ibid.

18. Martin Broszat, "Plädoyer für eine Historisierung des Nationalsozialismus" [Plea for a historicization of National Socialism], *Merkur,* 39 (1985), 373–385. Many of these findings have been stressed now for a decade or more. Broszat is best known for his concept of "polycracy," developed in *Der Staat Hitlers* (Frankfurt am Main: Deutscher Taschenbuch Verlag, 1969), translated by John Hiden as *The Hitler State* (London and New York: Longman, 1981); most recently he has directed a group of excellent studies concerning the impact of National Socialist rule in Bavaria.

19. Ernst Nolte, "Between Myth and Revisionism? The Third Reich in the Perspective of the 1980s," in *Aspects of the Third Reich,* ed. H. W. Koch (London:

Macmillan, 1985), pp. 36–37. The contributions of Koch himself, a German teaching at York University in Britain, were also revisionist.

20. For the major work of research see Andreas Hillgruber, *Hitlers Strategie: Politik und Kriegsführung 1940–41* (1965: 2d ed., Munich: Bernard & Graefe, 1987); see also idem, "Die Endlösung und das deutsche Ostimperium," *Vierteljahrshefte für Zeitgeschichte*, 20 (1972), 133–153. For an English-language assessment see Holger Herwig, "Andreas Hillgruber: Historian of 'Grossmachtpolitik' 1871–1945," *Central European History*, 15 (1982), 186–198.

21. Of course, to come to terms with their terrible mission in June 1941 is also a major challenge; the German authors of the federal Military History Research Office in Boog et al., who honestly attempted it in *Der Angriff auf die Sowjetunion*, have been sharply criticized for their exemplary synthesis. (Concerning the recent claims that Hitler's attack was a preventive war, see Bianka Pietrow, "Deutschland im Juni 1941—Opfer sowjetischer Aggression? Zur Kontroverse über die Präventivkriegsthese," *Geschichte und Gesellschaft*, 14 [1988], 116–135.) Hillgruber cites the Soviet murder of civilians in the East Prussian town of Nemmersdorf (briefly retaken by the Germans) as a sign of what the German defenders knew they must fear from the Red Army. He certainly understands that such a threatening "orgy of revenge" was a response to "everything of a criminal nature that was committed by whatever agency in the areas of Russia occupied by German troops from 1941 to 1944"; *Zweierlei Untergang. Die Zerschlagung des deutschen Reiches und das Ende des europäischen Judentums* (Berlin: Corso bei Siedler, 1986), p. 21. Still, the entire emotional force of the narrative is stacked in favor of the German military. For a harsh (I think excessive) critique of Hillgruber, which appeared at the same time as Habermas's major attack, see Michael Brumlik, "Neuer Staatsmythos Ostfront" [New myth of state—Eastern Front], *Tageszeitung*, July 12, 1986: "For the first time a conservative, famous, and respected historian openly declares that under certain conditions the extermination of the Jews and the Sinti, if not approved, can at least be accepted in a legitimating way."

22. For a compilation of the hardships inflicted on the Germans in the East see Alfred-Maurice de Zayas, *Anmerkungen zur Vertreibung der Deutschen aus dem Osten* (Stuttgart: Kohlhammer, 1986). Zayas is an American historian whose specialization in the sufferings of the Germans at the end of World War II has made him a favorite in right-wing circles of the Federal Republic. This is not to deny that the deportations and deaths he reports took place.

23. Hillgruber, *Zweierlei Untergang*, p. 24.

24. It has also had (and still has) a left-wing or neutralist analogue, according to which Germany can serve as a buffer between capitalism and socialism, the West and revolutionary Russia. In the postwar era such a mystique motivated Social Democrats and Christian Democrats (Jakob Kaiser) alike, until the Cold War and Adenauer's triumph made it apparently utopian. It has recently found echoes in the peace movement and the left of the Social Democratic Party (SPD).

25. Ernst Nolte, *Der Faschismus in seiner Epoche* (Munich: Piper, 1963); translated by Leila Vennevitz as *Three Faces of Fascism* (New York: Holt, Rinehart & Winston, 1966).

26. It is difficult but important to distinguish Nolte's "transcendence" from the left's notion of "emancipation." Transcendence is clearly a historical and social

process; emancipation is usually a spiritual or pedagogical program, although in post–Frankfurt school philosophy it is tied to certain social requisites. Transcendence implies a psychological uprooting that the notion of emancipation need not entail: it is politically problematic. For Nolte's reflection on the term see his "Philosophische Geschichtsschreibung heute?" *Historische Zeitschrift,* 242 (1986), 265–289—a remarkable self-eulogy in which Nolte explains his role as apparently the only contemporary practitioner of philosophical history.

27. Ernst Nolte, *Marxismus und Industrielle Revolution* (Stuttgart: Klett-Cotta, 1983); this work is discussed in Chapter 3.

28. Ernst Nolte, *Deutschland und der kalte Krieg* (Munich: Piper, 1976), p. 29.

29. Ibid., p. 39.

30. Ibid., pp. 330–339.

31. Ibid., pp. 589–598.

32. Ibid., p. 601.

33. Nolte, "Between Myth and Revisionism?" p. 21.

34. Ibid., p. 27. Nolte later said that this statement was taken out of context: that he was only quoting what David Irving (notorious for the argument that Hitler never endorsed the Final Solution) had written about Hitler. In fact, Nolte argued, he had wanted to distance himself from the remark about Weizmann, although he also wanted to point out that such reports should not be ignored merely because the right-radical literature might compress or distort them. See Ernst Nolte, "Die Sache auf den Kopf gestellt. Gegen den negativen Nationalismus in der Geschichtsbetrachtung" [Looking at the matter backward: Against negative nationalism in historical treatments], *Die Zeit,* October 31, 1986. Even supposing that Nolte's translator may have obscured the author's "distancing himself" (perhaps by ignoring German use of the subjunctive), Nolte's self-interpretation does not seem supported by the text. He was clearly not paraphrasing Irving, when he wrote: "But it can hardly be denied that Hitler had good reasons to be convinced of his enemies' determination to annihilate him," etc. Nolte apparently pressed the argument on his dinner guest Saul Friedländer, the Israeli historian then doing research at the Berlin Wissenschaftskolleg, who finally excused himself from the evening. Nolte's charges about Weizmann are discussed further in Chapter 3.

35. Hildebrand praised Nolte's essay for its extraordinary capacity "to contextualize historically the destructive capacity of the ideology and the regime" in the "mutually interacting connection of Russian and German history"; see his review of Koch's *Aspects of the Third Reich* in *Historische Zeitschrift,* 242 (1986), 465–466.

36. Halfway through his article Nolte switches the referent of "the past that will not pass away" from Germany's Nazi past to Hitler's perception in the 1940s of the Red terror after 1917. Hitler's 1943 citation of the Soviets' "rat cage," Nolte argues, refers to the torturing of political prisoners, much as depicted in the famous Room 101 scene of Orwell's *1984,* which though written later was supposedly—like Hitler's fantasy—based on earlier reports of Soviet prisons. Such reports and memories allegedly became Hitler's personal "past that would not pass away." (In fact later references to the rat cage in Hitler's conversation seem clearly to confirm that he was referring to Lubianka prison, not to exotic tortures.) Likewise the image of the past as overhanging sword of judgment, Nolte insists,

referred to Hitler's view of history, not to the monitory example of National Socialist crimes for today's generation. See Nolte, "Die Sache auf den Kopf gestellt." A plain reading of Nolte's *FAZ* article (June 6, 1986), however, hardly supports his own later reading. Hans-Ulrich Wehler has traced the "rat cage" references (alleged tortures carried out in 1919 Kiev by Chinese and Jewish Bolsheviks) to their émigré sources, which Nolte apparently garbled. See Wehler, *Entsorgung der deutschen Vergangenheit? Ein polemischer Essay zum "Historikerstreit"* (Munich: C.H. Beck, 1988), pp. 147–154, 237–238.

37. Nolte, "Vergangenheit, die nicht vergehen will." Nolte added that "the so-called annihilation of the Jews during the Third Reich was a reaction or a distorted copy, but not an unprecedented procedure or an original."

38. Joachim Fest, "Die geschuldete Erinnerung. Zur Kontroverse über die Unvergleichbarkeit der nationalsozialistischen Massenverbrechen" [Indebted memory: Concerning the controversy about the incomparability of National Socialist mass crimes], *FAZ*, August 29, 1986. See also idem, *Hitler. Eine Biographie* (Frankfurt am Main: 1973) and *The Face of the Third Reich,* trans. Michael Bullock (New York: Pantheon, 1970).

39. The two major psychobiographical interpretations are Rudolf Binion, *Hitler among the Germans* (New York: Elsevier, 1976), which emphasizes the 1918 crisis; and Robert G. L. Waite, *The Psychopathic God: Adolf Hitler* (New York: Basic Books, 1977). See the latter, pp. 186–190, on the prewar onset of anti-Semitism.

40. Klaus Hildebrand, "Wer dem Abgrund entrinnen will, muss ihn aufs genaueste ausloten. Ist die neue deutsche Geschichtsschreibung revisionistisch?" [Whoever wants to escape the precipice must take its precise measure: Is the new German history revisionist?], *Die Welt,* November 22, 1986.

41. Nolte, "Die Sache auf den Kopf gestellt."

42. See Mommsen, "Suche nach der 'verlorenen Geschichte'?" for a political reading of the debates.

43. Nolte, "Die Sache auf den Kopf gestellt."

44. See Josef Joffe's concept of a "war of the German succession" in "The Battle of the Historians: A Report from Germany," *Encounter,* 69 (June 1987), 72–77 (esp. 76).

2. Habermas among the Historians

Epigraph: Thomas Nipperdey, "Unter der Herrschaft des Verdachts. Wissenschaftliche Aussagen dürfen nicht an ihrer politischen Funktion gemessen werden," *Die Zeit,* October 17, 1986.

1. Fritz Fischer, *Griff nach der Weltmacht* (Düsseldorf: Droste, 1961), published in English as *Germany's War Aims in the First World War* (New York: Norton, 1967). For an account of the dispute that ensued see John A. Moses, *The Politics of Illusion: The Fischer Controversy in German Historiography* (London: G. Prior, 1975). Hans Gatzke had made many of the same points in *Germany's Drive to the West: A Study of Germany's Western War Aims in the First World War* (Baltimore: Johns Hopkins, 1950), but Gatzke's monograph was overlooked by German

readers and did not have the sensational documentary find (Bethmann Hollweg's September Program) that Fischer had. The point here is not the correctness of Fischer's interpretation—I have many reservations—but how quickly it became a political football.

2. See Klaus Hildebrand's bitter attack on Wehler's idea of an aggregating history of society: "Geschichte oder 'Gesellschaftsgeschichte'? Die Notwendigkeit einer politischen Geschichtsschreibung von den internationalen Beziehungen," *Historische Zeitschrift*, 223 (1976), 328–357; and Wehler's response, "Kritik und kritische Antikritik," ibid., 225 (1977), 347–384; for similar conservative defenses of an autonomous history of international politics, see Andreas Hillgruber, "Politische Geschichte in moderner Sicht," ibid., 216 (1973), 529–552; also Walther Hubatsch, *Kaiserliche Marine* (Munich: Lehmann, 1975), pp. 76–78.

3. Heinrich Boehme, *Deutschlands Weg zur Grossmacht* (Cologne and Berlin: Kiepenheuer & Witsch, 1966); Hans-Ulrich Wehler, *Bismarcks Imperialismus* (Cologne and Berlin: Kniepenheuer & Witsch, 1969) (an English-language précis is available as "Bismarck's Imperialism, 1862–1890," *Past & Present*, 48 [1970], 119–155). There were some very fine monographs, such as Peter-Christian Witt's work on the financial crises of the empire, *Die Finanzpolitik des deutschen Reiches von 1903 bis 1914* (Lübeck: Historische Studien, 1970), but their methodological impact was limited. For Immanuel Geiss's earlier work see *Der polnische Grenzstreifen 1914–1918* (Lübeck: Matthiesen, 1960) and his edition of documents *July 1914* (New York: Norton, 1971). For a good survey of German historiography since the 1960s see George Iggers, ed., "Introduction," in *The Social History of Politics: Critical Perspectives in West German Historical Writing since 1945* (Leamington Spa: Berg, 1985), pp. 1–48.

4. Hans-Ulrich Wehler, "Historiography in Germany Today," in *Observations on "The Spiritual Situation of the Age,"* ed. Jürgen Habermas, trans. Andrew Buchwalter (Cambridge, Mass.: MIT Press, 1985), p. 241.

5. Hans-Ulrich Wehler, *Das deutsche Kaiserreich* (Göttingen: Vandenhoeck & Ruprecht, 1973); now available in English as *The German Empire, 1871–1918,* trans. Kim Traynor (Leamington Spa: Berg, 1985). For the major critique, see Thomas Nipperdey, "Wehlers 'Kaiserreich.' Eine kritische Auseinandersetzung," *Geschichte und Gesellschaft,* 1 (1975), 539–560. Some of the original members of the "organized capitalism" group were politically preoccupied. Heinrich August Winkler, who has completed an authoritative history of working-class politics during the Weimar Republic, *Arbeiter und Arbeiterbewegung in der Weimarer Republik,* 3 vols. (Berlin and Bonn: J.H.W. Dietz, 1984–87), became a spokesman for the centrist position of the SPD against the "alternatives" of the Greens and the peace movement.

6. David Blackbourn and Geoffrey Eley, *The Peculiarities of German History: Bourgeois Society and Politics in Nineteenth-Century Germany* (Oxford: Oxford University Press, 1984); also Richard Evans, "Introduction," in *Society and Politics in Wilhelmine Germany* (London: Croom Helm, 1978); idem, "The Myth of Germany's Missing Revolution," *New Left Review,* no. 149 (January/February 1985), 67–94. For a significant critique of Kehr's own work, which sharply undermined an essay that had been important in presenting the primacy of internal politics, see Margaret L. Anderson and Kenneth Barkin, "The Myth of the Putkammer Purge

and the Reality of the *Kulturkampf*: Some Reflections on the Historiography of Imperial Germany," *Journal of Modern History*, 54 (1982), 647–686.

7. For an admittedly sharp critical discussion of the problematic aspects of *Alltagsgeschichte* see Hans-Ulrich Wehler, "Königsweg zu neuen Ufern oder Irrgarten der Illusionen? Die westdeutsche Alltagsgeschichte: Geschichte 'von Innen' und 'von Unten'" (Paper presented at Fernuniversität, Hagen, 1985), a revision of Wehler's contribution at the German Historical Congress in Berlin in October 1984. Cf. idem, "Geschichte—von unten gesehen. Wie bei der Suche nach dem authentischen Engagement mit Methodik verwechselt wird," *Die Zeit*, May 10, 1985; Jürgen Kocka's critique, "Historische-anthropologische Fragestellungen—ein Defizit der historischen Sozialwissenschaft," in *Historische Anthropologie*, ed. Hans Süssmuth (Göttingen: Vandenhoeck & Ruprecht, 1984), 73–83; and *Geschichte und Gesellschaft*, 10 (1984), including Hans Medick's defense of anthropologically informed history, " 'Missionäre im Ruderboot'? Ethnologische Erkenntnisweisen als Herausforderung an die Sozialgeschichte," pp. 295–319. By pointing out the problematic aspects of "everyday history," I do not mean to deny its contribution to reconstruction of the experienced past; its best practitioners, moreover, have not sought to evade questions of authority and power. See the work collected in Jürgen Reulecke and Wolfhard Weber, eds., *Fabrik—Familie—Feierabend: Beiträge zur Sozialgeschichte des Alltags im Industriezeitalter* (Wuppertal: Hammer Verlag, 1978), also, for the Nazi period, Detlev Peuckert and Jürgen Reulecke, eds., *Die Reihen fast geschlossen: Beiträge zur Sozialgeschichte des Alltags unterm Nationalsozialismus* (Wuppertal: Hammer Verlag, 1981). The title is a pun on the "Horst Wessel Lied": "fast geschlossen" (nearly serried) replacing "fest geschlossen" (firmly serried) ranks.

8. See Knut Borchardt, *Wachstum, Krisen, Handlungsspielräume der Wirtschaftspolitik* (Göttingen: Vandenhoeck & Ruprecht, 1982), which unites several of the major essays. The essays provoked considerable argument. For my own dissent see Charles S. Maier, "Die Nicht-Determiniertheit ökonomischer Modelle. Überlegungen zu Knut Borchardts These von der 'kranken Wirtschaft' der Weimarer Republik," *Geschichte und Gesellschaft*, 11 (1985), 275–294, an issue devoted to critical responses.

9. Wehler, "Historiography in Germany Today," p. 246.

10. Thomas Nipperdey, *Deutsche Geschichte 1800–1866* (Munich: C. H. Beck, 1983); Reinhard Koselleck, *Preussen zwischen Reform und Revolution. Allgemeines Landrecht, Verwaltung und soziale Bewegung von 1791–1848* (Stuttgart: Klett, 1967); Klaus Tenfelde, *Sozialgeschichte der Bergarbeiterschaft an der Ruhr im 19. Jahrhundert* (Bad Godesberg: Verlag Neue Gesellschaft, 1977).

11. Jürgen Habermas, "Introduction," in *Observations on "The Spiritual Situation of the Age,"* esp. pp. 20–25.

12. Jürgen Habermas, "Neoconservative Culture Criticism in the United States and West Germany: An Intellectual Movement in Two Political Cultures," trans. Russell A. Berman, *Telos*, 56 (1983), 75–89; reprinted in Richard J. Bernstein, *Habermas and Modernity* (Cambridge, Mass.: MIT Press, 1985), pp. 78–94 (quotation p. 93).

13. Habermas, "Neoconservative Culture Criticism," in Bernstein, *Habermas and Modernity*, p. 87.

14. Jürgen Habermas, *Erkentnisse und Interesse* (Frankfurt am Main: Suhr-kamp, 1968); translated by Jeremy Shapiro as *Knowledge and Human Interests* (Boston: Beacon, 1971).

15. Jürgen Habermas, *Theorie des kommunikativen Handelns*, 2 vols. (Frank-furt am Main: Suhrkamp, 1981); vol. 1 translated by Thomas McCarthy as *The Theory of Communicative Action: Reason and the Rationalization of Society* (Boston: Beacon, 1984).

16. See Anthony Giddens, "Reason without Revolution: Habermas's *Theorie des kommunikativen Handelns*," in Bernstein, *Habermas and Modernity*, esp. pp. 114–117. "Once we admit the principle of the critical evaluation of beliefs, how can anything be exempt?"

17. Thomas McCarthy, *The Critical Theory of Jürgen Habermas* (Cambridge, Mass.: MIT Press, 1981), pp. 305–317, and critique of the position, pp. 320–325. Why should entry into a conversation, Anthony Giddens also asked ("Reason without Revolution"), express the intention of reaching unconstrained consensus? On the other hand, Richard Rorty's implied criticism that Habermas believes "we converse in order to make further conversation unnecessary" seems an unfair characterization: Habermas insists on procedures, not on outcomes. See Richard Rorty, "Pragmatism, Relativism, and Irrationalism," in *Consequences of Pragmatism (Essays: 1972–1980)* (Minneapolis: University of Minnesota Press, 1982), p. 170.

18. Jürgen Habermas, *Strukturwandel der Öffentlichkeit. Untersuchungen zu einer Kategorie der bürgerlichen Gesellschaft* (Berlin: Luchterhand, 1962). See also the fundamental *Knowledge and Human Interests* and Habermas's essays in his *Zur Rekonstruktion des historischen Materialismus* (Frankfurt am Main: Suhrkamp, 1976). Habermas's effort to support his evolutionary views with psychological theories of individual development, such as those of Jean Piaget and Lawrence Kohlberg, is less convincing. It also makes him a ready target for those who would dismiss his criticisms as based upon a utopian belief in human perfectibility. See Jean-François Lyotard's critique, *The Postmodern Condition: A Report on Knowledge*, trans. Geoff Bennington and Brian Massumi (Minneapolis: University of Minnesota Press, 1984), pp. 65–66, 72–73.

19. I am thinking here primarily of Jacques Derrida's treatment of Rousseau in *Of Grammatology*, trans. G. C. Spivak (Baltimore: Johns Hopkins University Press, 1979), pt. 2.

20. See Lyotard, *The Postmodern Condition*; also Richard Rorty, "Habermas and Lyotard on Postmodernity," in Bernstein, *Habermas and Modernity*, pp. 161–175. On Habermas's response to the postmodern left or the late Adorno see Al-brecht Wellmer, "Reason, Utopia, and the *Dialectic of Enlightenment*," reprinted in Bernstein, *Habermas and Modernity*, esp. pp. 48–49. See also Peter U. Hohendahl, "The Dialectic of Enlightenment Revisited: Habermas's Critique of the Frankfurt School," *New German Critique*, 35 (Spring/Summer 1985), 3–26.

21. Gadamer rejected the privileged role of "critical reflection" and also re-sponded that political and economic structures were themselves mediated by the linguistic understanding of the participants. For an account of the debate, see McCarthy, *Critical Theory of Habermas*, pp. 169–193. Habermas's position is in *Zur Logik der Sozialwissenschaften* (Frankfurt am Main: Suhrkamp, 1970), pp. 251–290; see also his 1965 Frankfurt inaugural lecture, published as a postscript to *Erkentnisse*

und Interesse (*Knowledge and Human Interests,* pp. 301–317); for Gadamer's position, see his major work, *Wahrheit und Methode* (Tübingen: J.C.B. Mohr, 1960), translated by William Glen Doepel as *Truth and Method* (New York: Crossroad, 1982), pp. xvi–xxiii, 305–366; and, for a response to Habermas, idem, *Philosophical Hermeneutics,* trans. David E. Linge (Berkeley: University of California Press, 1976), pp. 18–43.

22. See Michael Stürmer, *Koalition und Opposition in der Weimarer Republik 1924–1928* (Düsseldorf: Droste, 1967); idem, *Regierung und Reichstag im Bismarckstaat 1871–1880. Cäsarismus oder Parlamentarismus* (Düsseldorf: Droste, 1974); idem, *Das ruhelose Reich: Deutschland 1866–1918* (Berlin: Siedler, 1983), which argues that the mass democratic impulses, inadequately contained within traditional structures, were responsible for many of the Reich's veerings in foreign policy. Stürmer's work also includes a massive output of edited collections and a series of studies on artisanal furniture craftsmanship in the eighteenth century. For a critical commentary from a defender of the "primacy of domestic policy," see Volker Berghahn, "Geschichtswissenschaft und grosse Politik," *Aus Politik und Zeitgeschichte,* supplement to *Das Parlament,* B 11/87 (March 14, 1987), 25–37.

23. Michael Stürmer, "Geschichte in geschichtslosem Land" [History in a land without a history], *FAZ,* April 25, 1986. This and other essays are collected in idem, ed., *Dissonanzen des Fortschritts: Essays über Geschichte und Politik in Deutschland* (Munich: Piper, 1986). For an earlier lament of historical disorientation see Alfred Heuss, *Verlust der Geschichte?* (Göttingen: Vandenhoeck & Ruprecht, 1959). Heuss later prefigured Hillgruber's concern with the loss of German influence in the East. See Heuss, *Versagen und Verhängnis. Vom Ruin deutscher Geschichte und ihres Verständnisses* (Berlin: Siedler, 1984).

24. Stürmer argued at the September 1987 Leeds Castle conference that he himself does not believe history can produce "identity." Identity is in demand by the masses, but historians can offer orientation at best.

25. William H. McNeill, "Mythistory, or Truth, Myth, History, and Historians," *American Historical Review,* 91 (February 1986), 1–10.

26. Stürmer, "Geschichte in geschichtslosem Land." On the immaturity of Antifa concepts see idem, "Was Geschichte wiegt," *FAZ,* November 26, 1986; also idem, "The Do's and Don't's of Deutschlandpolitik," in *Aspects of the German Question,* ed. Peter R. Weilemann (Sankt Augustin: Konrad Adenauer Stiftung, 1986), esp. pp. 19–22.

27. Stürmer, "Geschichte in geschichtslosem Land."

28. Cf. the claim in Habermas, "Neoconservative Culture Criticism," p. 93.

29. Jürgen Habermas, "Eine Art Schadensabwicklung. Die apologetischen Tendenzen in der deutschen Zeitgeschichtsschreibung" [One sort of compensation: Apologetic trends in German historiography], *Die Zeit,* July 11, 1986. The term *Schadensabwicklung* is not easy to translate; it refers to a compensatory payment for damages, as in an insurance settlement.

30. "In dieser Tiefendimension, in der alle Katzen grau sind, wirbt er dann um Verständnis für die antimodernistischen Impulse, die sie sich gegen 'eine vorbehaltlose Affirmation der praktischen Transcendenz' richten. Darunter versteht Nolte die angeblich ontologisch begründete 'Einheit von Weltwirtschaft, Technik,

Wissenschaft und Emanzipation.' Das alles fügt sich trefflich in heute dominierende Stimmungslagen—und in den Reigen der kalifornischen Weltbilder, die daraus hervorspriessen"; ibid.

31. Habermas's quotations, ibid., of Nolte's "Philosophische Geschichtsschreibung Heute?" *Historische Zeitschrift*, 242 (1986), 265–289. Habermas scornfully cited Nolte's statement, " 'The "monstrous deed" [*Untat*] was determined not by [National Socialism's] ultimate intentions, but by the ascription of guilt, leveled against a human group that was itself so hard hit by the process of emancipation that some of its significant representatives declared it to be in mortal danger.' " That is, Nazism's worst crime did not follow from what it really wanted, but from its reaction to a group whose leaders were so panicked by emancipation that they declared themselves threatened.

32. Habermas, "Eine Art Schadensabwicklung."

33. The pillorying to which they referred, however, was rather that of Rudolf Augstein, editor of the weekly *Der Spiegel*, who had asserted that whoever could write Hillgruber's jacket copy (he did not accuse Hillgruber directly, as was sometimes later claimed) "is a constitutional Nazi," and that if a high school teacher had claimed that the extinction of the Jews was " 'tied in' " with the collapse of the Reich, he or she would be removed from teaching. See Rudolf Augstein, "Die neue Auschwitz-Lüge" [The new Auschwitz lie], *Der Spiegel*, October 6, 1986.

34. Andreas Hillgruber, "Jürgen Habermas, Karl-Heinz Janssen und die Aufklärung Anno 1986" [Jürgen Habermas, Karl-Heinz Janssen, and the Enlightenment of year 1986], *Geschichte in Wissenschaft und Unterricht*, 37 (December 1986), 725–738. The salient cases included one place where Hillgruber had argued that forced emigration was not the Nazis' preferred policy from 1938 to 1941. Habermas took him to suggest that most Nazis did not desire so drastic a measure; Hillgruber clearly meant that they would have preferred extermination. A second instance involved Habermas's waxing clever over Hillgruber's omission of the subjunctive that German employs to distance the writer from the opinion he is reporting, in this case Hitler's notion that only extermination of the Jews could secure German world power. Habermas later declared himself satisfied that this view was not shared by Hillgruber, but the thrust had been gratuitous.

Hillgruber's article was his second response to Habermas. The first had been a quick, anguished, but not very effective letter to the *FAZ*, August 23, 1986: "Mangel an elementarer Redlichkeit beim Zitieren." "With justice a senior colleague has written in a letter to me: 'Hasn't the man ever attended a history proseminar?' Apparently not."

35. Klaus Hildebrand, "Wer dem Abgrund entrinnen will, muss ihn aufs genaueste ausloten. Ist die neue deutsche Geschichtsschreibung revisionistisch?" *Die Welt*, November 22, 1986: "The threatening loss of public resonance seems to have drawn Jürgen Habermas to the attack against what scholars have long established and/or discussed. It appears that it is a question not of truth but of *influence*." Habermas had already scornfully replied to Hildebrand's first article, "Das Zeitalter der Tyrannen. Geschichte und Politik: Die Verwalter der Aufklärung, das Risiko der Wissenschaft und die Geborgenheit der Weltanschauung. Eine Entgegnung auf Jürgen Habermas" [History and politics: The administrators of the Enlightenment, the risk of scholarship, and the security of ideology: A response to

Jürgen Habermas], *FAZ,* July 31, 1986, with a scornful letter to *FAZ* on August 11, 1986.

36. Hillgruber, "Jürgen Habermas," pp. 733–736. Cf. Habermas's 1983 critique of the German neoconservatives: "All phenomena which do not correspond to a compensatorily immobilized modernity are personalized and moralized, i.e., blamed on Left intellectuals, who allegedly are carrying on a cultural revolution in order to insure their own authority, the 'priestly rule of a new class' "; "Neoconservative Culture Criticism," p. 87.

37. Gian Enrico Rusconi, "L'intervista: Habermas in Germania," *L'indice,* no. 1 (1987), 34–35.

38. Hagen Schulze, "Fragen, die wir stellen müssen. Keine historische Haftung ohne nationale Identität" [Questions that must be posed: No historical liability without national identity], *Die Zeit,* September 26, 1986. Against Schulze, however, it might be argued that Weimar's democrats had hardly sought to create a *Verfassungspatriotismus.* Instead they had actually tended to compete on the grounds of traditional national identity. Given the fact that Germany was left an intact nation-state after World War I but felt aggrieved by the Versailles Treaty, was another reaction likely? One powerful reason for the potential viability of a patriotism of the constitution today, in contrast to the difficulty of creating such a sentiment after 1918, is the simple division of the fatherland.

39. Habermas had warmed to this theme at an SPD hearing in Bonn on July 2, 1986, convened to discuss government plans for a national historical museum. There he allegedly condemned Hillgruber's book as "a scandal." See Tina Stadlmayer, "Verfassungspatriotismus gegen Nationalgeschichte," *Tageszeitung,* July 14, 1986, p. 9.

40. Thomas Nipperdey, "Unter der Herrschaft des Verdachts," *Die Zeit,* October 17, 1986.

41. Chancellor Kohl was reported to feel that helping Germans to feel easy with their long-run history was a major achievement of his administration. See James M. Markham, "Election Eve Talk with Kohl: Sure of Victory and All Smiles," *New York Times,* January 21, 1987.

42. Augstein, "Die neue Auschwitz-Lüge." Another *Der Spiegel* editor, Wolfgang Malanowski, had attacked the Hillgruber book in the September 1 issue (" 'Vergangenheit, die nicht vergehen will,' Das politische Buch"). Nolte, however, remained the prime target: "His intention is unmistakable. The noncomparable is to be made comparable so that the past is forgiven [by itself] . . . He pushes inane analogies to the point of perfidious apologia."

43. Immanuel Geiss, "Auschwitz, 'asiatische Tat,' " *Der Spiegel,* October 20, 1986.

44. Hildebrand, "Das Zeitalter der Tyrannen."

45. "Pankraz," "Pankraz, die Quellen und der neue Gesslerhut" [Pankraz, the sources and the new Gessler hat], *Die Welt,* August 11, 1986. "Pankraz" went on to note: "How illuminating, if depressing, to establish that more victims were claimed in the kulak pogrom [*sic*] of 1932–33 than in the Nazi concentration camps from 1933 through 1945. How undisputable the fact that in Western Europe, from France to Denmark, more people ('collaborators') were killed during the liberation after [May] 1945 than during the whole German occupation."

46. Joachim Fest, "Die geschuldete Erinnerung," *FAZ,* August 29, 1986.

47. Eberhard Jäckel, "Die elende Praxis der Untersteller. Das Einmalige der nationalsozialistischen Verbrechen lässt sich nicht leugnen" [The wretched practice of insinuation: The uniqueness of National Socialist crimes cannot be denied], *Die Zeit,* September 12, 1986. It is unclear, however, in what sense the National Socialists announced that they would kill the Jews, since the existence of the extermination camps was to be kept secret.

48. Schulze, "Fragen die wir stellen müssen."

49. Jürgen Kocka, "Hitler sollte nicht durch Stalin und Pol Pot verdrängt werden. Über Versuche deutscher Historiker, die Ungeheuerlichkeit von NS-Verbrechen zu relativieren" [Hitler is not to be repressed by means of Stalin and Pol Pot: Concerning the efforts of German historians to relativize the monstrosity of National Socialist crimes], *Frankfurter Rundschau,* September 23, 1986.

50. Christian Meier, *Die Entstehung des Politischen unter den Griechen* (Frankfurt am Main: Suhrkamp, 1980).

51. In addition to his interventions in the controversy, see also Christian Meier, *40 Jahre nach Auschwitz. Deutsche Geschichtserinnerung Heute* (Munich: Deutscher Kunstverlag, 1987), for a highly conscientious, almost agonized effort to draw a balance of the *Historikerstreit* and come to terms with German responsibilities.

52. Ernst Nolte, letter to *FAZ,* December 6, 1986.

53. Hillgruber, "Habermas und die Aufklärung 1986."

54. Hildebrand, "Wer dem Abgrund entrinnen will, muss ihn aufs genaueste ausloten," *Die Welt,* November 22, 1986. Restating his position, Hildebrand insisted that of course Nazism, like all historical phenomena, was unique. But to state that it was more destructive than, say, Stalinism was only one opinion and, in the case of Christian Meier, not even an expert opinion. "Connected with each other and related to each other in an antagonistic way, Hitler's and Stalin's regimes matched each other in the extent and the intensity of their policies of annihilation." In fact Meier had compared Germany with countries of the West in the passage that offended Hildebrand. And, as Meier insisted, if only contemporary historians were qualified to enter such a debate, then any civic consciousness would be impossible in a modern democracy. As Habermas wrote in his reply, Hildebrand combined a curious piety toward guild professionalism with an exploitation of murky conservative cliches.

55. Jürgen Habermas, "Vom öffentlichen Gebrauch der Historie," *Die Zeit,* November 7, 1986. At the end of his article Habermas reviewed the criticisms of his first intervention and conceded only that he should have referred to the destruction, not to the deportation, of the kulaks. But he maintained his charges against Nolte and Fest. They undermined a political morality that was established in accordance with Western concepts of freedom, responsibility, and self-determination only after the Allies had liberated the Germans "without action on our part."

56. Habermas, "Vom öffentlichen Gebrauch der Historie." The Jaspers reference is to Karl Jaspers, *Die Schuldfrage. Zur politischen Haftung Deutschlands,* translated by E. B. Ashton as *The Question of German Guilt* (New York: Dial, 1947).

57. Habermas, "Vom öffentlichen Gebrauch der Historie."

58. See Thomas McCarthy's introduction to his translation of Habermas, *The*

Theory of Communicative Action: Reason and the Rationalization of Society (Boston: Beacon, 1984), pp. xx–xxxvii; and Bernstein, *Habermas and Modernity,* pp. 22–25.

59. The detective is an analogy urged in different ways by Carlo Ginsburg, *Miti, emblemi, spie: morfologia e storia* (Turin: Einaudi, 1986), and Piero Redondi, *Galileo Heretic,* trans. Raymond Rosenthal (Princeton: Princeton University Press, 1987); it accords with a postmodernist rejection of synthesis and the taste of the past decade for fragmentary evidence and anthropologically revealing clues or vignettes. I believe it is an insufficient description of the historian's role. Historians have to weigh significance as well as follow clues; otherwise they exaggerate the importance of the merely picturesque. In his most recent book Ernst Nolte has also used the courtroom metaphor to justify "revision": "Isn't nonpartisanship . . . in a juridical sense nothing else than the demand that regular procedures will take the place of show trials or courts-martial, that is, judicial processes in which witnesses for the defense can be earnestly heard and judges are not separated by mere formality from the prosecutors?" *Der europäische Bürgerkrieg. Nationalsozialismus und Bolschewismus* (Frankfurt am Main: Propyläen, 1987), p. 26. This is just another version of the demand that no answer (as well as no question) be excluded a priori. Not all witnesses, however, need be accepted with equal credulity.

60. Hedley Bull, *The Anarchical Society: A Study of Order in World Politics* (New York: Columbia University Press, 1977), pp. 26–27, 40–46.

61. One reason is a practical pedagogical one. Enough people believe their charges so that they must be argued in a rational forum, not just dismissed as bad faith. In the wake of an earlier article on the current controversy (*New Republic,* December 1, 1986) I had correspondence from non-historians who had had to contend in their community with those arguing that the Holocaust was a Jewish fraud. They needed arguments, not just my endorsement that this view was obnoxious.

62. Leopold von Ranke, "A Dialogue on Politics," included as appendix to Theodore H. von Laue, *Leopold Ranke: The Formative Years* (Princeton: Princeton University Press, 1950), p. 165.

3. A Holocaust like the Others?

Epigraphs: Christa Wolf, *A Model Childhood,* trans. Ursule Molinaro and Hedwig Rappolt (London: Virago Press, 1980), p. 334. Ernst Nolte, "Die Ausschau nach dem Ganzen: Wissenschaftliches Ethos und Historisierung" [The view of the whole: Scientific ethos and historicization], *FAZ,* July 18, 1987.

1. Wolf, *A Model Childhood,* p. 334.

2. Nolte, "Die Ausschau nach dem Ganzen." The argument is also in idem, *Der europäische Bürgerkrieg. Nationalsozialismus und Bolschewismus* (Frankfurt am Main: Propyläen, 1987), pp. 25–26. The draft of his book, which had been completed by the spring of 1986, formed the basis for Nolte's celebrated article, but according to Nolte the controversy kept him from completing revisions until early 1987. The sort of neoplatonic argumentation found in the passage cited here has become characteristic for Nolte. He sets up ideal-type normative commitments: man as moralist is defined by observance of the golden rule; man as politician is defined by dedication to his "group" even at the cost of others; man as historian is

defined by his willingness to understand all behavior. The distinction may have derived from Weber's last essays concerning politics and science as vocations. But Weber never claimed, as Nolte does, that the social scientist or historian must understand all behavior or else ascribe it to the utopian realm of absolute good or evil, which Nolte assigns as the exclusive domain of the moralist. Nolte also implies that since most of us accept that absolute good is utopian, absolute evil is equally utopian, so whatever has really existed cannot be absolutely evil. But not even the moralist has a need to declare Auschwitz "absolutely" evil—whatever that may mean. One murder can also be "absolutely" evil; a moralist needs to make distinctions. And, *pace* Nolte, the historian, who must after all write under some commitment to truth, must share the moralist's stake and cannot say that the evil concerns only his off-hours persona. For a dissent from the Noltean view that we can understand everything, see Cornelius Castoriadis, "The Destinies of Totalitarianism," *Salmagundi,* no. 60 (1983), 109: "we can understand the Parthenon or Macbeth; but there is not and cannot be any 'understanding' of Auschwitz or of the Gulag."

3. Klaus Hildebrand, "Wer dem Abgrund entrinnen will, muss ihn aufs genaueste ausloten," *Die Welt,* November 22, 1986.

4. Joachim Fest, "Die geschuldete Erinnerung," *FAZ,* August 29, 1986.

5. Alfred Schickel, "Die Vergangenheitsbewältigung entlässt ihre Kinder," cited in Arno Klönne, "Die deutsche Geschichte geht weiter," *Das Argument,* no. 161 (January/February 1987). Troubling for the same reasons is the statement of Terrence Des Pres, who certainly had no apologetic agenda when he wrote: "And what, really, is the difference if Buchenwald was not classified as an extermination camp and had no gas chamber, but had special rooms for mass shooting and a level of privation so severe that prisoners died in hundreds every day?" Des Pres, *The Survivor* (Oxford: Oxford University Press, 1976), p. 114. Des Pres wanted to suggest that Buchenwald should be deemed as evil as Auschwitz, but the argument can be exploited to suggest that Auschwitz was as "good" as Buchenwald.

6. But then, too, no difference would remain between Auschwitz and the tactics of the 1904–1908 German war in Southwest Africa against the Herero, who were forced into desert areas, where they must starve. To equate the evils, though, would be wrong no matter how reprehensible the colonial repression. Historians must make distinctions even among murderous policies; they must record intentions as well as results. Seeing a genocide as a brutal by-product of repression rather than as totally deliberate will not restore the victims, and perhaps should not mitigate responsibility. But a serviceable legal order does depend upon this casuistic fine-tuning.

7. See Nolte, *Der europäische Bürgerkrieg,* p. 466; also Nolte's Israeli interview reproduced in idem, *Das Vergehen der Vergangenheit. Antwort an meine Kritiker im sogennanten Historikerstreit* (Berlin: Ullstein, 1987), p. 109. With characteristic negative phrasing Nolte wrote: "One cannot exclude or omit from discussion in advance the possibility that the war, though 'a war of extermination and enslavement,' was nonetheless objectively a preventive war" (pp. 108–109).

8. This was the astonishing implication in Nolte's "Between Myth and Revisionism? The Third Reich in the Perspective of the 1980s," in *Aspects of the Third Reich,* ed. H. W. Koch (London: Macmillan, 1985), pp. 36–37.

9. Fest, "Die geschuldete Erinnerung." For a classic specimen of neo-Nazi apologetics, see Thies Christophersen, *Die Auschwitz-Lüge: Ein Erlebnisbericht* (Möhrkirch: Kritik-Verlag, 1975).

10. See Nolte, *Das Vergehen der Vergangenheit,* pp. 109–110; on the Weizmann citation, see the letter to the Israeli historian Dov Kulka, June 18, 1986, ibid., p. 129. Nolte's readers also found especially offensive his implications that Kurt Tucholsky's admittedly objectionable statement about the value of gassing the German bourgeoisie was a precedent for Hitler: "It is, for example, a weakness, not a virtue, of the established literature that it frequently cites the *völkisch* press's shameful comments about the murder of Walter Rathenau, but not Kurt Tucholsky's even worse comments of 1927, which vividly wished for the death of the children and wives of the German educated classes"; Nolte, "Die Sache auf den Kopf gestellt," *Die Zeit,* October 31, 1986. See Nolte's letters to Dov Kulka of December 8, 1986 (*Das Vergehen der Vergangenheit,* pp. 136–138), and to the publisher Gershom Schocken of March 4–May 11, 1987 (ibid., pp. 142–145), among other defenses of the citation. In his December 8, 1986, letter to Kulka, Nolte also disagreed with those historians (such as Robert Faurisson) who deny the Holocaust took place, but he suggested that their motivation was primarily a criticism of Israel and an expression of sympathy for the Palestinians—"Is the latter necessarily an unworthy motive?"—and he commented that the right-radical Munich *Nationalzeitung,* despite his fears, had not exploited his arguments: "It would really be paradoxical if Munich displayed a more correct instinct than Jerusalem." However one judges Israeli policy toward the Palestinians, it seems that at best this correspondence represents a persistent effort to push back the limits of taste and respect for historical suffering. Nolte has indeed decreed the end of the *Sperrfrist.*

11. In fact Weizmann said that Jews would stand on the side of the democracies; he did not mention England specifically. See Hans-Ulrich Wehler's extensive discussion of the Weizmann citation in *Entsorgung der deutschen Vergangenheit? Ein polemischer Essay zum "Historikerstreit"* (Munich: C.H. Beck, 1988), pp. 83–84 and 227, n. 41.

12. Joachim C. Fest's own biography, *Hitler,* trans. Richard and Clara Winston (New York: Vintage Books, 1975), underlines the prewar formation. For insights into the origins of Hitler's anti-Semitism, see the psychobiographical efforts by Rudolf Binion, *Hitler among the Germans* (New York: Elsevier, 1976), and Robert G. L. Waite, *The Psychopathic God: Adolf Hitler* (New York: Basic Books, 1977). Other revealing approaches are J. P. Stern's study of Hitler's rhetoric, *Hitler: The Führer and the People* (Berkeley: University of California Press, 1975); and Sebastian Haffner, *The Meaning of Hitler,* trans. Ewald Osers (London: Weidenfeld & Nicolson, 1979).

13. Ernst Nolte, *Der Faschismus in seiner Epoche* (Munich: Piper, 1963); translated by Leila Vennewitz as *Three Faces of Fascism* (New York: Holt, Rinehart & Winston, 1966). See Nolte, *Der europäische Bürgerkrieg,* p. 548, for the relationship between his concepts of the "epoch of fascism" and "the European civil war."

14. See the discussion of Nolte's problematic exegesis of the "rat cage" in Chapter 1.

15. Lothar Gruchmann, "Euthanasie und Justiz im Dritten Reich," *Viertel-jahrshefte für Zeitgeschichte*, 20 (1972), 235–279; Ernst Klee, *"Euthanasie" im NS-Staat. Die "Vernichtung lebensunwerten Leben"* (Frankfurt am Main: S. Fischer, 1983); I have not yet been able to consult what promises to be the authoritative summary: H.-W. Schmuhl, *Rassenhygiene, Nationalsozialismus, Euthanasie* (Göttingen: Vandenhoeck & Ruprecht, 1987).

16. In a trivial sense everything can be compared: even the class of unique events must share the property of uniqueness. But to impose a purely logical or semantic attribute as the common element is mere scholasticism. In the historical or natural world, comparison makes sense only if the common categories have some initial basis in the objects under scrutiny.

17. Hannah Arendt, *The Origins of Totalitarianism*, 2d ed. (New York: Meridian, 1958).

18. See Helmut Krausnick and Hans-Heinrich Wilhelm, *Die Truppe des Welt-anschauungskrieges. Die Einsatzgruppen der Sicherheitspolizei und des SD 1938–1942* (Stuttgart: Deutsche Verlags-Anstalt, 1981).

19. For a useful attempt to reflect on the motivation by examining one who backed down, see Daniel Goldhagen, "The 'Cowardly' Executioner: On Disobedience in the SS," *Patterns of Prejudice*, 19, no. 2 (1985), 19–32; for Hannah Arendt's problematic effort to think through the commitment to genocide, see *Eichmann in Jerusalem: A Report on the Banality of Evil* (New York: Viking Press, 1963).

20. Marc Bloch, "Pour une histoire comparée des sociétés européennes," in *Mélanges historiques* (Paris: S.E.V.P.E.N., 1963), pp. 16–40. See also Karl Dietrich Bracher, "Zeitgeschichtliche Erfahrungen als aktuelles Problem," in *Aus Politik und Zeitgeschichte*, supplement to *Das Parlament*, B 11/87 (March 14, 1987): B 11: "Comparisons are not merely a permissible, but a necessary, scholarly method. Only thus can similarities *and* differences be brought out [*ermittelt*] . . . Moreover, a causality between gulag and concentration camps, even were it provable, could effect no moral unburdening."

21. Peter Gay pointed out Nolte's recourse to "comparative trivialization" as early as the appearance of the latter's *Deutschland und der kalte Krieg* (Munich: Piper, 1976). See Gay, *Freud, Jews, and Other Germans* (New York: Oxford University Press, 1978), pp. xi–xiv.

22. For the responses see Nolte, *Das Vergehen der Vergangenheit*. This includes some direct rebuttals, later interviews, and letters to publishers who chose not to accept his new book, *Der europäische Bürgerkrieg*. The exchange with a third critical publisher—like the other two unidentified but, to judge from the letters I have seen, apparently Wolff Jobst Siedler—is not reproduced. My own summary report—"Immoral Equivalence" (not my title, however), *New Republic*, December 1, 1986, pp. 36–41—is criticized by Nolte (*Das Vergehen der Vergangenheit*, pp. 40–41) as written in a style that war correspondents might employ. See, too, *Der europäische Bürgerkrieg*, p. 548: resistance to the thesis that the gulag was "more original" than Auschwitz "in the last analysis can be explained only by political motives." According to Nolte, the reaction to his essay has been a series of continuing distortions and misunderstandings. Nolte also characterizes the controversy as one that pitted realistic, antiutopian intellectuals and historians against the left—a

left, he implies, that courted the danger of approving the most massive killings if they served "progress" and "socialism"; *Das Vergehen der Vergangenheit,* p. 59. Surely the debate should have moved beyond these tired allegations.

23. Nolte, *Der europäische Bürgerkrieg.* For Nolte's ambitions for the book, see his letter to publisher "Y," who faulted the effort: "What is true is merely that today I find myself in a stronger opposition to the dominant trends of the time and that a completely new and unusual challenge—to give the theory of totalitarianism a historical-genetic dimension that it has hitherto lacked—is presumably not to be accomplished without some partisanship and exaggeration"; *Das Vergehen der Vergangenheit,* p. 154. Whether the exaggeration must be the tactic of the author or the critic is not clear.

24. Nolte, *Der europäischer Bürgerkrieg,* p. 516. Hedged though it is with negatives, this statement is correct. The stakes of the controversy consist of which aspects are more important and for what reasons—the singular, or the comparable.

25. Fest, "Die geschuldete Erinnerung"; Jürgen Kocka, "Hitler sollte nicht durch Stalin und Pol Pot verdrängt werden," *Frankfurter Rundschau,* September 23, 1986.

26. Elizabeth Becker, *When the War Was Over* (New York: Simon and Schuster, 1987), pp. 195–298. The Cambodian terror combined a racialist effort against minorities; large-scale resettlement of city dwellers in the countryside, with forced labor; then imprisonment, torture, and execution of former cadres, reminiscent of Stalin's purges and hallmarked by the demand for written autobiographies, or confessions. Becker's account attempts no overall numerical estimate of casualties among the population of about 7 million. Victims would include the presumably thousands of executions immediately following seizure of power, the deaths attendant upon the shipping of city dwellers into rural areas and the mistreatment involved in their forced labor, and the successive political purges—one of thirty-three districts produced a supposed 34,000 executions (p. 298)—including a final 1978 purge in the eastern zone that took about 100,000 lives (pp. 320–322).

27. The literature is fragmentary and usually written from a nationalist perspective; but see Richard G. Hovannasian, *The Armenian Genocide in Retrospect* (New Brunswick, N.J.: Transaction, 1986); Gérard Chalian and Yves Ternon, *Le génocide des arméniens: 1915–1917* (Brussels: Editions Complèxe, 1980); Dickran H. Boyajian, *Armenia: The Case for a Forgotten Genocide* (Westwood, N.J.: Educational Book Crafters, 1972); Jean Mederian, *Le génocide du peuple arménien* (Beirut: Imprimerie Catholique, 1965); and the reports collected by James Bryce, *The Treatment of Armenians in the Ottoman Empire, 1915–1916, Documents Presented to Viscount Grey of Fallodon by Viscount Bryce* (London: Sir Joseph Causton, 1916). Most sources claim that there were 1.5 million victims, but the estimates are not independent.

28. On the famine see Robert Conquest, *The Harvest of Sorrow: Soviet Collectivization and the Terror-Famine* (New York: Oxford University Press, 1986); and, for a personal account, Miron Dolot, *Execution by Hunger: The Hidden Holocaust* (New York: Norton, 1987). Too often, the controversies over the number of victims have led to an invidious competition. Each terror has its champions, and the result is a competition for victimhood. Non-Jewish victims of either the Germans or the Russians resent the Jewish claim to a more transcendent level of

suffering. Jewish writers fear that their credentials of martyrdom will be impugned. The Epilogue will return to this theme; for now let it be said that one requires differentiations that do not need to downplay the sufferings of other groups.

29. Robert Conquest, *The Great Terror: Stalin's Purge of the Thirties* (London and New York: Macmillan, 1968), p. 532.

30. Eugene Kogon, *Der SS Staat* (Stockholm: Bermann-Fischer Verlag, 1947), p. 168. Bruno Bettelheim, *The Informed Heart* (Glencoe, Ill.: Free Press, 1960), reports that a third of new prisoners died at Buchenwald, which, like some other camps, had different blocks with different levels of punishment and lethal treatment.

31. The figures for Soviet victims are based on Conquest, *The Great Terror,* pp. 525–535; and idem, *Harvest of Sorrow,* pp. 299–307. I do not have figures for the postwar purges. But see Mikhail Heller and Aleksandr Nekrich, *Utopia in Power: The History of the Soviet Union from 1917 to the Present,* trans. Phyllis B. Carlos (New York: Summit Books, 1986), pp. 379–382, 492–497. For the ethnic deportations see Robert Conquest, *The Soviet Deportation of Nationalities* (London: Macmillan, 1960).

32. The estimate of 16,560 executions is that of Walter Wagner, *Der Volksgerichtshof im nationalsozialistischen Staat* (= *Die Deutsche Justiz und der Nationalsozialismus,* vol. 3) (Stuttgart: Deutsche Verlags-Anstalt, 1974), pp. 799–805. For the estimate of 200 Resistance conspirators executed in the wake of the July 20, 1944, plot and the number of victims for 1944 (5,764) and 1945 (c. 800), see Peter Hoffmann, *Widerstand. Staatsstreich. Attentat. Der Kampf der Opposition gegen Hitler* (Munich: Piper, 1969), pp. 630 and 871, n. 123. For the estimate of 40,000–50,000 executions of German soldiers by their own military tribunals see Manfred Messerschmidt and Fritz Wüllner, *Die Wehrmachtsjustiz im Dienste des Nationalsozialismus—Zerstörung einer Legende* (Baden-Baden: Nomos, 1988).

33. Kogon, *Der SS Staat,* pp. 36, 170. Kogon stresses the very approximate nature of these estimates. Martin Broszat suggests lower figures for victims of weakness and disease, but at least 500,000 during the war years; see "The Concentration Camps 1933–45," trans. Marian Jackson, in Helmut Krausnick, Hans Buchheim, Martin Broszat, and Hans-Adolf Jacobsen, *Anatomy of the SS State* (New York: Walker, 1968), pp. 459, 504.

34. Raul Hilberg, in what still seems the most authoritative and cautious compilation, estimates the total of Jewish slain at 5 million rather than the 6 million allegedly mentioned by Adolf Eichmann. These include 800,000 killed by ghettoization and general deprivation; over 1.3 million in open-air shootings; and up to 3 million in camps, including 1 million at Auschwitz, 750,000 at Treblinka, over half a million at Sobibor. By country of origin the tolls included up to 3 million Polish Jews, over 700,000 from the USSR; over 260,000 each from Rumania and Czechoslovakia; over 180,000 from Hungary; 120,000 from Germany (other sources suggest about 135,000); over 100,000 from the Netherlands; 75,000 from France; and 200,000 from the Baltic republics. See Raul Hilberg, *The Destruction of the European Jews,* rev. ed., 3 vols. (New York: Holmes & Meier, 1985), III, 1201–20.

35. As the general of one panzer corps told his troops a week after the inva-

sion, "In spite of my instructions . . . still more shootings of POWs and deserters have been observed, conducted in an irresponsible, senseless and criminal manner. This is murder! The German Wehrmacht is waging this war against Bolshevism, not against the united Russian peoples. We want to bring back peace, calm and order to this land which has suffered terribly for many years from the oppression of a Jewish and criminal group. The instruction of the Führer calls for ruthless action against Bolshevism (political commissars) and any kind of partisan! People who have been clearly identified as such should be taken aside and shot only by order of an officer"; quoted in Omer Bartov, *The Eastern Front, 1941–1945: German Troops and the Barbarisation of Warfare* (London: Macmillan & St. Antony's College, 1985), p. 117. On the atrocities of the Eastern Front see also Christian Streit, *Keine Kameraden* (Stuttgart: Deutsche Verlags-Anstalt, 1978).

36. Hilberg, *Destruction of the European Jews*, II, 291–317.

37. Eberhard Jäckel, "Die elende Praxis der Untersteller," *Die Zeit*, September 12, 1986.

38. The view that the actual murder of European Jewry was Hitler's firm plan from the beginning seems unprovable. On the other hand, the often very sophisticated argumentation that traces how the circumstances of rapid conquest presented Hitler with a Jewish problem that he could no longer solve merely by expulsions, downplays the preparatory role of Nazi discourse. There is a related argument between those who stress Hitler's central role and those who emphasize the role of the bureaucratic agents surrounding him. For polarized presentations of these issues see Lucy Dawidowicz, *The War against the Jews, 1933–1945* (New York: Bantam Books, 1986); and Hans Mommsen, "Die Realisierung des Utopischen: Die 'Endlösung der Judenfrage' im 'Dritten Reich,'" *Geschichte und Gesellschaft*, 9 (1983), 381–420. Cf. Karl A. Schleunes, *The Twisted Road to Auschwitz* (Urbana: University of Illinois Press, 1970). David Irving's exculpatory account, *Hitler's War* (New York: Viking Press, 1977), is clearly invalid; see Martin Broszat, "Hitler und der Genesis der Endlösung," *Vierteljahrshefte für Zeitgeschichte*, 25 (1977), 739–775. For an informed and balanced treatment that both allows for Hitler's primary role and stresses the murderous competition to implement his wishes see Christopher R. Browning, "The Decision concerning the Final Solution," in *Fateful Months: Essays on the Emergence of the Final Solution* (New York: Holmes & Meier, 1985), pp. 8–38. For a valuable recent survey of Holocaust issues—treating both the German and the Jewish issues—see Michael R. Marrus, *The Holocaust in History* (Toronto: Lester and Orpen Dennys, 1987). See also note 89, below.

39. Marrus, *The Holocaust in History*, p. 24.

40. Tadeusz Borowski, *This Way for the Gas, Ladies and Gentlemen*, trans. Barbara Vedder (Harmondsworth: Penguin, 1976), 39.

41. Alexsandr I. Solzhenitsyn, *The Gulag Archipelago, 1918–1956: An Experiment in Literary Investigation* (New York: Harper & Row, 1974), pp. 489–499, 565–587.

42. Evgenia S. Ginzburg, *Journey into the Whirlwind*, trans. Paul Stevenson and Max Hayward (New York: Harcourt, Brace & World, 1967); Vasily Grossman, *Life and Fate: A Novel*, trans. Robert Chandler (New York: Harper & Row, 1987); Nadezhda Mandelstam, *Hope against Hope: A Memoir*, trans. Max Hayward

(New York: Atheneum, 1976); and idem, *Hope Abandoned,* trans. Max Hayward (New York: Atheneum, 1973).

43. Raymond Aron, *Clausewitz* (New York: Simon and Schuster, 1986), p. 369.

44. For the list of offenses that "special boards" (irregular tribunals) could try, see Solzhenitsyn, *Gulag Archipelago,* p. 284.

45. Hoffmann, *Widerstand. Staatsstreich. Attentat,* pp. 600, 871, n. 123.

46. Solzhenitsyn, *Gulag Archipelago,* pp. 438–439.

47. Arendt, *Origins of Totalitarianism,* pp. 466, 468.

48. Ibid., p. 474.

49. Ibid., pp. 450–451.

50. Mandelstam, *Hope against Hope,* p. 11.

51. Franz Kafka, *Der Prozess* (New York: Schocken, 1946), p. 264; translated by Edwin Muir as *The Trial* (New York: Schocken, 1968).

52. *Night and Fog,* adopted as the title of Alan Resnais's postwar film, was the term applied to the December 7, 1941, decree establishing arbitrary arrest, deportation, and trial in Germany for any opponents of Nazi rule in the occupied territories. See Olga Wormser-Migot, *Le système concentrationnaire nazi (1933–1945)* (Paris: Presses Universitaires de France, 1968), pp. 203–213.

53. Mandelstam, *Hope against Hope,* p. 243.

54. It might appear that the Nazi ambition to hunt down Jews from every territory possible—including those of their allies such as Hungary, as well as all the lands they occupied directly—was also unique. But then Stalin's fixation with extirpating any possible opposition also extended outside the Soviet Union: witness the preoccupation with liquidating Trotskyites and POUM adherents in Spain.

55. Arendt, *Origins of Totalitarianism,* p. 6.

56. Ibid., pp. 308–309. Arendt recognized that Mussolini (or, more precisely, Alfredo Rocco) had first used the concept of totalitarianism, but in reference to the monopoly of political power by the state—not to the power to mold all aspects of life and opinion. Although the very low number of death sentences (but not of beatings that led to death during the period before the consolidation of power), the absence of concentration camps, the special privileges granted to the Roman Catholic church, and the continuing political role of the king and his entourage all suggest that Italian Fascism was not totalitarian, it should be recognized that Mussolini and Rocco did envisage a new type of political control, qualitatively different from ordinary dictatorship in its effort to sway hearts as well as minds, mold youth, and reinvigorate national existence. It is a mistake and a disservice to make too light of Italian Fascism.

57. Karl Dietrich Bracher, "Zeitgeschichtliche Erfahrungen als aktuelles Problem," *Aus Politik und Zeitgeschichte,* supplement to *Das Parlament,* B 11/87 (March 14, 1987), 3–14.

58. Ibid., p. 9.

59. Ibid., pp. 8–9.

60. Nolte, *Three Faces of Fascism,* pp. 4, 453.

61. Ibid., p. 457.

62. Nolte, *Der europäische Bürgerkrieg,* p. 549.

63. Ernst Nolte, *Marxismus und Industrielle Revolution* (Stuttgart: Klett-Cotta, 1983), p. 488.

64. Ibid., p. 532.

65. Ibid., pp. 280–285, 533. Nolte repeatedly uses the concept of *Vernichtung* (annihilation or extermination) to link the wiping out of occupational categories with physical murder—whether of kulaks or of Jews.

66. Ibid., pp. 478–479.

67. Nolte, *Deutschland und der kalte Krieg.*

68. Karl Dietrich Bracher, *Die deutsche Diktatur* (Cologne: Kiepenheuer & Witsch, 1969); translated by Jean Steinberg as *The German Dictatorship* (New York: Praeger, 1970). For the continuities of the NPD with the Nazi past, see *The German Dictatorship*, pp. 479–488.

69. Reinhard Kühnl, *Formen bürgerlicher Herrschaft. Liberalismus-Faschismus* (Reinbek bei Hamburg: Rowohlt, 1971). For a thoughtful résumé of this literature in general see Richard Saage, *Faschismustheorien* (Munich: C.H. Beck, 1976).

70. The typology of state monopoly capitalism could help to orient some detailed investigations. For some sample works: Kurt Gossweiler, *Grossbanken, Industriemonopole, Staat. Ökonomie und Politik des staatsmonopolistischen Kapitalismus in Deutschland 1914–1932* (E. Berlin: Deutscher Verlag der Wissenschaften, 1971); Dietrich Eichholtz, "Probleme einer Wirtschaftsgeschichte des Faschismus in Deutschland," *Jahrbuch für Wirtschaftsgeschichte*, 3 (1963), 97–117; Dietrich Eichholtz and Kurt Gossweiler, "Noch einmal: Politik und Wirtschaft 1933–1945," *Das Argument*, no. 47 (1968), 210–227; Eberhard Czichon, *Wer verhalf Hitler zur Macht? Zum Anteil der deutschen Industrie an der Zerstörung der Weimarer Republik* (Cologne: Pahl-Rugenstein, 1967).

71. For a strong Marxist-Leninist attack on liberal interpretations of fascism presented at the University of Tübingen in the mid-1960s, see Wolfgang Fritz Haug, *Der hilflose Antifaschismus*, 3d rev. ed. (Frankfurt am Main: Suhrkamp, 1970). The author was cheered that by 1970 a revolutionary student movement, albeit a minority in the society as a whole, had at least rendered the academics' "helpless anti-fascism" a thing of the past (p. 143).

72. Gilbert Allardyce, "What Fascism Is Not: Thoughts on the Deflation of a Concept," *American Historical Review*, 84 (1979), 367–388, with comments and a reply, pp. 389–398. Cf. Henry Ashby Turner, Jr., *German Big Business and the Rise of Hitler* (New York: Oxford University Press, 1965), pp. 349–359.

73. Lübbe closed by evoking (but by no means clarifying) the themes that occupied Stürmer and Nolte a few years later: "Now identity is a historically influenced quantity dependent on the past, [penetrating] deep into our political community; and subjects who find their past difficult have only one possibility: gradually to become freer of it. This one possibility consists in so arranging the present that when the present has finally become past, it will be reckoned with that part of the past that commands assent"; "Der Nationalsozialismus im politischen Bewusstsein der Gegenwart," in *Deutschlands Weg in die Diktatur. Internationale Konferenz zur nationalsozialistischen Machtübernahme im Reichstagsgebäude zu Berlin*, ed. Martin Broszat et al. (Berlin: Siedler Verlag, 1983), p. 345. See also Hermann Lübbe, *Politischer Moralismus. Der Triumph der Gesinnung über die Urteilskraft* (Berlin: Siedler Verlag, 1987). Cf. Christian Meier's far different dating of

the coming to terms with Nazism from the early 1960s in *40 Jahre nach Auschwitz. Deutsche Geschichtserinnerung Heute* (Munich: Deutscher Kunstverlag, 1987), pp. 36–37.

74. Carola Stern, response to Lübbe, in Broszat, *Deutschlands Weg in die Diktatur*, p. 355.

75. Hermann Rudolf, response to Lübbe, in ibid., pp. 355, 360–362.

76. Bracher, "Zeitgeschichtliche Erfahrungen als aktuelles Problem," p. 10.

77. See Nipperdey's response to Lübbe in Broszat, *Deutschlands Weg in die Diktatur*, pp. 368–371, that there was a certain "perversion" in the confrontation with the past, which was often designed to throw others under suspicion.

78. See Walter Hofer's comment, Jürgen Kocka's reply, and the interventions of Gerhard Schulz and J. Isensee in ibid., pp. 220–226.

79. See Nolte, "Die Ausschau nach dem Ganzen."

80. See Joachim Fest's "Afterword" in Rudolph Augstein et al., *Historikerstreit. Die Dokumentation der Kontroverse um die Einzigartigkeit der nationalsozialistischen Judenvernichtung* (Munich: Piper, 1987), p. 390; also the article by Martin Broszat, "Plädoyer für eine Historisierung des Nationalsozialismus," *Merkur*, 39 (1985), 373–385.

81. Dan Diner, ed., *Ist der Nationalsozialismus Geschichte? Zu Historisierung und Historikerstreit* (Frankfurt am Main: Fischer, 1987), p. 9.

82. Saul Friedländer, "Überlegungen zur Historisierung des Nationalsozialismus," in Diner, *Ist der Nationalsozialismus Geschichte?* pp. 34–50 (quotation p. 47). To show that historicization could verge toward apologia, Friedländer cited (p. 46) Hillgruber's effort to equate his effort at identification with the Eastern Front soldiers with the method of *Alltagsgeschichte*; see Andreas Hillgruber, "Für die Forschung gibt es kein Frageverbot," *Rheinischer Merkur*, October 31, 1986. An English-language version of Friedländer's article appears in the *Tel Aviver Jahrbuch für Deutsche Geschichte*, 16 (1987), 310–324. See also the exchange of letters between Broszat and Friedländer, "Um die Historisierung des Nationalsozialismus," *Vierteljahrshefte für Zeitgeschichte*, 36 (1988), 339–372.

83. Dan Diner, "Zwischen Aporie und Apologie," in *Ist der Nationalsozialismus Geschichte?* p. 73.

84. Detlev J. K. Peukert, "Alltag und Barbarei. Zur Normalität des Dritten Reiches," in ibid., pp. 51–61. Peukert argues that "critical historicization" hardly justifies Friedländer's foreboding. In fact it allows the historian to widen his focus from a few criminal leaders in order to understand what broad social and cultural roots sanctioned a national agenda of terror, war, and mass murder. But Peukert's own citation of the repressive potential of industrial capitalism or of abusive eugenic doctrines from the nineteenth century is not persuasive. The United States, after all, shared these contradictions. See Daniel J. Kevles, *In the Name of Eugenics* (New York: Knopf, 1985).

85. See Klaus Tenfelde, "Workers' Opposition in Nazi Germany: Recent West German Research," in *The Rise of the Nazi Regime*, ed. Charles S. Maier, Stanley Hoffmann, and Andrew Gould (Boulder, Colo.: Westview Press, 1985), pp. 107–114; also Tenfelde, *Proletarische Provinz: Radikalisierung und Widerstand in Penzburg/Oberbayern 1900–1945*, 2d ed. (Munich: Oldenbourg, 1982); idem, *Alltagsgeschichte der NS-Zeit: Neue Perspektive oder Trivialisierung* (Munich: Kollo-

quien des Instituts für Zeitgeschichte, 1984). See also Martin Broszat and Elke Fröhlich, *Alltag und Widerstand—Bayern im Nationalsozialismus* (Munich: Piper, 1987). Cf. the discussion by Ian Kershaw, *Popular Opinion and Political Dissent in the Third Reich: Bavaria 1933–1945* (Oxford: Clarendon Press, 1983), pp. 2–4. Kershaw chooses the term *dissent* rather than *opposition* or *resistance* to categorize the spectrum of disapproving opinion.

86. In this regard Marie Luise Recker, *Nationalsozialistische Sozialpolitik im Zweiten Weltkrieg* (Munich: Oldenbourg, 1985), has been cited for its documentation of Nazi welfare schemes. Why, however, welfare policies should be cited as remarkable is not clear. See my own essay, "The Economics of Fascism and National Socialism," in *In Search of Stability: Explorations in Historical Political Economy* (Cambridge: Cambridge University Press, 1987), for common trends under the impact of the Great Depression.

87. Martin Broszat, *The Hitler State*, trans. John W. Hiden (New York and London: Longman, 1981); see also Peter Hüttenberger, "Nationalsozialistische Polykratie," *Geschichte und Gesellschaft*, 2 (1976), 417–442.

88. Timothy W. Mason, "Intention and Explanation: A Current Controversy about the Interpretation of National Socialism," in *Der Führerstaat: Mythos und Realität*, ed. Gerhard Hirschfeld and Lothar Kettenacker (Stuttgart: Klett-Cotta, 1981), pp. 21–40. For the intentionalist view see Klaus Hildebrand, "Monokratie oder Polykratie? Hitlers Herrschaft und das Dritte Reich," in ibid., pp. 43–70. Cf. the contributions by Friedländer, Caplan, Geyer, and Kater and my own comments in Maier, Hoffmann, and Gould, *Rise of the Nazi Regime*, pp. 25–78.

89. The most pronounced functionalist contributions as they concerned the Final Solution were in Martin Broszat's response to David Irving's "Hitler und der Genesis der Endlösung" and Hans Mommsen's "Die Realisierung des Utopischen," both cited with other relevant works in note 38, above; also Uwe Dietrich Adam, *Judenpolitik im Dritten Reich* (Düsseldorf: Droste, 1972); Kurt Pätzold, "Von der Vertreibung zum Genozid. Zu den Ursachen, Triebkräften und Bedingungen der antijüdischen Politik des faschistischen deutschen Imperialismus," in *Faschismusforschung: Positionen, Probleme, Polemik* (Cologne: Pahl-Rugenstein, 1980), pp. 181–208; the intentionalist side, Gerald Fleming, *Hitler und die Endlösung. "Es ist des Führers Wunsch . . ."* (Wiesbaden and Munich: Limes Verlag, 1982)—clearly intentionalist; Schlomo Aronson, "Die dreifache Falle: Hitlers Judenpolitik, die Alliierten und die Juden," *Vierteljahrshefte für Zeitgeschichte*, 32 (1984), 28–65. The more intentionalist the historian, usually the earlier he or she dates the decision to murder. For a good summary see Marrus, *The Holocaust in History*, pp. 31–54; also Konrad Kwiet, "Zur historischen Behandlung der Judenverfolgung im Dritten Reich," *Militärgeschichtliche Mitteilungen*, 27 (1980), 149–192. Browning, "The Decision concerning the Final Solution," proposes some form of authorization (not a formal written order) from Hitler to Himmler and Heydrich in the summer of 1941, but emphasizes that the different agencies of the regime wanted to share in the prestige of this important assignment.

90. Cf. Recker, *Nationalsozialistische Sozialpolitik*. Unlike those who cite her work, Recker herself is not using her research for a "historicizing" purpose.

91. The good historian will not lose sight of the more general character of the regime: no discussion of Nazi marriage and family policy can neglect the concept

of the family as a nucleus of racial health; but not every marriage license need be seen as a prelude to Treblinka. See Heinz Holzhauer, "Die Scheidungsgründe in der nationalsozialistischen Familienrechtsgesetzgebung," in *NS-Recht in historischer Perspektive,* Kolloquien des Instituts für Zeitgeschichte (Munich: Oldenbourg, 1981), pp. 58–60.

92. Recker, *Nationalsozialistische Sozialpolitik,* pp. 109–121. A recent documentary of Keynesian policies in Germany starts with the Weimar Republic, then jumps to the postwar era without any consideration of the important work-creation programs of 1933–1936: see G. Bombach, K.-B. Netzband, H. J. Ramswer, and M. Timmermann, eds., *Der Keynesianismus IV. Die beschäftigungspolitische Diskussion in der Wachstumsepoche der Bundesrepublik Deutschland* [The discussion about employment policy during the growth era of the Federal Republic of Germany] (Berlin and New York: Springer-Verlag, 1983). The reader is unable to evaluate whether National Socialist deficit financing and public works were radically different from earlier programs or not, or whether or not the Finance Ministry's technical personnel conceived a continuing effort at countercyclical policy. In this sense the burden of the Third Reich has imposed a taboo on a more adequate evaluation and has hampered "historicization."

93. Jean-Paul Sartre, "Portrait of the Anti-Semite," trans. Mary Guggenheim, *Partisan Review,* 13 (1946), 163–178.

94. For help on the question of identity (with resolution attempted in this case by a concept of the closest continuer) see Robert Nozick, *Philosophical Explanations* (Cambridge, Mass.: Harvard University Press, 1981), pp. 27–114; and, from the viewpoint of psychology, Erik Erickson, "Identity, Psychosocial," in *International Encyclopedia of the Social Sciences,* vol. 7 (1968), 61–65; idem, *Childhood and Society,* 2d ed. (New York: Norton, 1963), pp. 42–44, 261–263, 281–402. See also Chapter 5 of this volume.

95. Philosophers have proposed a concept of "metapreferences" to provide consistency when personal preferences change (the terminally ill patient who may once have wanted no life support but might have changed his or her mind; the classic example of Odysseus, who asks to be unbound from the mast when he hears the sirens). See Jon Elster, *Ulysses and the Sirens: Studies in Rationality and Irrationality* (New York: Cambridge University Press, 1979). Is there an analogous "metamorality"? If so, how do we determine it?

96. Walter Benjamin, "Über den Begriff der Geschichte," in *Gesammelte Schriften,* 6 vols. in 12 (Frankfurt am Main: Suhrkamp, 1974–1985), I, 2, 695.

4. German History as Case History

1. Karl Dietrich Bracher, *Die deutsche Diktatur* (Cologne: Kiepenheuer & Witsch, 1969); translated by Jean Steinberg as *The German Dictatorship* (New York: Praeger, 1970).

2. Karl Dietrich Bracher, "Das Gemeinsame wurde ausgeblendet" [What is common was glossed over], *FAZ,* September 6, 1986.

3. See Karl Dietrich Bracher, *Die Auflösung der Weimarer Republik* (Villingen: Ring Verlag, 1955) and (with Gerhard Schulz and Wolfgang Sauer) *Die*

Nationalsozialistische Machtergreifung (Frankfurt am Main: Ullstein Verlag, 1974). For useful surveys of historiographic trends and social-science influences from the war to the *Tendenzwende* see Wolfgang J. Mommsen, "Gegenwärtige Tendenzen in der Geschichtsschreibung der Bundesrepublik," *Geschichte und Gesellschaft* 7 (1981), 149–188; also George C. Iggers, ed., "Introduction," in *The Social History of Politics: Critical Perspectives in West German Historical Writing since 1945* (Leamington Spa: Berg, 1985).

4. See Martin Broszat, "Die Ambivalenz der Forderung nach mehr Geschichtsbewusstsein," in *Nach Hitler, Der schwierige Umgang mit unserer Geschichte. Beiträge von Martin Broszat,* ed. Hermann Graml and Klaus-Dietmar Henke (Munich: Oldenbourg, 1986); also Martin Broszat, "Plädoyer für eine Historisierung des Nationalsozialismus," *Merkur,* 39 (1985), 373–385. Broszat's demand does raise the other problem of whether too much historicization may finally divest the Nazi experience of all overtones of abnormality.

5. Michael Stürmer, "Weder verdrängen noch bewältigen. Geschichte und Gegenwartsbewusstsein der Deutschen," *Schweizer Monatshefte,* 66 (September 1986), 689–694. Stürmer is sometimes ambiguous on this point: in addition to saying that German history cannot always be an *Unheilsgeschichte* (history of illness), he also cites Jakob Burckhardt that modern history is "essentially pathological." See Stürmer, "Deutsche Identität: Auf der Suche nach der verlorenen Nationalgeschichte," *Neue Züricher Zeitung,* May 28/29, 1983; reprinted in Stürmer, *Dissonanzen des Fortschritts: Essays über Geschichte und Politik in Deutschland* (Munich: Piper, 1986), pp. 208–209.

6. Thomas Mann, *Reflections of a Nonpolitical Man,* trans. Walter D. Morris (New York: Ungar, 1987), p. 33. For a nuanced review of the *Sonderweg* debate see Helga Grebing, *Der "deutsche Sonderweg" in Europa 1806–1945. Eine Kritik* (Stuttgart: Kohlhammer, 1986).

7. Karl Marx [actually Friedrich Engels], *Revolution and Counter-Revolution or Germany in 1848* (London: Allen and Unwin, 1952), p. 8.

8. Max Weber, "Der Nationalstaat und die Volkswirtschaftspolitik. Akademische Antrittsrede," in *Gesammelte politische Schriften,* ed. Johannes Winckelmann, 3d ed. (Tübingen: J.C.B. Mohr, 1971), p. 19. See also Wolfgang J. Mommsen, *Max Weber und die deutsche Politik 1890–1920,* 2d ed. (Tübingen: J.C.B. Mohr, 1959).

9. Thorstein Veblen, *Imperial Germany and the Industrial Revolution* (New York: Macmillan, 1915).

10. Kehr was encouraged by Charles A. Beard and in 1932 won a Rockefeller fellowship for research. He died prematurely of a heart attack in Washington, D.C., in May 1933. Hans-Ulrich Wehler, a student of Beard's own student William Appleman Williams, collected the essays for German publication—*Der Primat der Innenpolitik* (Frankfurt am Main: Ullstein, 1970). Not surprisingly, Kehr's own work has now come under scrutiny; see Margaret L. Anderson and Kenneth Barkin, "The Myth of the Putkammer Purge and the Reality of the *Kulturkampf*: Some Reflections on the Historiography of Imperial Germany," *Journal of Modern History,* 54 (1982), 647–686.

11. Alexander Gerschenkron, *Bread and Democracy in Germany* (Berkeley: University of California Press, 1943); Hans Rosenberg's "Political and Social Con-

sequences of the Great Depression of 1873–96 in Central Europe," *Economic History Review*, 13 (1943), 58–73, became the basis for his book *Grosse Depression und Bismarckzeit* (Berlin: Ullstein, 1967).

12. Among other works emphasizing intellectual divergence from a Western norm, see Fritz Stern, *The Politics of Cultural Despair* (Berkeley: University of California Press, 1961), which diagnosed a "Germanic ideology" among cultural conservatives; Leonard Krieger, *The German Idea of Freedom* (Boston: Beacon, 1957), a rich and difficult treatment of a handicapped German liberalism; and Fritz Ringer, *The Decline of the German Mandarins: The German Academic Community, 1890–1933* (Cambridge, Mass.: Harvard University Press, 1969), discussing the defects of the academic establishment.

13. Ralf Dahrendorf, *Society and Democracy in Germany* (Garden City, N.Y.: Doubleday, 1967). The reimportation of Max Weber deserves a book in its own right. Weber's legacy to the social sciences was ambiguous: stressing reason and rational science on the one hand; despairing, on the other, that subjectivity must always govern the scholar's choice of subjects, his ethical values, and political preferences. American interpreters such as Talcott Parsons and the émigré scholar Reinhard Bendix emphasized the rationalist legacy; and American social science—itself heavily influenced by Parsonian models of modernization—were brought back into Germany after 1945 (although conservative critiques continued). Habermas, on the left, reemphasized the murkier aspects of Weber. Cf. David Blackbourn and Geoff Eley, *The Peculiarities of German History: Bourgeois Society and Politics in Nineteenth-Century Germany* (Oxford: Oxford University Press, 1984), pp. 65–68.

14. James Sheehan could talk of a "new orthodoxy." Gordon Craig resisted the trend and embraced it at the same time. The Bielefeld school felt engaged in a heady campaign to clear the deadwood from the profession, although they have become more receptive in retrospect of the work of such earlier conservative social patrons of social history as Werner Conze. See Thomas Nipperdey's review, "Wehlers 'Kaiserreich.' Eine kritische Auseinandersetzung," *Geschichte und Gesellschaft*, 1 (1975), 539–560; Geoff Eley, "Die 'Kehrites' und das Kaiserreich. Bemerkungen zu einer aktuellen Kontroverse," ibid., 4 (1978), 90–107; and Hans-Jürgen Puhle, "Die Legende der Kerschen Schule," ibid., pp. 108–119.

16. Heinrich August Winkler, *Mittelstand, Demokratie und Nationalsozialismus* (Cologne: Kiepenheuer & Witsch, 1972).

17. Jürgen Kocka, *Angestellte zwischen Faschismus und Demokratie* (Göttingen: Vandenhoeck & Ruprecht, 1977); translated by Maura Kealey as *White Collar Employees in America, 1890–1940* (Beverly Hills, Calif.: Sage, 1980). On premodern patterns for industrial management, see idem, *Unternehmensverwaltung und Angestelltenschaft am Beispiel Siemens. Zum Verhältnis von Kapitalismus und Bürokratie in der deutschen Industrialisierung* (Stuttgart: Klett, 1969).

18. For specimens see Hans-Ulrich Wehler, *Geschichte als Sozialwissenschaft* (Frankfurt am Main: Suhrkamp, 1973) and *Historische Sozialwissenschaft und Geschichtsschreibung* (Göttingen: Vandenhoeck & Ruprecht, 1980). For a somewhat more measured but still affirmative statement, see Wolfgang Mommsen's inaugural lecture at Düsseldorf in 1981, "Geschichtswissenschaft jenseits des Historismus."

19. Blackbourn and Eley, *Peculiarities of German History*. The original German edition was *Mythen deutscher Geschichtsschreibung. Die gescheiterte bürgerliche Revolution von 1848* (Frankfurt am Main: Ullstein, 1980); the English-language edition discusses the reactions of the 1980 volume.

20. Cf. the attention given to Martin J. Wiener, *English Culture and the Decline of the Industrial Spirit 1850–1980* (New York: Cambridge University Press, 1981).

21. Blackbourn and Eley express disappointment that their arguments were apparently misread by almost every critic except Dieter Langewiesche; see his review in *Archiv für Sozialgeschichte*, 21 (1981), 527–531. I do not think they were misread. The argument does imply that British and French Revolutions represented no decisive transformation, that German bourgeois hegemony was as decisive as the British, that it influenced all political spheres. They attacked their professed friends with gusto; they should hardly have expected to be loved for their revision. Questions of intellectual style have also dismayed some readers; although the book makes some very important points, such as stressing the distinction between right-wing manipulation from above and grass-roots, popular chauvinism, Eley sometimes overemphasizes points of disagreement. For more on this aspect see Geoff Eley, *Reshaping the German Right: Radical Nationalism and Political Change after Bismarck* (New Haven: Yale University Press, 1980).

22. See Fritz Fischer, *Griff nach der Weltmacht* (Düsseldorf: Droste, 1961); also idem, *Krieg der Illusionen. Die deutsche Politik von 1911 bis 1914* (Düsseldorf: Droste, 1969). See also J. A. Moses, *The Politics of Illusion: The Fischer Controversy in German Historiography* (London: G. Prior, 1975).

23. In part this was because Hans-Ulrich Wehler's interpretation crystallized discussion. But see Werner Conze, "Das Kaiserreich von 1871 als gegenwärtige Vergangenheit im Generationswandel der deutschen Geschichtsschreibung," in *Staat und Gesellschaft im politischen Wandel,* ed. Werner Pöls (Stuttgart: Klett, 1979), pp. 383–405.

24. See the preface to Gerhard Ritter's magisterial work, *Staatskunst und Kriegshandwerk. Das Problem des Militarismus in Deutschland,* 4 vols. (Munich: Oldenbourg, 1959–68).

25. For a criticism of Wehler's indictment and a denial that Germany represented a deviant case, see Nipperdey, "Wehlers 'Kaiserreich.' "

26. For accounts of favorable British working-class development or the unfortunate German outcomes, see Gerhard A. Ritter, *Arbeiterbewegung, Parteien und Parlamentarismus* (Göttingen: Vandenhoeck & Ruprecht, 1976); Dieter Groh, *Negative Integration und revolutionärer Attentismus: Die deutsche Sozialdemokratie am Vorabend des Ersten Weltkrieges* (Frankfurt am Main: Propyläen, 1973); Klaus Saul, *Staat, Industrie, Arbeiterbewegung im Kaiserreich. Zur Innen- und Aussenpolitik des Wilhelminischen Deutschlands 1903–1914* (Düsseldorf: Droste, 1974).

27. See H. A. Winkler, ed., *Organisierter Kapitalismus. Voraussetzungen und Anfänge* (Göttingen: Vandenhoeck & Ruprecht, 1974), collecting the contributions to a series of panels at the 1972 Regensburg Historikertag. The authors included Wehler, Kocka, Hans-Jürgen Puhle, Gerald Feldman (who expressed reservations), and myself (examining the 1920s from a similar perspective). The concept of organized capitalism itself was derived from the analysis of Social

Democratic theorist Rudolf Hilferding, who envisaged that such an intertwining of state bureaucracies and capitalist enterprises would allow a painless transition to socialism. When Winkler, Kocka, and others revived it in the early 1970s, the notion beckoned primarily as a typological alternative to the "state-monopoly capitalism" (Stamokap) model that was currently popular in the German Democratic Republic and had found adherents among the far left at the West German universities. Organized capitalism was the historiographic echo of the SPD's heyday. Its exponents hardly expected that the doctrinaire left-wing interpretations they opposed would ebb so quickly, and that the new challenge to their effort at an integrative sociopolitical history (*Gesellschaftsgeschichte*) would emerge from conservative interpreters.

28. See Klaus Hildebrand's sharp attack on Wehler: "Geschichte oder 'Gesellschaftsgeschichte'? Die Notwendigkeit einer politischen Geschichtsschreibung von den internationalen Beziehungen," *Historische Zeitschrift*, 223 (1976), 328–357.

29. See, among others, Michel Crozier, Stanley Hoffmann, and Laurence Wylie, *In Search of France* (Cambridge, Mass.: Harvard University Press, 1963); also the Swiss journalist Herbert Luethy, *France against Herself* (New York: Meridian, 1955).

30. Arno J. Mayer, *The Persistence of the Old Regime: Europe to the Great War* (New York: Pantheon, 1981), p. 4.

31. Despite their useful recognition of this point, when Blackbourn and Eley evoke "the spheres of property relations, the rule of law, associational life . . . that more truly deserve the label 'bourgeois revolution' " (*Peculiarities of German History*, p. 16), they echo the old German critics of the French Revolution.

32. Among the works that restored a lively interest in the old regime were those of American and British historians: Mack Walker, *German Home Towns* (Ithaca: Cornell University Press, 1971); T. C. W. Blanning, *Reform and Revolution in Mainz, 1743–1803* (New York: Cambridge University Press, 1974); and the Germans' own work: Reinhard Koselleck, *Preussen zwischen Reform und Revolution* (Stuttgart: Klett, 1967); Helmut Berding, *Napoleonische Herrschafts- und Gesellschaftspolitik im Königreich Westfalen 1807–1813* (Göttingen: Vandenhoeck & Ruprecht, 1973).

33. Thomas Nipperdey, *Deutsche Geschichte 1800–1866* (Munich: C.H. Beck, 1986). On associations see idem, "Verein als soziale Struktur in Deutschland im späten 18 und frühen 19. Jahrhundert," in *Gesellschaft, Kultur, Theorie: Gesammelte Aufsätze zur neueren Geschichte* (Göttingen: Vandenhoeck & Ruprecht, 1976), pp. 174–205.

34. Although he criticized the historians of social structure, Nipperdey's interpretation itself owed an indirect debt to earlier leftist history and theory. One of the influential stimuli to rethinking the political legacy of the German Enlightenment was Habermas's 1962 sketch of bourgeois cultural political development, with its concept of a "public sphere." See Jürgen Habermas, *Strukturwandel der Öffentlichkeit. Untersuchungen zu einer Kategorie der bürgerlichen Gesellschaft* (Berlin: Luchterhand, 1962).

35. "German History before Hitler: The Debate about the German 'Sonderweg' " (Paper presented at the conference "Germany's Singularity? The 'Sonderweg' Debate," Hebrew University of Jerusalem, March 30–31, 1987).

36. Marc Bloch, "Pour une histoire comparée des sociétés européennes," reprinted in *Mélanges historiques* (Paris: S.E.V.P.E.N., 1963), pp. 16–40.

37. Paul Kennedy, *The Rise of the Anglo-German Antagonism, 1860–1914* (London: Allen and Unwin, 1982), p. 436.

38. What about notorious German anti-Semitism? it might be asked. Did it not set Germany apart, and in light of later history should it not be given special emphasis? However, although anti-Semitism in Germany, Austria-Hungary, and Russia was certainly more oppressive than in Britain or Italy, Germany's was not so different in kind from everywhere else that one could have predicted the final outcome. Traveling in France during the Dreyfus Affair, Freud was appalled by the virulence of anti-Jewish attitudes. The key in France, and periodically in Germany, lay in the political mobilization of the often dormant sentiments. No predominantly Christian society was free of the conviction that Jews never quite belonged. Liberals could work to make that feeling politically and culturally irrelevant; the new right-wing populists could exploit it as a basis of demagogic success. Who would win depended more upon general political factors than upon the strength of the prejudice appealed to.

39. For German observers, see Theodor Schieder, "The Theory of the Political Party in Early German Liberalism," in *The State and Society in Our Times,* trans. C. A. M. Syme (London: Nelson, 1962).

40. Ironically, British and American reformers around 1900 deplored the role of parties and looked enviously at German municipal politics and bureaucratic welfare institutions. Richard Eley, Charles A. Beard, the Fabians, and others studied German innovations; they appealed to German patterns of local governance to try to roll back party influence, to recover a "progressive" but often elitist governmental role against the rule of parties.

41. Max Weber's 1917 article, "Parlament und Regierung im neugeordneten Deutschland," in *Gesammelte politische Schriften,* p. 340.

42. This is the basis for the argument that conservative elites wagered on war, or at least ran the risk of nationalistic crises, precisely to preclude further democratization. See Arno J. Mayer's tentative "Internal Causes and Purposes of War in Europe, 1870–1956," *Journal of Modern History,* 41 (1969), 291–303. Elements of this go-for-broke risk taking are discernible, but so too is an acute awareness that war might mean revolution. In any case, during the crisis of July 1914 the international system clearly overwhelmed the players.

43. For a discussion of these reformist possibilities see Blackbourn and Eley, *Peculiarities of German History,* pp. 98–117.

44. Weber, "Der Nationalstaat und die Volkswirtschaftspolitik," p. 22.

45. In my book *Recasting Bourgeois Europe* (Princeton: Princeton University Press, 1975) I tried to suggest that what once seemed exclusively premodern elements of German social structure in some ways prefigured modern "postliberal" elements more than did their absence in France and Britain. But this argument would not in its own right be applicable against the proponents of a *Sonderweg* that ended in 1945. It suggested only that from the post-1945 perspective, it is not clear which development in the early twentieth century was backward, and which represented "modernity."

46. There is a growing consensus here (which Kocka has explicitly recog-

nized). Thomas Childers, *The Nazi Voter* (Chapel Hill: University of North Carolina Press, 1983); Richard F. Hamilton, *Who Voted for Hitler?* (Princeton: Princeton University Press, 1982); and Jürgen W. Falter, Thomas Lindenberger, and Siegfried Schumann, *Wahlen und Abstimmungen in der Weimarer Republik* (Munich: C.H. Beck, 1986), disagree among themselves on methods and particular interpretative points—but all see Nazism as a far wider protest than earlier interpretations allowed.

47. Hagen Schulze, *Wir sind was wir geworden sind. Vom Nutzen der Geschichte für die deutsche Gegenwart* (Munich: Piper, 1987), pp. 169–170. The phrase "between Meuse and Memel, Adige and Belt [the Danish sound]" evokes the first stanza of *Deutschland über Alles,* officially demoted as national anthem since 1945, with its references to the outermost boundaries of the German states in the Holy Roman Empire. Why Schulze considers rivers an impediment to national communication is not apparent.

48. The term recapitulates the title of Hellmuth Rössler's popular apologia for Germany's international record, *Deutsche Geschichte. Schicksal des Volkes in Europas Mitte* (Güterloh: C. Bertelsmann, 1961).

49. Michael Stürmer, "Mitten in Europa: Versuchung und Verdammung der Deutschen," in *Dissonanzen des Fortschritts,* p. 314.

50. For these trends see above all Stern, *The Politics of Cultural Despair,* and idem, *The Failure of Illiberalism: Essays on the Political Culture of Modern Germany* (New York: Knopf, 1972).

51. Peter Bender, "Mitteleuropa—Mode, Modell, oder Motiv?" *Die Neue Gesellschaft, Frankfurter Hefte,* 34 (April 1987), 297–304; I have paraphrased from p. 302.

52. The current president of the German Historians' Association, Christian Meier, has insisted on the self-motivating sources of political conflict in his depiction of antiquity; *Die Entstehung des politischen unter den Griechen* (Frankfurt am Main: Suhrkamp, 1980), p. 258.

53. Peter Kriedte, Hans Medick, and Jürgen Schlumbohm, *Industrialisierung vor der Industrialisierung: Gewerbliche Warenproduktion auf dem Land in der Formationsperiode des Kapitalismus* (Göttingen: Vandenhoeck & Ruprecht, 1977); translated by Beate Schempp as *Industrialization before Industrialization: Rural Industry in the Genesis of Capitalism* (Cambridge: Cambridge University Press, 1981). This valuable study of protoindustrialization emphasized the role of rural family formation and of production. The focus on the rural household then facilitated the bridge to more strictly cultural and anthropological concerns. For an important American contribution see David Sabean, *Power in the Blood: Popular Culture and Village Discourse in Early Modern Germany* (New York: Cambridge University Press, 1984). On the importance of historical anthropology, see Hans Medick, " 'Missionäre im Ruderboot'? Ethnologische Erkenntnisweisen als Herausforderung an die Sozialgeschichte," *Geschichte und Gesellschaft,* 10 (1984), 295–319. But see Jürgen Kocka's response, "Historische-anthropologische Fragestellungen—ein Defizit der historischen Sozialwissenschaft," in *Historische Anthropologie,* ed. Hans Süssmuth (Göttingen: Vandenhoeck & Ruprecht, 1984), pp. 73–83.

54. For an early example that is still a model, see William Sheridan Allen, *The*

Nazi Seizure of Power: The Experience of a Small German Town (Chicago: Quadrangle, 1964); also the essays in Detlev Peukert and Jürgen Reulecke, eds., *Die Reihen fast geschlossen: Beiträge zur Sozialgeschichte des Alltags unterm Nationalsozialismus* (Wuppertal: Hammer Verlag, 1981); also some of the contributions to the Institut für Zeitgeschichte's multivolume study of Bavaria under National Socialism, including, in English, Ian Kershaw, *Popular Opinion and Political Dissent in the Third Reich: Bavaria 1933–1945* (New York: Oxford University Press, 1984).

55. For critiques of the Reitz film see Miriam Hansen, "Dossier on *Heimat*," and Michael Geisler, "*Heimat* and the German Left: The Anamnesis of a Trauma," both in *New German Critique,* 36 (1985), 3–24.

56. For American statements see Eric Nordlinger, *On the Autonomy of the Democratic State* (Cambridge, Mass.: Harvard University Press, 1981): Peter B. Evans, Dietrich Rueschemeyer, and Theda Skocpol, eds., *Bringing the State Back In* (New York: Cambridge University Press, 1985).

57. David Abraham, *The Collapse of the Weimar Republic: Political Economy and Crisis* (Princeton: Princeton University Press, 1981; 2d ed., New York: Holmes and Meier, 1987).

58. See Michael Stürmer, *Regierung und Reichstag im Bismarckstaat 1871–1880. Cäsarismus oder Parlamentarismus* (Düsseldorf: Droste, 1974).

59. Nipperdey, *Deutsche Geschichte,* p. 11.

60. Louis Hartz, *The Liberal Tradition in America* (New York: Harcourt, Brace, 1955). Hartz's view of American history presupposed an American exceptionalism. *Amerika du hast es besser:* in this case, no feudalism, therefore no aristocracy, no traditionalist conservatism, no powerful socialism—liberal democracy by happy default. The interpretation had to downplay the range of inequality that did exist, the labor violence, the role of ethnic conflict in attenuating class stratification. For a syncretic attempt to stipulate American identity, see Seymour Martin Lipset, *The First New Nation: The United States in Historical and Comparative Perspective* (New York: Basic Books, 1963).

5. A Usable Past?

Epigraph: Jonathan Spence, *The Memory Palace of Matteo Ricci* (New York: Viking-Penguin, 1984), pp. 1–2.

1. Speech by Chancellor Helmut Kohl, "Bericht der Bundesregierung zur Lage der Nation," February 27, 1985, in *Verhandlungen des deutschen Bundestages,* 10. Wahlperiode, vol. 131, p. 9017.

2. There has been much less discussion of the Bonn plans, which were announced in 1984. For the proposal see the memorandum by Lothar Gall, Klaus Hildebrand, Ulrich Löber, and Horst Möller, *Überlegungen und Vorschläge zur Errichtung eines Hauses der Geschichte der Bundesrepublik Deutschland in Bonn* (Bonn: Bundesminister des Innern, 1984). For the SPD critique: " 'Soll es dem Volk dienlich sein, muss das Volk in ihm vorkommen' " (Bonn: Materialien der Arbeitsgruppe Kunst und Kultur der SPD-Bundestagsfraktion, 1984); Ulrich Löber, " 'Haus der Geschichte' in Bonn," *Museumskunde,* 49 (1984), 189–196. For a collection of critical essays concerning the museum plans see Geschichtswerkstatt Berlin, ed., *Die Nation als Ausstellungsstück* (Hamburg: VSA-Verlag, 1987).

3. Joachim Fest, "Nachwort, 21 April 1987," in Rudolph Augstein et al., *Historikerstreit. Die Dokumentation der Kontroverse um die Einzigartigkeit der nationalsozialistischen Judenvernichtung* (Munich: Piper, 1987), p. 389.

4. Cf. Jürgen Habermas, "Eine Art Schadensabwicklung," *Die Zeit*, July 11, 1987: "Seeing the composition of the committees that have worked out the conceptions for the museums planned by the federal government, the German Historical Museum in Berlin and the House of History of the Federal Republic, one cannot entirely resist the impression that the ideas of the new revisionism are to be translated into a structure of exhibits and objects displayed for effective popular didactic purposes."

5. Not surprisingly, one of the main neoconservative participants in the debate welcomed the new museums as places of refuge against the increasingly rapid modernization in flux around him. See Hermann Lübbe, "Der Fortschritt und das Museum," *Dilthey-Jahrbuch für Philosophie und Geschichte der Geisteswissenschaften*, 1 (1983), 39–56; cited in Alfred G. Frei and Walter Hochreiter, "Der neue Museumsboom—Kultur für alle?" *Neue Politische Literatur*, 31 (1986), 385–397.

6. Frei and Hochreiter, "Der neue Museumsboom," p. 385.

7. See the accompanying catalogue, *Fragen an die deutsche Geschichte. Ideen, Kräfte, Entscheidungen von 1800 bis zur Gegenwart*, 12th ed. (Bonn: Deutschen Bundestag, 1986).

8. Hartmut Boockmann, "Weder Lehrbuch noch Posterschau: Möglichkeiten und Grenzen eines Deutschen Historischen Museums," *FAZ*, Nov. 27, 1986.

9. Gall, Hildebrand, and Möller, *Überlegungen und Vorschläge*.

10. I am drawing on Hans Mommsen's "Zum Projekt eines 'Deutschen Historischen Museums' in West-Berlin," *Geschichtsdidaktik. Probleme, Projekte, Perspektiven*, 11 (1986), 310–328. For the origins see also Werner Knopp, "Deutsches Historisches Museum—eine Chance für Berlin," *Der Tagesspiegel*, November 23, 1986, p. B10; also Boockmann, "Weder Lehrbuch noch Posterschau." Knopp, as director of the Stiftung Preussischer Kulturbesitz, was chairman of the Committee of Experts; Boockmann was a member and one of the drafters of the 1982 project.

11. Hans Mommsen, "Stellungnahme zur Errichtung eines Historischen Museums in Berlin" (Memorandum provided by the author).

12. Ibid.

13. Quoted in Mommsen, "Zum Projekt eines 'Deutschen Historischen Museums,'" p. 312.

14. Sachverständigenkommission für die Konzeption des geplanten Deutschen Historischen Museum in Berlin, *Konzeption für ein "Deutsches Historisches Museum" überreicht am 21. April 1986* (Bonn: Bundesminister für Raumordnung, Bauwesen und Städtebau, 1986), p. 6. A revised version was submitted on June 24, 1987. For a summary see also Hartmut Boockmann, "Die Konzeption für ein 'Deutsches Historisches Museum,'" *Geschichte in Wissenschaft und Unterricht*, 37 (1986), 294–310.

15. "'Im Märchenwald des deutschen Gemüts,' SPIEGEL-Interview mit dem Historiker Arnulf Baring über die geplanten Museen für Geschichte," *Der Spiegel*, May 1, 1987, pp. 24–25.

16. Sachverständigenkommission, *Konzeption für ein "Deutsches Historisches*

208 Notes to Pages 131–135

Museum," pp. 7–8. How a historical museum can deal with controversy, how it can anticipate future controversies, and what differences of opinion it chooses to display are issues unresolved in the document. But in fairness, few of the models available have really attempted such resolutions either. The Washington museum exhibits conflicting contemporary opinions about some issues (industrial development, race relations), but it does not usually impose retrospective interpretations.

17. Frank Thomas Gatter, "Kolonisation der Geschichte und warum wir daran teilnehmen sollen," in Geschichtswerkstatt Berlin, *Die Nation als Ausstellungsstück*, p. 90.

18. Sachverständigenkommission, *Konzeption für ein "Deutsches Historisches Museum,"* p. 17.

19. *Der Spiegel* interview with Arnulf Baring, " 'Im Märchenwald des deutschen Gemuts.' "

20. Konrad Adam, "Wo bleiben die Verschwörer?" *FAZ*, October 10, 1986. The article defended a meeting of the conservative historians at the Hans Martin Schleyer Foundation in Berlin against the reproaches of Martin Broszat and the left.

21. The résumé of the hearings is in "Vermerk betr. Deutsches Historisches Museum: Offentliche Anhörung der SPD zum Deutschen Historischen Museum . . . 2. Juli 1986" (Manuscript provided by Jürgen Kocka). See also Tina Stadlmayer, "Verfassungspatriotismus gegen Nationalgeschichte. SPD-Hearing zum Geschichtsbewusstsein und zur Gründung des Deutschen Historischen Museums . . . ," *Tageszeitung*, July 14, 1986, p. 9. For Kocka's justification see "Ein Jahrhundertunternehmen zum 750. Geburtstag," *Das Parlament*, May 17, 1986.

22. Mommsen, "Zum Projekt eines 'Deutschen Historischen Museums,' " pp. 316–320. For Mommsen's other pieces, see idem, "Betrachtungen zur 'Konzeption für ein "Deutsches Historisches Museum" ' in Berlin" (Manuscript provided by the author); idem, "Die Last der Vergangenheit wird weitgehend ausgeklammert," *Frankfurter Rundschau*, March 29, 1986; idem, "Suche nach der 'verlorenen Geschichte'?" *Merkur*, 40 (1986), 864–874, esp. 873–874; idem, "Ein Museum für die Geschichte der Deutschen in Europa. Ein Rückfall in die Chronologie des Nationalstaates," *Der Tagesspiegel*, November 23, 1986; idem, "Die Bürde der Vergangenheit: Auseinandersetzung mit dem unbequemen historischen Erbe der Deutschen," in *Gegen den Versuch, Vergangenheit zu verbiegen*, ed. Hilmar Hoffmann (Frankfurt am Main: Athenäum, 1987), pp. 94–104.

23. Mommsen, "Zum Projekt eines 'Deutschen Historischen Museums,' " p. 327.

24. Sibylle Wirsing, "Die unerlöste Nation. Deutsche Geschichte im Museum. Nachtrag zu einer Berliner Tagung in Reichstagsgebäude," *FAZ*, October 11, 1986.

25. Quoted in Gustav Seibt, "Monologue über Räume. Der 36. Deutsche Historikertag in Trier," *FAZ*, October 14, 1986.

26. Quoted in Brigitte Mohr, "Zu viel gewollt. Die Anhörung zum Deutschen Historischen Museum," *FAZ*, December 11, 1986.

27. Ibid.

28. Wirsing, "Die unerlöste Nation."

29. Manfred Sack, "Das drohende Geschenk. (K)ein Platz für Helmut Kohls Geschichtsmuseum in Berlin," *Die Zeit*, August 15, 1986.

30. Wirsing, "Die unerlöste Nation."

31. Boockmann, "Weder Lehrbuch noch Posterschau"; Jürgen Habermas, "Vom öffentlichen Gebrauch der Historie," *Die Zeit*, November 7, 1986.

32. Cf. Alfred G. Frei, "Geschichtswerkstätten als Zukunftswerkstätten. Plädoyer für eine aufklärische Geschichtsarbeit," in *Die andere Geschichte*, ed. Gerhard Paul and Bernhard Schossig (Cologne: Bund Verlag, 1986), pp. 258–280.

33. For a critique of German trends from a West German Marxist critic, see Reinhard Kühnl, *Nation, Nationalismus, Nationale Frage. Was ist das und was soll das?* (Cologne: Pahl-Rugenstein, 1986).

34. See most recently Jürgen Habermas, "Geschichtsbewusstsein und post-traditionale Identität. Die Westorientierung der Bundesrepublik," in *Eine Art Schadensabwicklung. Kleine politische Schriften VI* (Frankfurt am Main: Suhrkamp, 1987), esp. pp. 173–174.

35. Quoted in the summary minutes of the Römerberg transcript in Dieter Krämer, "Die Diskussion der 'Römerberggespräche' 1986," in Hoffmann, *Gegen den Versuch, Vergangenheit zu verbiegen*, p. 109.

36. Geoffrey Hartman's translation of Theodor Adorno's "Was bedeutet: Aufarbeitung der Vergangenheit" (1959) is now included in Hartman's collection, *Bitburg in Moral and Political Perspective* (Bloomington: Indiana University Press, 1986), pp. 114–130.

37. Ranke: "Jede Epoche steht unmittelbar vor Gott"; Nipperdey: "Jede Epoche ist mittelbar zu Hitler. Mittelbar auch zur Bundesrepublik"; "Unter der Herrschaft des Verdachts," *Die Zeit*, October 17, 1986.

38. Andreas Hillgruber, "Politische Geschichte in moderner Sicht," *Historische Zeitschrift*, 216 (1973), 529–552; similar statements are found in Hildebrand, "Geschichte oder 'Gesellschaftsgeschichte'?" ibid., 223 (1976), 328–357. See Georg C. Iggers, *The German Conception of History*, rev. ed. (Middletown, Conn.: Wesleyan University Press, 1986), p. 290, for these views and for a useful orientation to the continuing methodological disputes. I agree that international relations remains an important field of history and that it suffered from undue neglect during the heyday of social history. Nonetheless, the fault often lay with the field's own practitioners. See Charles S. Maier, "Marking Time: The Historiography of International Relations," in *The Past before Us: Contemporary Historical Writing in the United States*, ed. Michael Kammen (Ithaca: Cornell University Press, 1980), pp. 355–387.

39. The history of antiquity permitted more wide-ranging an approach, and the class struggles of the ancient world were an object lesson for conservatives. See Robert von Pöhlmann, *Geschichte der sozialen Frage und des Sozialismus in der antiken Welt*, 2 vols. (Munich: C.H. Beck, 1912); also Arnaldo Momigliano on the historiography of the "agrarian law," "New Paths of Classicism in the Nineteenth Century," *History and Theory Beiheft*, 21 (1982), esp. 3–16.

40. Eckart Kehr, "Neuere deutsche Geschichtsschreibung," in *Der Primat der Innenpolitik*, ed. Hans-Ulrich Wehler (Frankfurt am Main: Ullstein, 1970), p. 259; cited in Iggers, *German Conception of History*, p. 236.

41. Cf. the revealing judgment on Herder: "In the last analysis, Herder's awareness of the historical world, and of the character of the nation as well, followed from his ideal of humanity, and it was this ideal that in turn imposed limitations on that awareness"; Friedrich Meinecke, *Cosmopolitanism and the National State,* trans. Robert B. Kimber (Princeton: Princeton University Press, 1970), p. 29.

42. Ibid., p. 207. In contrast to Meinecke, Leonard Krieger's *Ranke: The Meaning of History* (Chicago: University of Chicago Press, 1977) emphasizes the universalistic moment in Ranke's historiography.

43. Carl Schmitt, *The Concept of the Political,* trans. and ed. George Schwab (New Brunswick, N.J.: Rutgers University Press, 1976).

44. See Friedrich Meinecke, *Machiavellism: The Doctrine of Raison d'Etat and Its Place in Modern History,* trans. Douglas Scott (New Haven: Yale University Press, 1957); also idem, *The German Catastrophe,* trans. Sidney B. Fay (Cambridge, Mass.: Harvard University Press, 1946); also Iggers, *German Conception of History,* pp. 238–258. Meinecke was fair enough to recognize the outstanding merits of his doctoral student, Kehr.

45. "For most of my life, as I looked back on [the Germany of my youth], it seemed to be bathed in a kind of radiance that did not begin to darken until the outbreak of war in 1914. Now, at the twilight of my life, my probing eye finds shadows far deeper than my generation perceived—let alone my academic teachers"; Gerhard Ritter, *The Sword and the Scepter: The Problem of Militarism in Germany,* trans. Heinz Norden, 4 vols. (Coral Gables, Fla.: University of Miami Press, 1969–73), II, 2.

46. For accounts of the controversy see Iggers, *German Conception of History,* pp. 197–200; idem, "The 'Methodenstreit' in International Perspective: The Reorientation of Historical Studies at the Turn from the Nineteenth to the Twentieth Century," *Storia della storiografia,* 6 (1984), 21–32; also Hans-Josef Steinberg, "Karl Lamprecht," in *Deutsche Historiker,* ed. Hans-Ulrich Wehler (Göttingen: Vandenhoeck & Ruprecht, 1973), pp. 58–68; Luise Lorne-Schütte, *Karl Lamprecht. Kulturgeschichte, Wissenschaft und Politik* (Göttingen: Vandenhoeck & Ruprecht, 1984). By 1908 Meinecke could give Lamprecht his due in the hundredth-anniversary issue of *Historische Zeitschrift* and counsel that, although history must remain focused on the state, it should renew contact with philosophy and culture. See Iggers, *German Conception of History,* p. 200.

47. For the most recent argument that there was a chance for reunification as a neutral but democratic country during the Cold War see Rolf Steininger, *Eine vertane Chance. Die Stalin-Note vom 10. März 1952 und die Wiedervereinigung* (Berlin and Bonn: Dietz, 1986). These assertions prompted an intense debate. See Stürmer's scathing dismissal of this claim as well as of the other "specters of the past," such as "the legend of the Communists' noble will, of the failure of the German Social Democrats, and of the blessings of the Popular Front," in "Geschichte in geschichtslosem Land," *FAZ,* April 25, 1986.

48. Peter Schneider, *The Wall Jumper,* trans. Leigh Hafrey (New York: Pantheon, 1983), pp. 29–30.

49. The best appreciation of Hintze is now Jürgen Kocka, "Otto Hintze," in

Wehler, *Deutsche Historiker*, pp. 275–298; see also Felix Gilbert, ed., *The Historical Essays of Otto Hintze* (New York: Oxford University Press, 1975).

50. Kehr, "Neuere deutsche Geschichtsschreibung," pp. 259–260.

51. Hans-Ulrich Wehler, *Deutsche Gesellschaftsgeschichte*, vol. 1: *Vom Feudalismus des Alten Reiches bis zur defensiven Modernisierung der Reformära 1700–1815* (Munich: C.H. Beck, 1987), pp. 6–12.

52. Ibid., p. 16.

53. Habermas, "Geschichtsbewusstsein und posttraditionale Identität," p. 162.

54. I am indebted to Hans Betz's detailed unpublished paper on the West German "New Right" for citations and background. See also Henning Eichberg, *Nationale Identität* (Munich: Langen-Müller, 1978); Karl Lamers, ed., *Suche nach Deutschland. Deutsche Identität und die Deutschlandpolitik* (Bonn: Europa Union Verlag, 1983); Bernard Willms, *Die deutsche Nation* (Cologne-Lövenich: Hohenheim Verlag, 1982); *Idealismus und Nation. Zur Rekonstruktion des politischen Selbstbewusstseins der Deutschen* (Paderborn: Schoeningh, 1986); Wolfgang Seiffert (a DDR émigré), *Das ganze Deutschland* (Munich: Piper, 1986); Helmut Diwald, *Geschichte der Deutschen* (Berlin: Siedler, 1978). For a rightist view of the historians' controversy see Rolf Kosiek, *Historikerstreit und Geschichtsrevision* (Tübingen: Grabert Verlag, 1987).

55. Carl Pletsch, " 'The Socialist Nation of the German Democratic Republic' or the Asymmetry in Nation and Ideology between the Two Germanies," *Comparative Studies in Society and History*, 21 (1979), 323–345.

56. For an early sign of this reevaluation among East German historians see Horst Bartel, "Erbe und Tradition in Geschichtsbild und Geschichtsforschung der DDR," *Zeitschrift für Geschichtswissenschaft*, 29 (1981), 387–394; also Horst Bartel and Walter Schmidt, "Historisches Erbe und Traditionen—Bilanz, Probleme, Konsequenzen," ibid., 30 (1982), 816–829.

57. See Kurt Gossweiler, "Nur eine Historikerdebatte?" and Arno Klönne, "Historiker-Debatte und 'Kulturrevolution von rechts,' " in *Vergangenheit, die nicht vergeht: Die "Historiker-Debatte." Dokumentation, Darstellung und Kritik*, ed. Reinhard Kühnl (Cologne: Pahl-Rugenstein, 1987), pp. 292–316 and 317–330, respectively.

58. A useful survey is George C. Iggers, "Some Comments on Recent Historical Studies in the German Democratic Republic" (Manuscript provided by the author). Iggers singles out Ingrid Mittenzwei, *Friedrich II von Preussen, eine Biographie* (Cologne: Pahl-Rugenstein, 1980); and Hartmut Zwahr, *Zur Konstituierung des Proletariats als Klasse: Strukturuntersuchung über das Leipziger Proletariat während der industriellen Revolution* (E. Berlin: Akademie der Wissenschaften der DDR, 1978; reprint, Munich: C.H. Beck, 1981), as well as collective social-history studies of the early modern period, and of the Magdeburg region as exemplary. Other surveys of East German historiography include Andreas Dorpalen, *German History in Marxist Perspective: The East German Approach* (Detroit: Wayne State University Press, 1985); Gustavo Corni, "La storiografia nella Repubblica democratica tedesca tra dogmatismo e innovazione," *Studi storici*, 2 (1984), 569–591; and two survey volumes of the East German *Zeitschrift für Geschichtswis-*

senschaft: Historische Forschungen in der DDR 1960–1970 (E. Berlin: Deutscher Verlag der Wissenschaften, 1970) and *Historische Forschungen in der DDR 1970–1980* (E. Berlin: Deutschen Verlag der Wissenschaften, 1980).

59. Besides Mittenzwei, *Friedrich II*, see Ernst Engelberg, *Bismarck. Urpreusser und Reichsgründer* (Berlin: Siedler, 1985).

60. See Heinz Peperle's revision of the Marxist view of Nietzsche and the counterattack by the orthodox Wolfgang Harich, "Revision der Marxistischen Nietzschebildes?" *Sinn und Form*, 39 (September–October 1987), 1018–53, in turn criticized as "reactionary" by Hermann Kant and Stephen Hermlin at the November 1987 Congress of Writers' Associations; "Strange Bedfellows: Marxists Embrace Nietzsche," *New York Times*, November 28, 1987, p. 4. The debate is ironic, since the Marxist spokesman's effort to reestablish an orthodox East German view of Nietzsche criticized him from a perspective of liberal distaste for his antifeminist and anti-Jewish slurs.

61. Saul Friedländer, *When Memory Comes*, trans. Helen R. Lane (New York: Farrar, Straus, Giroux, 1979).

62. For an apologetic evocation of Weimar's conservative revolutionaries, but one that well conveys their moods, see Armin Mohler, *Die konservative Revolution in Deutschland 1918–1932* (Stuttgart: Friedrich Vorwerk Verlag, 1950). Mohler has remained an elder statesman of the far right. See the sources listed in note 59 above.

63. See Karl Dietrich Bracher, "Das Modewort Identität und die deutsche Frage," *FAZ*, August 9, 1986, supplement, "Bilder und Zeiten"; also Karl-Heinz Jeismann, " 'Identität' statt 'Emanzipation'?" *Aus Politik und Zeitgeschichte*, supplement to *Das Parlament*, B 20–21/86 (May 17, 1986), 3–16.

64. Jürgen Kocka, "Kritik und Identität. Nationalsozialismus, Alltag und Geographie," *Die Neue Gesellschaft, Frankfurter Hefte*, 33 (October 1986), 891–892.

65. Emancipation has been defended recently with greatest sophistication by the intellectual historian Jörn Rüsen. He advocates that historians follow a neo-Kantian program of "enlightenment," which envisages history "as a universal process of human self-liberation and simultaneously orients current activity to drive this process further along." Emancipation means the negation of domination, but it does not propose a naive reading of the past simply as a history of liberation. It mandates the study of political rule to see how it can be made more consonant with a view of citizens as mature and autonomous. See Jörn Rüsen, "Geschichte als Aufklärung? Oder: Das Dilemma des historischen Denkens zwischen Herrschaft und Emanzipation," *Geschichte und Gesellschaft*, 7 (1981), 189–218 (quotation p. 195). For a dissenting, nonhistoricist view, see Thomas Nipperdey, "Historismus und Historismuskritik heute," in *Gesellschaft, Kultur, Theorie: Gesammelte Aufsätze zur neueren Geschichte* (Göttingen: Vandenhoeck & Ruprecht, 1976), pp. 59–73.

66. Habermas, "Geschichtsbewusstsein und posttraditionale Identität," p. 166. At the same time good history must dissolve collective myths.

67. Hagen Schulze, *Wir sind was wir geworden sind. Vom Nutzen der Geschichte für die deutsche Gegenwart* (Munich: Piper, 1987), p. 12. German allows two terms for history: *Geschichte* (what has happened) and *Historie* (how we study it; sometimes with the belletristic overtone of how we write it). Unfortunately, there is little consistency in usage; and the fact that our approach to what has happened affects our version of what has happened makes the distinction of limited help.

68. Analogue, of course, is not equivalence. What happens when the two sorts of identity are implied to be more than an analogue is shown by the furor evoked by Hillgruber's bracketing of physical identity and national identity in *Zweierlei Untergang. Die Zerschlagung des deutsches Reiches und das Ende des europäischen Judentums* (Berlin: Corso bei Siedler, 1986). Even though the title suggested "kinds of" annihilation, readers felt that he was claiming that the end of a nation-state was tantamount to the physical destruction of a people, and that the difference was being trivialized. Destruction of life is not the same as destruction of a nation-state.

69. See, for example, a work useful for its synthetic approach, Seymour Martin Lipset, *The First New Nation: The United States in Historical and Comparative Perspective* (New York: Basic Books, 1963), esp. chaps. 2 and 3.

70. The concept of identity, as Habermas defines it, owes much to models from psychology. But the idea of individual identity in general has important roots in German idealism and subsequent philosophy. For some recent explorations of the problem see Jon Elster, *Ulysses and the Sirens: Studies in Rationality and Irrationality* (New York: Cambridge University Press, 1979); and Richard Wollheim, *The Thread of Life* (Cambridge, Mass.: Harvard University Press, 1984), esp. chap. 1. To move from the already-problematic notion of personal identity to that of a collective identity adds new dimensions of difficulty.

71. Habermas, "Eine Art Schadensabwicklung"; idem, "Vom öffentlichen Gebrauch der Historie." Habermas had cautioned earlier against oversimplifying any national identity. See idem, "Können komplexen Gesellschaften eine vernünftige Identität ausbilden?" in *Zur Rekonstruktion des historischen Materialismus* (Frankfurt: Suhrkamp, 1976).

72. Habermas, "Geschichtsbewusstsein und posttraditionale Identität," p. 166.

73. It would be unfair to overlook the fact that Stürmer also insists on the need for the critical destruction of myth and the application of scholarly methods. But his essays emphasize the role of history in the production of identity. See Stürmer, "Geschichte in Geschichtslosem Land."

74. Habermas, "Geschichtsbewusstsein und posttraditionale Identität," p. 171.

75. Habermas, "Vom öffentlichen Gebrauch der Historie." Habermas argues that the analogy with Kierkegaard cannot be taken too far. Kierkegaard demands moral responsibility from the individual; but the moral responsibility demanded of the present generation for Nazi crimes is less compelling: "for those born later there results only a sort of intersubjective liability" ("Geschichtsbewusstsein und posttraditionale Identität," p. 174)—a sort of regret or melancholy in the face of sacrifices that cannot be made good.

76. Habermas, "Geschichtsbewusstsein und posttraditionale Identität," p. 173.

77. In this regard see Habermas's explanation that Kierkegaard realized he had to presuppose Kantian ethics and "offer an alternative to Hegel's effort to 'concretize' Kantian universalist morality in a questionable way." In his criticism of a facile Hegelian compromise, Habermas proposes, Kierkegaard can be compared with Marx; ibid., p. 172.

78. Ibid., p. 176.

79. Ibid., p. 178.

80. Claude Lévi-Strauss, *The Savage Mind* (Chicago: University of Chicago Press, 1966), p. 255.

81. Ibid., pp. 255, 247. As Lévi-Strauss wrote mischievously, "As we say of certain careers, history may lead to anything, provided you get out of it"; ibid., p. 262.

82. For Habermas's revisions of Max Weber see Seyla Benhabib, *Critique, Norm, and Utopia: A Study of the Foundations of Critical Theory* (New York: Columbia University Press, 1986), esp. pp. 255–263.

83. Erik Erikson, *Childhood and Society,* 2d ed. (New York: Norton, 1963).

84. Schmitt, *The Concept of the Political*; Joseph W. Bendersky, *Carl Schmitt, Theorist for the Reich* (Princeton: Princeton University Press, 1983), pp. 88–103; Otto Kirchheimer, "Weimar—and What Then? Analysis of a Constitution," in *Politics, Law, and Social Change: Selected Essays of Otto Kirchheimer,* ed. Frederic S. Burin and Kurl L. Shell (New York: Columbia University Press, 1969), pp. 33–74.

85. See the debate concerning Ellen Kennedy's article, "Carl Schmitt and the Frankfurt School," *Telos,* no. 71 (Spring 1987), 37–66, with rejoinders by Martin Jay, Alfons Söllner, and Ulrich K. Preuss, ibid., pp. 67–110.

86. Jürgen Habermas, "Sovereignty and the Führerdemokratie," *Times Literary Supplement,* September 26, 1986, pp. 1053–54. Habermas concentrates discussion on Schmitt's *Leviathan* (1938) and tries to explain the fascination the author (along with Heidegger, Gottfried Benn, and Ernst Jünger)still exerts "in certain forgotten sub-cultures previously of left-wing provenance" (p. 1054).

87. Walter Benjamin, *The Origin of German Tragic Drama,* trans. John Osborne (London: Verso, 1977).

88. Walter Benjamin, "Über den Begriff der Geschichte," in *Gesammelte Schriften,* 6 vols. in 12 (Frankfurt am Main: Suhrkamp, 1974–1985), I, 2, 698. See also Susan Buck-Morss, *The Origin of Negative Dialectics: Theodor W. Adorno, Walter Benjamin, and the Frankfurt Institute* (New York: Free Press, 1977), p. 169.

Epilogue

1. Friedrich Nietzsche, "Vom Nutzen und Nachteil der Historie für das Leben," in *Unzeitgemässe Betrachtungen* (Munich: Goldmann Verlag, 1984), pp. 76, 79; translated by Peter Preuss as *On the Advantage and Disadvantage of History for Life* (Indianapolis: Hockett, 1980).

2. Judith Miller, "Erasing the Past: Europe's Amnesia about the Holocaust," *New York Times Magazine,* November 16, 1986, p. 30.

3. Renzo De Felice, *Mussolini il Duce, vol. 1: Gli anni di consenso 1929–1936* (Turin: Einaudi, 1974). The debate, however, should have been less over whether consensus prevailed by the 1930s and more over whether an acquiescence (and at times enthusiasm) built originally upon repression really deserved the same term as acceptance based upon democratic methods.

4. See the gorgeously illustrated catalogue *L'economia italiana tra le due guerre 1919–1939* (Milan: IPSOA, 1984); also the critiques by Tim Mason, "Modernità e gigantismo nella didattica della Storia," *Politica ed economia,* 16 (January 1985), 61–66; and Charles S. Maier, "Fascismo alla Fioriucci," *Politica ed economia,* 16 (April 1985), 49–51. A similar exhibit in the Milan train station contributed a

related impression. The Rome exhibit was sponsored by the IPSOA business school in Rome with some support from the Craxi government, at a time when that administration was also presenting itself as a modern, quasi-plebiscitary alternative to the parliamentary coalitions. Contributors to the catalogue included a whole range of historians, a few of whom were frankly quite sympathetic to corporativist economics.

5. Henry Rousso, *Le syndrome de Vichy 1944–18* . . . (Paris: Seuil, 1987).

6. Ibid., pp. 141–146, 248–251. Cf. Pascal Ory, "Retro satanas," *Le débat*, 16 (November 1981), now in *L'entre-deux-mai: Histoire culturelle de la France, mai 1968–mai 1981* (Paris: Seuil, 1983), pp. 118–127.

7. Saul Friedländer, *Reflections of Nazism: An Essay on Kitsch and Death*, trans. Thomas Weyr (New York: Harper & Row, 1984). He cites Hans-Jürgen Syberberg's film *Hitler*, Alain Tournier's *The Ogre*, trans. Barbara Bray (Garden City, N.Y.: Doubleday, 1972), and even George Steiner's novel, *The Portage to San Cristobal of A.H.* (Boston: Faber and Faber, 1981). In these cases memory is so fascinating that the authors seem to summon up spirits they do not fully control, in a process reminiscent of Nietzsche's fascination with an earlier "seducer": "He is distinguished by every ambiguity, every double sense, everything quite generally that persuades those who are uncertain without making them aware *of what* they have been persuaded . . . Music as Circe . . . He had the naïveté of decadence: this was his superiority. He believed in it, he did not stop before any of the logical implications of decadence. The others hesitate—that is what differentiates them. Nothing else"; Friedrich Nietzsche, *The Birth of Tragedy and the Case of Wagner*, trans. Walter Kauffmann (New York: Vintage, 1967), p. 186.

8. Dieter Stiefel, *Entnazifierung in Österreich* (Vienna, Munich, and Zurich: Europaverlag, 1981), pp. 327–328. Nonetheless, the author believes that denazification did have voluntary aspects and represented an active "mastery of the past." It confirmed, in effect, the modernization or revolution that the Nazis had carried out. See also Robert Knight, "The Waldheim Context: Austria and Nazism," *Times Literary Supplement*, October 13, 1986, pp. 1083–84. For a critical discussion of Austrian attitudes toward the past and toward Waldheim see Josef Haslinger, *Politik der Gefühle. Ein Essay über Österreich* (Darmstadt: Luchterhand, 1987).

9. I am grateful to Günter Bischof for having provided a copy of the letter from Peter Jankowitsch, dated on Foreign Ministry stationery, November 28, 1986. The provocation was Robert Knight's balanced and informed article concerning the limits of denazification in Austria (cited in the preceding note). For Austrian protests against this initiative see Hubertus Czernin, "Überaus Bedenklich. Peter Jankowitsch fordert Historiker zum Kampf gegen einen britischen Kollegen," *Profil*, December 15, 1976. See also the letter by Professor Gerald Stourzh (*Profil*, December 22, 1986), which said that Knight should have formulated his charges about continuing Austrian anti-Semitism and his dismissal of the Resistance record more cautiously, but defended Knight as a knowledgeable historian and his article as the basis for dialogue. For an attack on Knight's "perverse perspective" and on the general American "soap-opera" treatment of Germans and Nazis see Andreas Unterberger, "Die Vergangenheit als Seifenoper: Das Anhalten der Vorwürfe aus dem Ausland verunsichert die Alpenrepublik," *Die Presse*, December 29, 1986. Cf. Gerhard Botz, "Österreich und die NS-Vergangenheit," in *Ist der*

Nationalsozialismus Geschichte? Zu Historisierung und Historikerstreit, ed. Dan Diner (Frankfurt am Main: Fischer, 1987), pp. 140–152.

10. *Le monde,* special edition, *Le procès de Klaus Barbie,* July 1987, p. 8.

11. Cf. Jean-Marc Théolleyre, "Le verdict de la mémoire," *Le monde,* July 4, 1987. American coverage of the trial sometimes wrongly suggested that it would finally force the French for the first time to confront their own collaboration. In fact, that self-examination has been proceeding at least since the appearance of Marcel Ophuls's *The Sorrow and the Pity* (Le chagrin et la pitié) in 1971.

12. Richard C. Lukas, *Forgotten Holocaust: The Poles under German Occupation, 1939–1944* (Lexington: University Press of Kentucky, 1986), pp. ix, 1. Lukas is especially concerned to rebut the image of the Poles as accomplices of German anti-Semitism by showing their own suffering. Agreed: Poles were treated with egregious brutality, and had the Third Reich continued as master of Poland, many would have been wantonly starved, shot, and otherwise reduced to a sort of agrarian slavery. Agreed further: Polish Christian attitudes toward their Jewish populations are not usually treated with the careful differentiation merited. Still, the urgency and comprehensiveness of German extermination efforts toward the Jews distinguished them from the cruelty inflicted on the wider Polish nation. In any case, the historiography of Polish-Jewish relations is still mired in a mutual defensiveness that the German-Jewish historiography had superseded (at least until the *Historikerstreit*).

13. This is not to deny that leading young adults through Holocaust exhibits can produce a backfire effect. The pedagogical outcome needs to be thought through carefully.

14. Detlev J. K. Peukert, "Alltag und Barbarei: Zur Normalität des Dritten Reiches," in Diner, *Ist der Nationalsozialismus Geschichte?* esp. pp. 54, 57. For a less ambiguous survey see in the same volume Konrad Kwiet, "Judenverfolgung und Judenvernichtung im Dritten Reich. Ein historiographischer Überblick," pp. 237–264.

15. Adi Ophir, "On Sanctifying the Holocaust: An Anti-Theological Treatise," *Tikkun,* 2 (1987), 61–66 (quotations pp. 62, 63, 65).

16. Golo Mann, *Der Antisemitismus. Wurzeln, Wirkung und Überwindung* (Munich: Ner-Tamid-Verlag, 1961), p. 29; quoted in Dan Diner, "Fragments of an Uncompleted Journey: On Jewish Socialization and Political Identity in West Germany," in *Germans and Jews since the Holocaust: The Changing Situation in West Germany,* ed. Anson Rabinbach and Jack Zipes (New York: Holmes & Meier, 1986), p. 128.

17. See the essays by Diner, Detlev Claussen, and Zipes in Rabinbach and Zipes, *Germans and Jews since the Holocaust.* To be fair, much of the malaise expressed in these reflections seems to arise as much from the rupture with the New Left (over the Palestinian question) as from German conditions per se.

18. See Lily Gardner Feldman, *The Special Relationship between West Germany and Israel* (Boston: Allen and Unwin, 1984).

19. Andrei S. Markovits, "Was ist 'Deutsch' an den Grünen? Vergangenheitsaufarbeitung als Voraussetzung politischer Zukunftsbewältigung," in Otto Kallscheuer, ed., *Die Grünen—Letzte Wahl* (Berlin: Rotbuch Verlag, 1986), pp. 146–163 (quotation p. 148).

20. Rousso, *Le syndrome de Vichy*, p. 322.

21. For the range of Jewish artistic and historiographic responses see David G. Roskies, *Against the Apocalypse: Response to Catastrophe in Modern Jewish Culture* (Cambridge, Mass.: Harvard University Press, 1984).

22. See Chapter 2, "An 'Intellectual Civil War.'"

23. See Niklaus Luhmann, *Zweckbegriff und Systemrationalität* (Frankfurt am Main: Suhrkamp, 1973); also idem, "Evolution und Geschichte," answered by Jürgen Habermas, "Geschichte und Evolution," both in *Geschichte und Gesellschaft*, 2 (1976), and the latter reprinted in Habermas, *Zur Rekonstruktion des historischen Materialismus* (Frankfurt am Main: Suhrkamp, 1976).

Index